creativity
· annual · awards ·

Creativity 38
Annual Awards

Creativity 38
Annual Awards

COLLINS DESIGN

An Imprint of HarperCollins*Publishers*

HarperCollins books may be purchased for educational, business, or sales promotional use.
For information, please write: Special Markets Department, HarperCollins*Publishers*,
10 East 53rd Street, New York, NY 10022.

First published in 2009 by:
Collins Design
An Imprint of HarperCollins*Publishers*
10 East 53rd Street
New York, NY 10022
Tel: (212) 207-7000
Fax: (212) 207-7654
collinsdesign@harpercollins.com
www.harpercollins.com

Distributed throughout the world by:
HarperCollins*Publishers*
10 East 53rd Street
New York, NY 10022
Fax: (212) 207-7654

Book design by SW!TCH Studios • www.switchstudio.com
Photography, scanning & pre-press services provided by FCI Digital • www.fcidigital.com

Library of Congress Control Number: 2009923265

ISBN: 978-0-06-180833-3

Produced by Creativity Annual Awards, Louisville, KY.

Printed in China by Everbest Printing Company.

First Printing, 2009

contents

contents

foreword

Now in its thirty-ninth year, the Creativity Annual Awards is one of the oldest and most widely respected design competitions in the world. This book showcases the winners of the 2008 competition.

This year's book was created by SW!TCH Studio in Tempe, Arizona which developed a whole new look and feel. Once again, the best in category Platinum winners receive full-page treatments with the story behind the winning design. Creativity's international reach also doubled in 2008, proving that good design is being created in all parts of the globe.

We hope you enjoy reviewing these pages and continue to submit inspiring designs to future Creativity Annual Award competitions. We are proud to continue our tradition of bringing awareness and well-deserved recognition to the world's most imaginative design firms, both large and small.

acknowledgements

Thank you to the 2008 judges for donating their time and expertise: Von Glitschka – Glitschka Studios; Mark Kaufman – Vivitiv; Paula Jaworski – HSUS; Jim Nissen – SW!TCH Studio; Shane Luitjens – INK Publishing; Stanley Church – Wallace Church; Earl Gee – Gee + Chung; Richard Zeid – Zeid Designs; Greg Kihlstrom – Carousel30; Les Kollegian – Jacob Tyler Group; John Clark – Berman Printing; Joey Zornes – Resource Interactive and Jason Clark – VIA Studios. Thank you to Eve Lee for her outstanding copywriting skills and Diana Falvey for assisting with this year's competition.

medal designations

This symbol designates a **PLATINUM** award winning design. Our most prestigious award is reserved for the best in category.

This symbol designates a **GOLD AWARD** winning design. The top 10% of designs in each category are selected for the **GOLD AWARD**.

This symbol designates a **SILVER AWARD** winning design. The top 25% of designs in each category are selected for the **SILVER AWARD**.

CREATIVITY
Annual Awards

REGISTER ONLINE AT WWW.CREATIVITYAWARDS.COM

PRINT

CREATIVITY **38** ANNUAL AWARDS

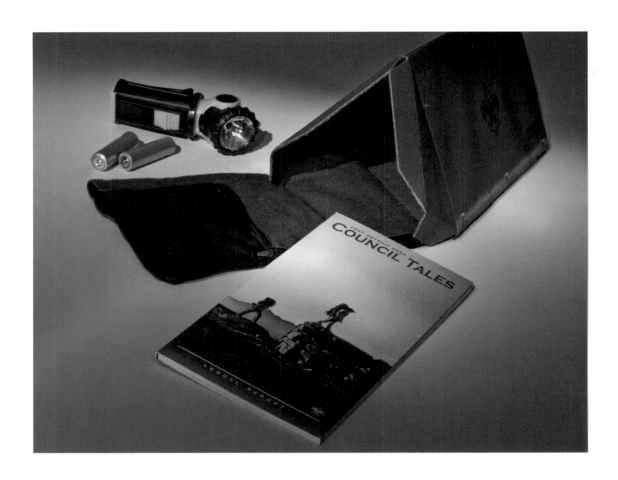

PLATINUM

CREATIVE FIRM: Latcha+Associates - Farmington Hills, MI

CREATIVE TEAM: Ken Suminski - Art Director; Bob Maas - Print Prod.; Preston Wertheimer - Copywriter

CLIENT: Boy Scouts cf America-Detroit Area Council

"Be Prepared" to have fun with this Annual Report

Think of Boy Scouts, and a few things come to mind: "Be Prepared." Helpfulness. And, a most traditional activity: camping.

"The primary purpose of the Boy Scouts of America Detroit Area Council's Annual Report is to communicate the Council's activities, achievements and fiscal health to its supporters," says area agency Latcha+Associates. "As most members of this audience are lifelong participants in Scouting, a secondary—yet no less important function—is to reinforce readers' emotional connection to their Scouting roots." To appeal to this feeling, Latcha used camping as the theme for the Detroit Area Council's 2007 report.

According to Mason Thomas, Southern Region Chief for the National Scoutreach program, "Without camping, Scouting as we know it would cease to exist." Each year, thousands of Scouts from the Detroit Area Council go camping; however, as not all can readily afford the financial expenditure of this experience, the Council awards many camp scholar-

ships to those in need. "Strategically," says the agency, "the report's theme ties in with ongoing efforts to keep the camping experience at the core."

The iconic Scout Field Tent serves as the enclosure, which also doubles as a sturdy mailer. The theme progresses naturally from an actual flashlight inside the report to the miniature sleeping bag that holds it all. Besides these extras, Latcha took care to make this report appealing enough that one would want to browse through it beside the fire, rather than discard it as another boring annual report fit only for kindling. "The design of the report incorporates a serif type, coloration and treated photography that combine to give it a vintage lithographic look," they say, "and the writing style uses story form to tell the Detroit Area Council's annual 'tales'—a selection of classic campfire stories at the close of the report."

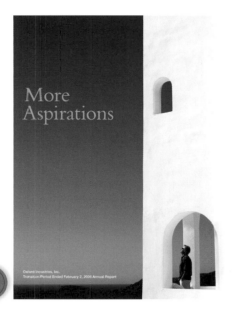

1

2

3

1 CREATIVE FIRM: Corporate Reports Inc. - Atlanta, GA CREATIVE TEAM: Brooke Fumbanks - President; Andy Lyons - Art Director; Drew Blakeney, Brandol Major - Computer Graphics; Don Chambers, Studio Chambers - Photographer CLIENT: Oxford Industries 2 CREATIVE FIRM: BCN Communications - Chicago, IL CREATIVE TEAM: Michael Neu - Creative Director; Michael O'Brien - Designer, Project Manager; James Schnepf - Photographer (portraits only); Ted Stoik - Writer CLIENT: General Motors Corporation 3 CREATIVE FIRM: BCN Communications - Chicago, IL CREATIVE TEAM: Michael Neu - Creative Director; Jim Pitroski - Designer, Project Manager; James Schnepf - Photographer CLIENT: PPL Corporation

1

A GOOD THING
More Mileage Through Teamwork

and another

COX
ENTERPRISES
2007 ANNUAL REPORT

One good thing leads to another   and another

2

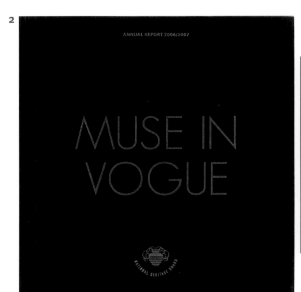

ANNUAL REPORT 2006/2007

MUSE IN
VOGUE

year in review

going
PLACES

*"The 10-year-old Singapore Art Museum (SAM) is home to some of
Southeast Asia's most impressive contemporary modern artworks, as well as
top-notch touring international exhibitions."*

Bringing the World to our Shores

3

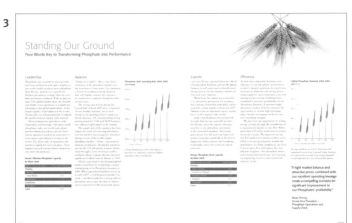

Standing Our Ground
Four Words Key to Transforming Phosphate into Performance

Mosaic   2007 ANNUAL REPORT

Groundbreaking Opportunity

---

1 CREATIVE FIRM: **Corporate Reports Inc. - Atlanta, GA** CREATIVE TEAM: **Brooke Fumbanks - President; Andy Lyons - Art Director; Drew Blakeney, Brandol Major - Computer Graphics; Eric Myer, John Madere - Photographers** CLIENT: **Cox Enterprises 2** CREATIVE FIRM: **Splash Productions Pte Ltd - Singapore** CREATIVE TEAM: **Norman Lai - Art Director; Terry Lee, Serene See - Copywriters; Joshua Tan - Photographer** CLIENT: **National Heritage Board 3** CREATIVE FIRM: **Corporate Reports Inc. - Atlanta, GA** CREATIVE TEAM: **Josh Dempsey - Executive Vice President; Andy Lyons, Erika Galloway, Ronda Davis - Art Directors; Brandol Major, Drew Blakeney - Computer Graphics** CLIENT: **The Mosaic Company**

1

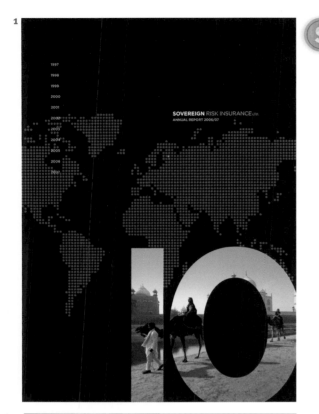

2

3

4

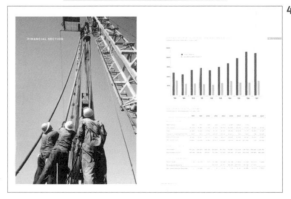

1 CREATIVE FIRM: Cosmic - St. Petersburg, FL CREATIVE TEAM: Sean Collier, David Scott - Designers CLIENT: Sovereign Risk Insurance 2 CREATIVE FIRM: MJE Marketing Services Inc. - San Diego, CA CREATIVE TEAM: Marlee Ehrenfeld - Creative Director; David Fielding - Art Director; Frank Rogozienski - Photographer; Diana Lucero - Project Manager; Nancy Mumford - Copywriter; Susan Smith - Editor CLIENT: San Diego County Regional Airport Authority 3 CREATIVE FIRM: Splash Productions Pte Ltd - Singapore CREATIVE TEAM: Kok Choon Ng - Art Director; Joshua Tan - Photographer; Serene See - Copywriter CLIENT: Eucon Holdings Limited 4 CREATIVE FIRM: Cosmic - St. Petersburg, FL CREATIVE TEAM: Sean Collier, David Scott - Designers CLIENT: Oil Casualty Insurance Limited

1

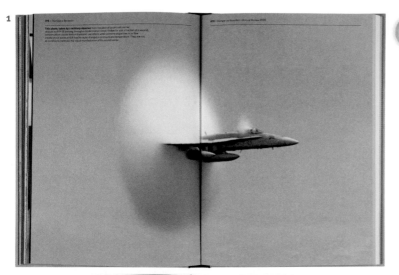

A CHEMICAL

CONVERSATION

logistics business

Each business unit has made significant progress over the last year in terms of building market leadership positions and achieving significant economies of scale.

MEMORIAL MEDICAL CENTER FOUNDATION
LONG BEACH MEMORIAL MEDICAL CENTER 2006-2007 ANNUAL REPORT
MILLER CHILDREN'S HOSPITAL

1 CREATIVE FIRM: **Dietwee design and communication - Utrecht, Netherlands** CREATIVE TEAM: **Tirso Francés - Art Director; Dirkjan Brummelman - Designer; Louise Hide, Charlie Errington - Copywriters of Aquarium Writers, London** CLIENT: **Bank Insinger de Beaufort NV 2** CREATIVE FIRM: **Credence Partnership Pte Ltd - Singapore** CREATIVE TEAM: **Wong Zhihong - Snr Designer; Francis Sim - Design Director** CLIENT: **CWT Limited 3** CREATIVE FIRM: **MedArt - Torrance, CA** CREATIVE TEAM: **Carol Beckerman - Med Art; Donna Reckseen - Memorial Medical Center Foundation; Michael Cunningham - Queen Beach Printers; Dann Froehlich - Dann Froehlich Design; Scott Windus - Scott Windus Photo** CLIENT: **Memorial Medical Center Foundation**

creativity 38 annual awards

_CONTENTS

1 CREATIVE FIRM: **Credence Partnership Pte Ltd - Singapore** CREATIVE TEAM: **Wong Zhihong - Snr Designer; Francis Sim - Design Director** CLIENT: **EnGro Corporation Limited** 2 CREATIVE FIRM: **Simon & Goetz Design GmbH & Co. KG - Frankfurt, Germany** CREATIVE TEAM: **Bernd Vollmöller - Creative Direction, Art Direction** CLIENT: **Sal. Oppenheim jr. & Cie.**

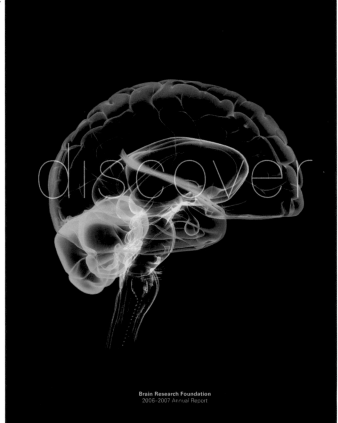

1 CREATIVE FIRM: **Liska + Associates - Chicago, IL** CREATIVE TEAM: **Vanessa Reu - Designer; Steve Liska - Creative Director, Photographer; Tom Maday - Photographer; Bonita Brodt - Writer** CLIENT: **Northwestern Memorial HealthCare** 2 CREATIVE FIRM: **Liska + Associates - Chicago, IL** CREATIVE TEAM: **Liz Johnson - Designer; Kim Fry - Creative Director; Tom Maday, Steve Liska - Photographers** CLIENT: **Brain Research Foundation**

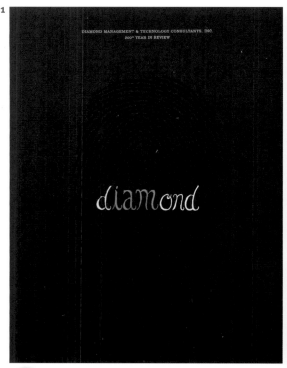

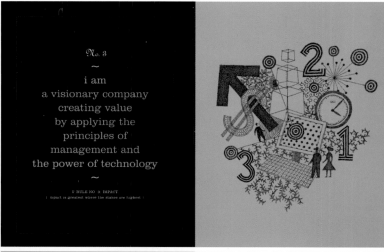

No. 3
~
i am
a visionary company
creating value
by applying the
principles of
management and
the power of technology
~
1 RULE NO. 3: IMPACT
[Impact is greatest where the stakes are highest]

No. 2
~
i am
a thriving business
delivering results
for clients
through the
execution of
innovative ideas
~
1 RULE NO. 2: INNOVATION
[Innovation is equal parts inspiration, preparation and application]

1 CREATIVE FIRM: **Paragraphs - Chicago, IL** CREATIVE TEAM: **Rachel Radtke, Cary Martin - Senior Vice Presidents; Meow Vatanatumrak - Senior Designer** CLIENT: **Diamond Management & Technology Consultants** 2 CREATIVE FIRM: **Mad Dog Graphx - Anchorage, AK** CREATIVE TEAM: **Kris Ryan-Clarke - Art Director** CLIENT: **Food Bank of Alaska**

1

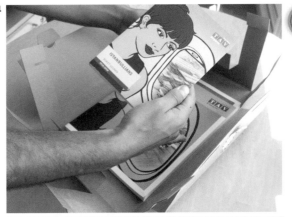

2

3

1 CREATIVE FIRM: **Finar Kurumsal - Istanbul, Turkey** CREATIVE TEAM: **Baki Kara - Creative Director; Tülay Demircan - Art Director; Mehmet Kutan - Copywriter** CLIENT: **TAV Airports** 2 CREATIVE FIRM: **Suka Design - New York, NY** CREATIVE TEAM: **Brian Wong - Creative Director; Lola Bernabe - Art Director; Bud Glick - Photographer** CLIENT: **Visiting Nurse Service of New York** 3 CREATIVE FIRM: **Caliber - Tucson, AZ** CREATIVE TEAM: **Rob Nicoletti - Art Director/Designer; Kerry Stratford - Creative Director; Kevin Anderson - Photographer** CLIENT: **Commerce Bank Of Arizona**

1

2

3

1 CREATIVE FIRM: **Suka Design - New York, NY** CREATIVE TEAM: **Brian Wong - Creative Director; Lola Bernabe - Art Director; Greg Kinch - Photographer (interior); David Prince - Photographer (cover)**
CLIENT: **Bessemer Trust** 2 CREATIVE FIRM: **Suka Design - New York, NY** CREATIVE TEAM: **Brian Wong - Creative Director; Maria Belfiore - Art Director** CLIENT: **Consumers Union, Consumer Reports**
3 CREATIVE FIRM: **Paragraphs - Chicago, IL** CREATIVE TEAM: **Rachel Radtke, Cary Martin - Senior Vice Presidents; Meow Vatanatumrak - Senior Designer** CLIENT: **Advanta**

1

h2Oo7

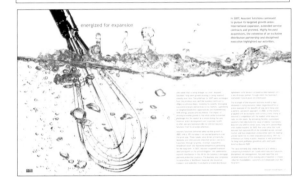

energized for expansion

picture of success

the perfect consumer experience
at every point of sale

winning execution

Coca-Cola FEMSA

2

selected financial data

Coca-Cola FEMSA's
presence in Latin America

9 countries serving more than
183 million people,
through more than
79 brands with a total of
1,190 SKUs

Total Revenues

our picture of success

3

Thriving

"I really do take
school seriously
because without
education I wouldn't
be anywhere."

Potential

Inner-City Scholarship Fund Annual Report 2007

4

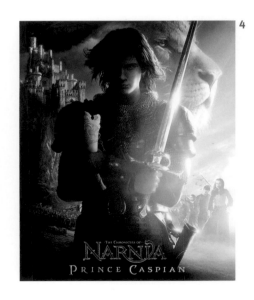

THE CHRONICLES OF
NARNIA
PRINCE CASPIAN

1 CREATIVE FIRM: **Paragraphs - Chicago, IL** CREATIVE TEAM: **Rachel Radtke, Cary Martin - Senior Vice Presidents; Carrie Ceresa - Senior Designer** CLIENT: **Assurant** 2 CREATIVE FIRM: **SIGNI - Mexico** CREATIVE TEAM: **Rene Galindo - Art Director; Odette Edwards - Designer** CLIENT: **Coca-Cola FEMSA** 3 CREATIVE FIRM: **Suka Design - New York, NY** CREATIVE TEAM: **Brian Wong - Creative Director; Matthew Carl - Designer; Bud Glick - Photographer** CLIENT: **Inner-City Scholarship Fund** 4 CREATIVE FIRM: **The Walt Disney Company - Burbank, CA** CREATIVE TEAM: **Steven Clark - Vice President, Disney Corporate Communications; Anne Taylor - Director, Disney Corporate Communications Resource** CLIENT: **The Walt Disney Company**

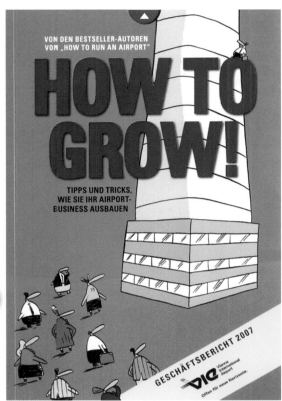

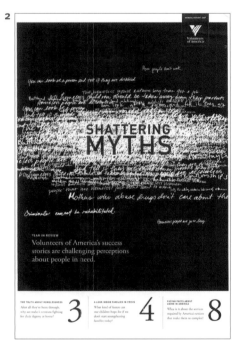

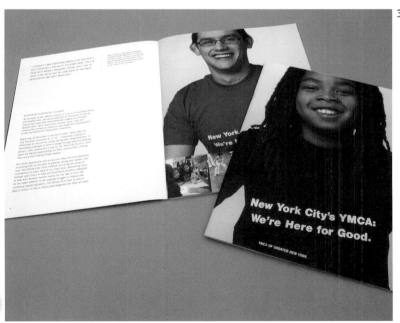

1 CREATIVE FIRM: Rosebud Inc. - Vienna, Austria CREATIVE TEAM: Ralf Herms - Creative Director, Art Director; Fritz Magistris - Creative Director; Lukas Müllner - Designer; Tom Krutt - Copywriter; Nikolaus Mahler - Illustrator CLIENT: Vienna International Airport 2 CREATIVE FIRM: Grafik Marketing Communications - Alexandria, VA CREATIVE TEAM: Hal Swetnum - VP of Creative Development; Melissa Wilets, Mila Arrisueno - Senior Designers; Ivan Hooker - Production Manager CLIENT: Volunteers of America 3 CREATIVE FIRM: Suka Design - New York, NY CREATIVE TEAM: Brian Wong - Creative Director; Jen Pressley-Thomas - Designer; Bud Glick - Photographer CLIENT: YMCA of Greater New York

1

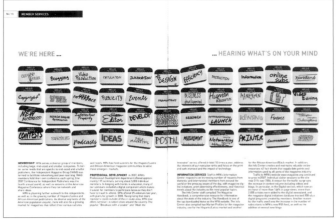

2

3

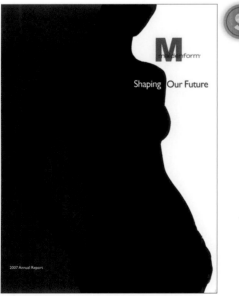

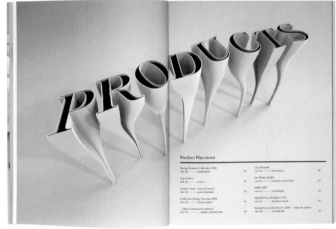

1 CREATIVE FIRM: **Rosebud Inc. - Vienna, Austria** CREATIVE TEAM: **Ralf Herms** - Creative Direction; **Sandra Berchthold** - Art Direction; **Bernd Preiml** - Photographer; **Tom Krutt** - Copywriter CLIENT: **Wien Energie GmbH** 2 CREATIVE FIRM: **Rosebud Inc. - Vienna, Austria** CREATIVE TEAM: **Ralf Herms** - Creative Director; **Raphael Drechsel** - Art Director; **Martin Stöbich, Michael Dürr** - Photographers; **Christoph Opperer** - Illustrator CLIENT: **departure wirtschaft, kunst und kultur gmbh** 3 CREATIVE FIRM: **Karacters Design Group DDB Canada - Vancouver, BC, Canada** CREATIVE TEAM: **Lisa Ma** - Designer; **James Bateman** - Creative Director; **Trish Beck** - Producer; **Marlowe Shearing** - Production Artist CLIENT: **Healthcare Benefit Trust**

1

2

1

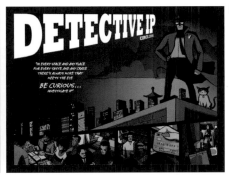

2

3

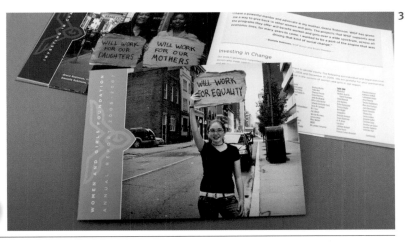

1 CREATIVE FIRM: **Sayles Graphic Design - Des Moines, IA** CREATIVE TEAM: **John Sayles, Bridget Drendel** CLIENT: **Mid-Iowa Health Foundation** 2 CREATIVE FIRM: **Epigram - Singapore** CREATIVE TEAM: **Caslyn Ong - Senior Designer; Nicholas Leong - Photographer; Andrew Tan (Drewscape) - Illustrator; Sharon Lam - Project Manager** CLIENT: **Intellectual Property Office of Singapore** 3 CREATIVE FIRM: **Fitting Group - Pittsburgh, PA** CREATIVE TEAM: **Travis Norris - Creative Director; Vanessa German - Photographer** CLIENT: **Women and Girls Foundation**

annual reports

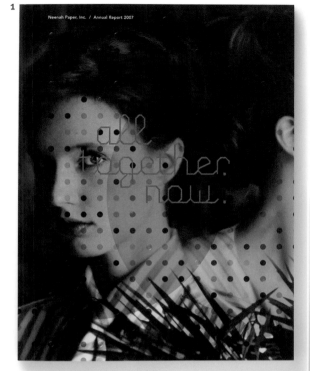

1 CREATIVE FIRM: **Addison - New York, NY** CREATIVE TEAM: **Richard Colbourne - Creative Director; Jason Miller - Art Director; Michelle Steg-Faranda - Account Director; Ioulex, Kyoko Hamada, Rick Burda, Burkhard Schittny, Nadav Kander - Photographers** CLIENT: **Neenah Paper, Inc.** 2 CREATIVE FIRM: **SIGNI - Mexico** CREATIVE TEAM: **Rene Galindo - Art Director; Odette Edwards - Designer** CLIENT: **GEO** 3 CREATIVE FIRM: **MediaConcepts Corporation - Assonet, MA** CREATIVE TEAM: **Greg Dobos - Creative Director, Designer** CLIENT: **Ocean Spray** URL: **www.mediaconceptscorp.corp.com**

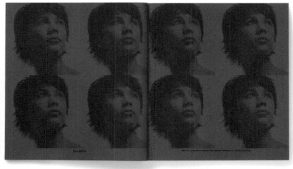

1 CREATIVE FIRM: **Ruder Finn Design - New York, NY** CREATIVE TEAM: **Lisa Gabbay - Creative Director; Salvatore Catania - Art Director; Kaven Lam - Designer** CLIENT: **New York Theatre Workshop**
2 CREATIVE FIRM: **Addison - New York, NY** CREATIVE TEAM: **David Kohler - Creative Director; Jason Miller - Art Director; Bryan Christie - Illustrator (Map); Ofer Wolberger - Photographer (Architecture); Jason Schmidt - Photographer (Portrait); Edward Keating - Photographer (Documentary)** CLIENT: **SL Green Realty Corp.** 3 CREATIVE FIRM: **Addison - New York, NY** CREATIVE TEAM: **Richard Colbourne - Creative Director; Christina Antonopoulos - Art Director; Renee Marmer - Account Director; Chris Jones - Photographer** CLIENT: **iStar Financial, Inc.**

1

2

Risk is an inherent part of business, it's unavoidable. But if you take the proper precautions, you can turn challenges into opportunities.

3

Our customers are central to everything we do.

ITT
Engineered for life

---

1 CREATIVE FIRM: **Addison - New York, NY** CREATIVE TEAM: **David Kohler - Creative Director; Rick Slusher - Art Director; Renee Marmer - Account Director; David Katzenstein - Photographer; Linda DeCosta - Writer** CLIENT: **AES Corporation** 2 CREATIVE FIRM: **Addison - New York, NY** CREATIVE TEAM: **Richard Colbourne - Creative Director; Aidan Giuttari - Art Director; Ginger Price - Account Director; Peter Young - Photographer** CLIENT: **Guardian Life Insurance Company of America** 3 CREATIVE FIRM: **Addison - New York, NY** CREATIVE TEAM: **Richard Colbourne - Creative Director; Jason Miller - Art Director; Ginger Price - Account Director; Carlos Serrao - Photographer (principal); Mark Peterson - Photographer (executives); Mike Hughes - Writer** CLIENT: **ITT Corporation**

1

2

"The real voyage of discovery consists not in seeking new landscapes, but in having new eyes."
— Marcel Proust

arcus
2007 Annual Report

3

MIGHTY

NATIONAL COUNCIL OF JEWISH WOMEN, LOS ANGELES SECTION
2006–2007 ANNUAL REPORT

4

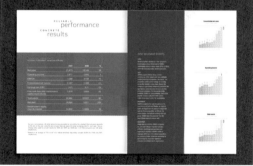

NCJ3

MISSION STATEMENT

The National Council of Jewish Women (NCJW), Inc., is a volunteer organization, inspired by Jewish values, that works through a program of research, education, advocacy, and community service to improve the quality of life for women, children, and families and strives to ensure individual rights and freedoms for all.

1

2

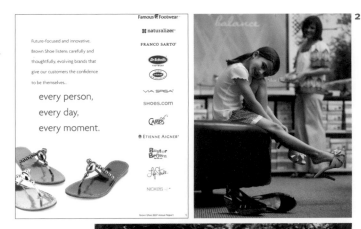

3

4

1 CREATIVE FIRM: RWI - New York, NY CREATIVE TEAM: Michael DeVoursney - Art Director; Lara Peso - Designer CLIENT: Research In Motion 2 CREATIVE FIRM: Kiku Obata & Company - St. Louis, MO CREATIVE TEAM: Joe Floresca - Designer; Carole Jerome - Writer CLIENT: Brown Shoe 3 CREATIVE FIRM: SIGNI - Mexico CREATIVE TEAM: Daniel Castelao - Art Director; Felipe Salas - Designer CLIENT: America Movil 4 CREATIVE FIRM: Object 9 - Baton Rouge, LA CREATIVE TEAM: Object 9 CLIENT: Baton Rouge Area Chamber

1

2

3

1 CREATIVE FIRM: **SIGNI - Mexico** CREATIVE TEAM: **Daniel Castelao - Art Director; Alicia Garcia - Designer** CLIENT: **Herdez** 2 CREATIVE FIRM: **Emerson Wajdowicz Studios Inc. - New York, NY** CREATIVE TEAM: **Lisa LaRochelle, Jurek Wajdowicz - Art Directors; Peter Biro, Gerald Martone, Melissa Winkler, David Guttenfelder - Photographers; Steven Manning - Editor** CLIENT: **International Rescue Committee** 3 CREATIVE FIRM: **SIGNI - Mexico** CREATIVE TEAM: **Rene Galindo - Art Director; Pablo Garcia - Designer** CLIENT: **Televisa**

34

CREATIVE FIRM: **Campbell-Ewald - Warren, MI**

CREATIVE TEAM: **Bill Ludwig - Vice Chairman, Chief Creative Officer; Duffy Patten - Writer; Bob Guisgand - Art Director; Kim Warmack - Print Production**

CLIENT: **Chevrolet**

1 CREATIVE FIRM: Futura DDB d.o.o. - Ljubljana, Slovenia CREATIVE TEAM: Zoran Gabrijan, Bostjan Napotnik - Creative Directors; Miha Grobler - Art Director; Saso Petek - Copywriter; Marko Omahen - Designer CLIENT: Perutnina Ptuj 2 CREATIVE FIRM: Keller Crescent Company - Evansville, IN CREATIVE TEAM: Randy Rohn - Executive Creative Director; Lee Bryant - Art Director; Nancy Kirkpatrick - Copywriter CLIENT: Hardin Memorial Hospital 3 CREATIVE FIRM: Keller Crescent Company - Evansville, IN CREATIVE TEAM: Randy Rohn - Executive Creative Director; Lee Bryant - Art Director; Nancy Kirkpatrick - Copywriter CLIENT: Hardin Memorial Hospital

1 CREATIVE FIRM: **Yellow Shoes Creative - Anaheim, CA** CREATIVE TEAM: **Scott Starkey - Art Director; Wes Clark - Copywriter; Greg Trombo - Illustrator; Marty Muller - Sr. VP Global Creative, Walt Disney Parks & Resort; Joe Schneider - VP Global Creative; Jacquelyn L. Moe - Director of Creative** CLIENT: **Disneyland Resort** 2 CREATIVE FIRM: **MultiCare Health Systems - Seattle, WA** CREATIVE TEAM: **Jenny Davidson - Project Manager; Julie Smith - Copywriter; Robin Pederson, Dean Driskell - Art Directors** CLIENT: **MultiCare Health Systems**

1

2

3

1 CREATIVE FIRM: **Yellow Shoes Creative** - Anaheim, CA CREATIVE TEAM: **Scott Starkey - Art Director; Wes Clark - Copywriter; Marty Muller - Sr. VP Global Creative, Walt Disney Parks & Resort; Joe Schneider - VP Global Creative; Jacquelyn L. Moe - Director of Creative** CLIENT: **Disneyland Resort** 2 CREATIVE FIRM: **DCC marketing d. o. o.** - Maribor, Slovenia CREATIVE TEAM: **Tine Lugaric - Copywriter; Matija Kocbek - Designer** CLIENT: **Kelly** 3 CREATIVE FIRM: **Yellow Shoes Creative** - Anaheim, CA CREATIVE TEAM: **Scott Starkey - Art Director; Wes Clark - Copywriter; Marty Muller - Sr. VP Global Creative, Walt Disney Parks & Resort; Joe Schneider - VP Global Creative; Jacquelyn L. Moe - Director of Creative** CLIENT: **Disneyland Resort**

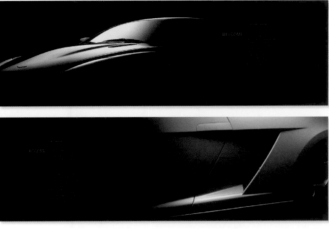

PLATINUM P

CREATIVE FIRM: **MiresBall - San Diego, CA**

CREATIVE TEAM: **Scott Mires - Creative Director; Dylan Jones - Designer; David Fried - Writer; Nick Nacca - Photographer; Kristi Jones - Project Manager; FreshForm Interactive - Developers**

CLIENT: **Vulcan Motor Club**

Vulcan Motor Club

Vulcan Motor Club, based in New York and New Jersey, offers its members access to some of the most luxurious, high-performance cars in the world. In early 2007, the company's founders came to MiresBall with a bold assignment: Create a brand that appeals to high-net-worth men.

Leveraging Vulcan's experience with other premium men's brands, the San Diego agency immediately focused on developing a brand that taps into men's desire for style, design and demand for utility and performance. Building on the company's key differentiator—concierge-style service—MiresBall positioned Vulcan Motor Club as the ultimate luxury car experience. Applied across flagship materials including a corporate Web site, product literature and print advertising, the new brand is stylish and substantive while maintaining a consistent ubiquity in the minds of its member enthusiasts.

"From a creative standpoint, we used design and messaging as a powerful one-two punch," says MiresBall. "The Vulcan iden-

tity conjures up the prestige and mystique of a classic car emblem, and a seductive photography style"—rich black backgrounds with a flash of platinum or gold as an automobile flies by—"shows just enough car to engage the imagination." To this luxurious image, MiresBall added an evocative narrative highlighting the facts and figures behind each car and the practical advantages of club membership.

1

Plein
Air
Past and
Present

Preston

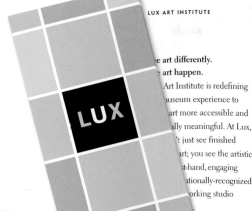

LUX ART INSTITUTE

...e art differently.
...e art happen.

...Art Institute is redefining
...useum experience to
...art more accessible and
...lly meaningful. At Lux,
...'t just see finished
...art; you see the artistic
...st-hand, engaging
...ationally-recognized
...orking studio

Welcome!

Lux
MEMBER BENEFITS

07/08
SEASON
RESIDENT ARTISTS

Tomás Rivas
IN STUDIO
NOVEMBER 1, 2007
through NOVEMBER 29, 2007
ON EXHIBIT
NOVEMBER 11, 2007
through JANUARY 16, 2008

Astrid Preston

LUX

2

3

CND e
ENHANCEMENTS
Retention+
Starter Pack

CND e
ENHANCEMENTS
Moxie
Starter Pack

CND e
ENHANCEMENTS
Radical SolarNail
Starter Pack

MANY CHOICES.
ONE LOCATION.

REAL KNOWLEDGE.

INNOVATION.
EDUCATION. INSPIRATION.

1 CREATIVE FIRM: MiresBall - San Diego, CA CREATIVE TEAM: John Ball - Creative Director; Jason Moll, Gale Spitzley, Beth Folkerth, Dylan Jones - Designers; David Fried - Writer CLIENT: Lux Art Institute
2 CREATIVE FIRM: KAA Design Group, Inc. - Brand Experience Studio - Los Angeles, CA CREATIVE TEAM: Melanie Robinson - Creative Director; Annette Lee, Alicia Nagel - Designers; Louis-Philippe
Carretta - Production Manager CLIENT: HOM Escape in Style 3 CREATIVE FIRM: MiresBall - San Diego, CA CREATIVE TEAM: John Ball - Creative Director; Jenny Goddard, Leslie Quinn, Ashley Kerns -
Designers; David Fried - Writer; Sarah Silver - Photographer CLIENT: CND

1

2

3

1 CREATIVE FIRM: **Stephen Longo Design Associates - West Orange, NJ** CREATIVE TEAM: **Stephen Longo - Art Director, Designer; Harvey Hirsch - Art Director, Copywriter** CLIENT: **The Art Directors Club of New Jersey** 2 CREATIVE FIRM: **Velocity Design Works - Winnipeg, MB, Canada** CREATIVE TEAM: **Lasha Orzechowski - Art Director; Velocity Team - Design** CLIENT: **Great Morning Eggs/Evergreen Poultry Farms** 3 CREATIVE FIRM: **STUDIO INTERNATIONAL - Zagreb, Croatia** CREATIVE TEAM: **Boris Ljubicic - Designer** CLIENT: **Croatian Tourist Board**

1

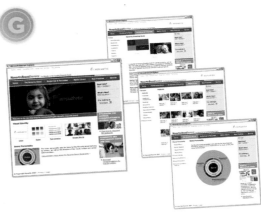

2

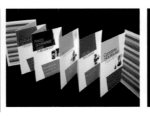

3

1 CREATIVE FIRM: **RUDER FINN DESIGN - New York, NY** CREATIVE TEAM: Lisa Gabbay - Creative Director; Diana Yeo - Art Director CLIENT: **Novartis** 2 CREATIVE TEAM: Yu-Fen Lin - Rego Park, NY 3 CREATIVE FIRM: **Scanad - Odense C, Denmark** CREATIVE TEAM: Henry Rasmussen - Creative Director, Copywriter; Jan Maack - Art Director; Soren Hald - Photographer CLIENT: **Copenhagen Theatre Association**

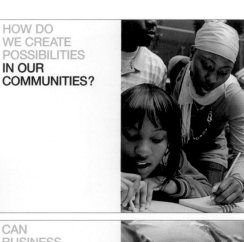

PLATINUM ℗

CREATIVE FIRM: **Cahan & Associates - San Francisco, CA**

CREATIVE TEAM: **Bill Cahan - Creative Director, Art Director; Sharrie Brooks - Art Director, Designer; Doug Adesko - Photographer; Thom Elkjer - Copywriter; Clare Rhinelander - Production Artist; Laura Bzdek - Account Director**

CLIENT: **Gap, Inc.**

Gap 2006 CSR

Clothing retailer The Gap recently has taken steps to address the issue of workers' rights, and their annual Social Responsibility reports seek to position them as leaders in "ethical sourcing"—ensuring that off-shore garment manufacturing is conducted responsibly for the people and environments involved.

"Gap wanted to convey that they, as a company, should go beyond the basics of ethical business practices and embrace their responsibility to people and the planet—that this would bring a sustained, collective value to their shareholders, their employees, their customers, and society," says San Francisco-based design and branding firm Cahan & Associates. "For its 2006 report, Gap wanted to go beyond disclosure of its practices and results to present its core challenge: How to balance a commitment to sustainability with market demands for low costs, high flexibility and fast turnarounds."

The tabloid-sized report's design expresses Gap's challenge in visual form—

balancing the fashion images of the company's other communications with stark black-and-white portraits of workers and factories. Posing questions such as, "Can business and human rights go hand in hand?" and "Why should companies invite customers to participate in their social responsibility efforts?" Cahan invited answers from employees, customers and objective industry observers, then integrated thirty comprehensive charts into reporting some of the important statistics on the company's ongoing efforts to improve their practices.

In an extension of social responsibility, Cahan designed the report to be completely renewable. "It's one hundred percent recycled post-consumer waste and manufactured with one hundred percent certified renewable, carbon neutral energy," they say.

1

THE WALL STREET JOURNAL BUSINESS SMARTKIT
A WAY TO HELP BUSINESS MINDS GROW.

THE BUSINESS MIND
CRAVES STIMULATION.
THE WALL STREET JOURNAL IN PRINT AND ONLINE.

The Wall Street Journal Business Smart Kit begins with the world's most authoritative coverage of business and global news. Employees receive both a print and online subscription to The Journal, encouraging them to broaden their business knowledge every day. It's a stimulating daily ritual that inevitably leads to better business decisions.

CULTIVATE SMART DAILY.

NOURISH THE MINDS OF YOUR EMPLOYEES TODAY.
Call 1-800-348-3555 or visit WSJSmartKit.com.

THE WALL STREET JOURNAL.
Business SmartKit

2

3

VALUE ADDED SERVICES

FIEGE FOR FASHION

---

1 CREATIVE FIRM: **Musto Kehoe/Struck - New York, NY** CREATIVE TEAM: **Mark Musto - Creative Director/Copywriter/Art Director; Kevin Kehoe - Creative Director/Art Director/Copywriter; Steve Driggs - Creative Director; Peder Singleton - Design Director; David Habben - Illustrator; Tatyana Ayrapetova - Account Manager** CLIENT: **The Wall Street Journal** 2 CREATIVE FIRM: **Levine & Associates - Washington, D.C.** CREATIVE TEAM: **Scott Miller - Designer; John Vance - Art Director** CLIENT: **American Chemical Society** 3 CREATIVE FIRM: **RTS Rieger Team Werbeagentur GmbH - Düsseldorf, Germany** CREATIVE TEAM: **Yvonne Wicht - Account Manager; Daniela Schäfer - Art Director; Luisa Lueg - Junior Art Director; Stefan Linder, Francisco Navarro Gomes - Copywriters** CLIENT: **Fiege Holding Stiftung & Co. KG**

1

2

Investing in
Digital Media

Velocity Interactive Group, L.P.

The New Era of
Media + Communications

DIGITAL
MEDIA

05_Investment Process

The core of Velocity's Connected Investing strategy is to develop or find exceptional **market opportunities** to pair with **accomplished executives**, who can devise and execute **winning strategies**. Velocity's task is to assist entrepreneurs in an early or growth stage, and work closely with them to capitalize on market conditions and technology advancements. Velocity will invest in all levels of digital media—from content and applications to platforms and infrastructure.

Connected Investing Approach
Velocity's thorough understanding of the evolving digital media industry allows us to take a thesis approach to investing. We develop an investment thesis in a category we identify for growth opportunities. We identify the voids, opportunities, challenges and trends in these select categories. We then flush out core investment ideas and companies in the sector. We seek to either invest in an emerging company or create a company from scratch that we believe will have a significant breakthrough. We then continue to make potentially synergistic investments to support the thesis and companies we build. Velocity's Connected Investing process assures companies can independently succeed and still support each other's accelerated growth as part of a distinctive ecosystem. The results can be impressive.

Implementing this strategy requires key capabilities and skills including:
• A keen understanding of market dynamics and global trends
• The ability to generate high quality privileged deal flow
• Developing a sound criteria and discriminating decision-making process
• Providing meaningful operating and strategic assistance to management
• Developing strategic partnerships and exit scenarios for each portfolio company

20   21

1 CREATIVE FIRM: **Sasges Inc. - Calgary, AB, Canada** CREATIVE TEAM: **Rita Sasges - Creative Director / Designer; Jeremy Miller - Designer** CLIENT: **Enbridge** URL: **www.sasgesinc.com** 2 CREATIVE FIRM: **Gee + Chung Design - San Francisco, CA** CREATIVE TEAM: **Earl Gee - Creative Director, Art Director, Designer, Illustrator; Fani Chung - Designer; Geoffrey Nelson - Photographer** CLIENT: **Velocity Interactive Group**

1

AT THE INTERSECTION OF
YESTERDAY, TODAY AND
TOMORROW

3

2

1 CREATIVE FIRM: **Neoscape, Inc. - Boston, MA** CREATIVE TEAM: **Travis Blake - Senior Graphic Designer; Leila Mitchell - Art Director; Jason Fiske - Graphic Designer** CLIENT: **L&L Holding Company, LLC**
2 CREATIVE FIRM: **Skidmore - Royal Oak, MI** CREATIVE TEAM: **Pete Nothstein - Designer** CLIENT: **Walbridge** 3 CREATIVE FIRM: **MVP Marketing + Design - Minneapolis, MN** CREATIVE TEAM: **MVP Marketing + Design** CLIENT: **Cincinnatus**

1

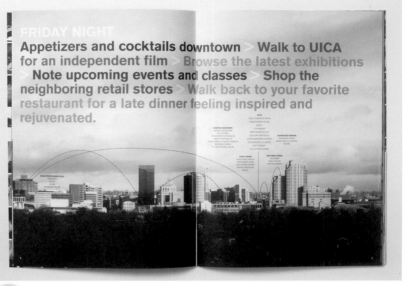

G

2

S

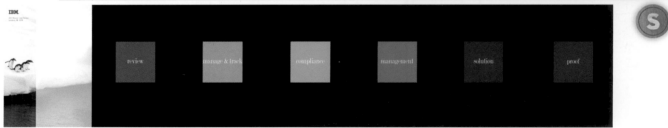

S

3

1 CREATIVE FIRM: **People Design Inc - Grand Rapids, MI** CREATIVE TEAM: **Michele Brautnick, Adam Rice - Designers; Yang Kim - Creative Director; Julie Ridl - Editor; Mitch Ranger - Photographer; Integra - Printer** CLIENT: **Urban Institute for Contemporary Arts** 2 CREATIVE FIRM: **IBM - Ponte Vedra Beach, FL** CREATIVE TEAM: **Thirza Duensing - Business Development Manager; Linda Soukop - Graphic Artist** CLIENT: **DAS** 3 CREATIVE FIRM: **Grafik Marketing Communications - Alexandria, VA** CREATIVE TEAM: **Mila Arrisueno - Senior Designer; Gregg Glaviano - Principal/Creative Director** CLIENT: **Susan Davis International/America Supports You**

1

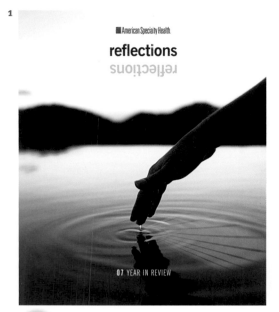

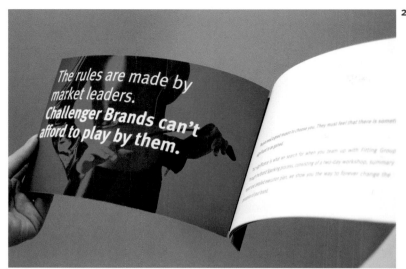

2

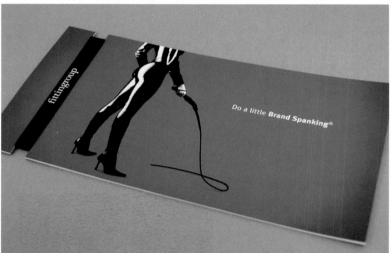

3

4

1 CREATIVE FIRM: **American Specialty Health - San Diego, CA** CREATIVE TEAM: **American Specialty Health** CLIENT: **clients, brokers & prospective clients.** 2 CREATIVE FIRM: **Fitting Group - Pittsburgh, PA** CREATIVE TEAM: **Travis Norris - Creative Director; Andrea Fitting - Copywriter** CLIENT: **Fitting Group** 3 CREATIVE FIRM: **Crawford Design - Chagrin Falls, OH** CREATIVE TEAM: **Crawford Design** CLIENT: **Sales Concepts, Inc.** 4 CREATIVE FIRM: **Paganucci Design, Inc. - New York, NY** CREATIVE TEAM: **Frank Paganucci** CLIENT: **AIG Investments**

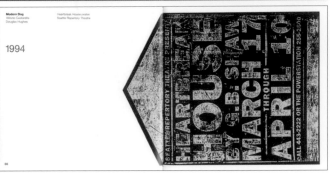

1993

VIRTUAL
TⱯⱯINE
METRIX
1 9 9 3
ANNUAL
REPORT

1998

1994

PLATINUM ⓟ

CREATIVE FIRM: **VSA Partners - Chicago, IL**

CREATIVE TEAM: **Dana Arnett - Creative Director; Michael Braley - Art Director; YanYan Zhang - Designer**

CLIENT: **Sappi Fine Paper**

The Best of AIGA

Sifting through seventy-five hundred pieces of graphic design can be daunting, as VSA Partners discovered when attempting to create a showcase of the best work from the AIGA Design Archives from the past three decades. Still, the show had to go on, as AIGA launched the book during the closing ceremony of the AIGA: Next conference, held at the collection's new home at the Denver Art Museum.

Choosing seventy-five pieces to represent the best of the best proved to be the hardest part: "The curation process was most challenging, as our selections had to be reviewed by [sponsor] Sappi and AIGA," the Chicago-based studio says, "and the incorporation of a range of media, not just print design, proved difficult."

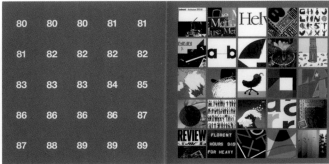

1

2

Step into the wave, don't fight it. The ultimate style.

LIMIT
NO LIMIT PROJECT
x-trail.net

X-TRAIL

www.nissan.co.jp

3

Home Equity
Line of Credit

Personal Banking
Irwin Union Bank

---

1 CREATIVE FIRM: **E-graphics communications** - Tokyo, Japan CREATIVE TEAM: **Tomohira Kodama** - Executive Creative Director; **Fuyuki Ogino** - Creative Director; **Yoshitaka Nonaka** - Art Director; **Masao Kumagami, Nobuhiro Yamaguchi** - Copywriters; **Keiichi Tuda** - Designer CLIENT: **Nissan Motor Company** 2 CREATIVE FIRM: **E-graphics communications** - Tokyo, Japan CREATIVE TEAM: **Tomohira Kodama** - Executive Creative Director; **Fuyuki Ogino** - Creative Director; **Yoshitaka Nonaka** - Art Director; **Hiroyuki Arai, Dan Kazaana** - Copywriters; **Junichi Sugawara** - Designer CLIENT: **Nissan Motor Company** 3 CREATIVE FIRM: **FACET Creative** - Los Angeles, CA CREATIVE TEAM: **Drew Fitzgerald** - Creative Director; **Jenifer Tracy** - Art Director CLIENT: **Irwin Union Bank**

1

All Aboard

"On the right track with Jack" was a catchy phrase that reflected many Americans' attitudes toward JFK during his 1960 Presidential campaign.

See Dick Run, See Dick Lose

Nixon's 1960 campaign used the expression "Keep Dick on the job," similar to Kennedy's "On the right track with Jack." On the other hand the outcomes of their campaigns were anything but similar. Jack won. Dick lost.

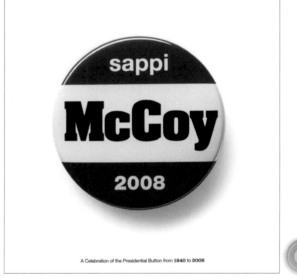

sappi
McCoy
2008

A Celebration of the Presidential Button from 1840 to 2008

2

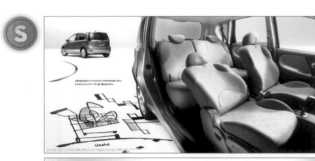

3

1 CREATIVE FIRM: **VSA Partners - Chicago, IL** CREATIVE TEAM: **Dana Arnett - Creative Director; Jason Kriegler - Art Director; Jonathan Turitz, Daniel Harmon - Writers; Mark Smalling - Photographer** CLIENT: **Sappi Fine Paper** 2 CREATIVE FIRM: **E-graphics communications - Tokyo, Japan** CREATIVE TEAM: **Tomohira Kodama - Executive Creative Director; Yasuhiko Yoshida - Creative Director; Reiko Tashiro - Copywriter; One or Eight Graphics - Design Production; Kouji Hirano - Illustrator** CLIENT: **Nissan Motor Company** 3 CREATIVE FIRM: **E-graphics communications - Tokyo, Japan** CREATIVE TEAM: **Tomohira Kodama - Executive Creative Director; Yasuyuki Nagato - Creative Director; Junichi Yokoyama - Art Director; Hiroyuki Arai - Copywriter; Naoya Miki - Designer** CLIENT: **Nissan Motor Company**

1

Opus: Environmental Responsibility

"It's not complicated. It's an overall trend. When specifying paper, my job is becoming less and less about the paper's press attributes and more and more about its environmental character."

It's a tough maze to navigate these days: preserving the integrity of your company's communications while being a responsible corporate citizen. Paper choice will always be a reflection of your company, your brand and your position on sustainability. As an environmentally responsible paper, Opus sheets feature 10% PCW content, FSC Chain of Custody and SFI Fiber Sourcing certifications and 100% of the electricity used to manufacture Opus sheets is Green-e certified renewable energy. Opus web features SFI Fiber Sourcing certification and can be manufactured with up to 30% PCW content, FSC Chain of Custody and Green-e certified renewable energy upon request.

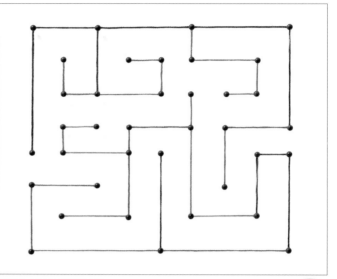

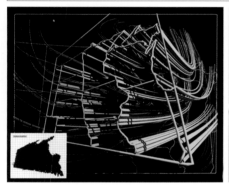

The time has come for one paper, indivisible, with quick turnaround, accurate color matching and environmental responsibility for all.

2

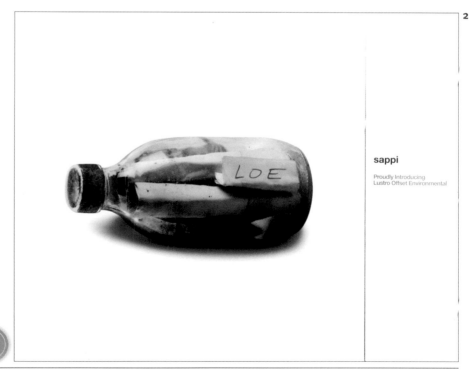

sappi

Proudly Introducing
Lustro Offset Environmental

1 CREATIVE FIRM: **VSA Partners - Chicago, IL** CREATIVE TEAM: **Dana Arnett - Creative Director; Jason McKean - Art Director; Jonathan Turitz - Writer; YanYan Zhang - Designer; Francois Robert - Photographer** CLIENT: **Sappi Fine Paper** 2 CREATIVE FIRM: **VSA Partners - Chicago, IL** CREATIVE TEAM: **Dana Arnett - Creative Director; Jason Kriegler - Art Director; Jonathan Turitz - Writer; Mark Smalling, Francois Robert - Photographers** CLIENT: **Sappi Fine Paper**

1

Magno

sappi

Tempo

sappi

Opus

sappi

LOE

sappi

Aero

sappi

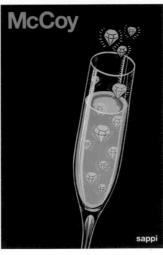

McCoy

sappi

When you want to be seen as a true leader, no other paper will make you look as good as **McCoy**. Infused with premium ingredients and backed by Sappi quality assurances, McCoy is the paper all others are judged by. Nothing else compares.

Gloss Silk Matte

2

Sappi Fine Paper North America

On-Product Environmental Label Guide

sappi

Stuck in the maze of sustainability?

To help you navigate through the confusion, we've created a simple chart that provides details on the environmental logos available for inclusion on your Sappi print projects. For further assistance please consult your Sappi sales representative, or call **800.882.4332.**

ECF

3

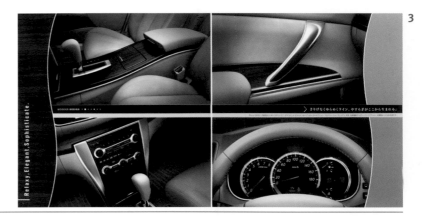

1 CREATIVE FIRM: **VSA Partners - Chicago, IL** CREATIVE TEAM: **Dana Arnett - Creative Director; Jason McKean - Art Director; YanYan Zhang - Designer; Nick Dewar - Illustrator** CLIENT: **Sappi Fine Paper**
2 CREATIVE FIRM: **VSA Partners - Chicago, IL** CREATIVE TEAM: **Dana Arnett - Creative Director; Jason McKean - Art Director; YanYan Zhang, John Foust - Designers** CLIENT: **Sappi Fine Paper** 3 CREATIVE
FIRM: **E-graphics communications - Tokyo, Japan** CREATIVE TEAM: **Tomohira Kodama - Executive Creative Director; Yasuhiko Yoshida - Creative Director; Yoshitaka Nonaka, Ryuji Ishimatsu - Art Directors; Hiroyuki Arai - Copywriter; Nobuko Murakami - Designer** CLIENT: **Nissan Motor Company**

1

2

1 CREATIVE FIRM: KNOCK inc. - Minneapolis, MN CREATIVE TEAM: Todd Paulson - Creative Director; KNOCK inc. - Art Direction/Design; Buck Holzmer, Jeff Johnson, Bob McNamara - Photographers; Jill Palmquist - Copy CLIENT: Children's Theatre Company 2 CREATIVE FIRM: Liska + Associates - Chicago, IL CREATIVE TEAM: Jenn Cash - Designer; Tanya Quick - Creative Director; Sarah Silver, Beth Galton - Photographers; Joi Rudd, Nichole Robertson - Copywriters CLIENT: Primavera

1

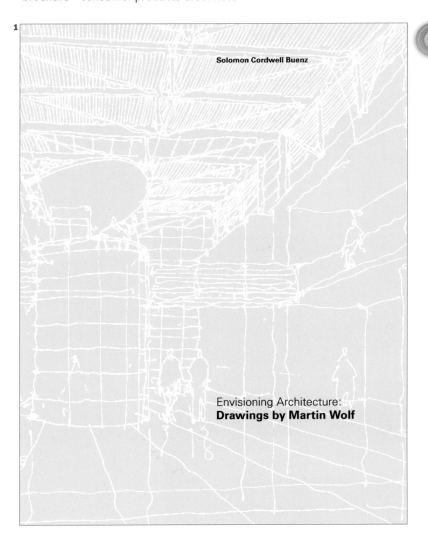

Solomon Cordwell Buenz

Envisioning Architecture:
Drawings by Martin Wolf

G

2

---

1 CREATIVE FIRM: **Liska + Associates - Chicago, IL** CREATIVE TEAM: **Laura Kesselring - Designer; Steve Liska - Creative Director; Martha Thorne - Writer** CLIENT: **Solomon Cordwell Buenz** **2** CREATIVE FIRM: **Davis Design Partners - Holland, OH** CREATIVE TEAM: **Matt Davis, Karen Davis - Designers; Joseph W. Darwal, Various Stock Agencies - Photographers** CLIENT: **University School (Ohio)**

1 CREATIVE FIRM: Hornall Anderson - Seattle, WA CREATIVE TEAM: Lisa Cerveny - Art Director; Julie Lock - Art Director; Lauren DiRusso, Andi Pihl - Designers; Vu Nguyen - Designer and Illustrator; Pamela Mason Davey - Copywriter CLIENT: Holland America 2 CREATIVE FIRM: Hornall Anderson - Seattle, WA CREATIVE TEAM: Kathy Saito, Jack Anderson - Art Directors; Yuri Schvets, Leo Raymundo, Andrew Well - Designers CLIENT: CitationShares 3 CREATIVE FIRM: Leibowitz Communications - New York, NY CREATIVE TEAM: Rick Bargmann - Creative Director; Dana Hager - Sr. Art Director/Designer CLIENT: Merrill Corporation

1

G

3

A PERFECT GATHERING PLACE.

S

2

---

1 CREATIVE FIRM: **Hornall Anderson - Seattle, WA** CREATIVE TEAM: **Michael Connors - Art Director; Jana Nishi, Chang Ling Wu, Jeff Wolff - Designers; Nancy Levine - Photographer** CLIENT: **Rainier Investment Management** 2 CREATIVE FIRM: **Franke+Fiorella - Minneapolis, MN** CREATIVE TEAM: **Craig Franke - Creative Director; Leslie McDougall - Senior Graphic Designer** CLIENT: **MacPhail Center for Music** 3 CREATIVE FIRM: **Brown-Forman - Louisville, KY** CREATIVE TEAM: **Nicole Walton - Senior Designer; Rob Thomas - Copywriter and Editor** CLIENT: **Jack Daniel Distillery**

PLATINUM Ⓟ

CREATIVE FIRM: **Yu-Shan Su - Taipei City, Taiwan**
CREATIVE TEAM: **Yu-Shan Su - Freelance Graphic Designer**
CLIENT: **Yu-Shan Su**

Made in Taiwan

Designer Yu-Shan Su was made in Taiwan, and her choice of self-promotional medium reflects that—with a combination of familiar labelling and graphic whimsy. "I wanted to demonstrate my personal image," she says. "A business card is not just a piece of paper displaying contact information—it's a representation of your or your organization's personality."

To this end, Su designed cards explicitly suggesting labels, like those found inside an article of clothing. It was a decidedly inspired idea, right down to the embossed monkey motif on the cards. "Many people have asked me, 'What's in your head?' after seeing my design," she says of the monkey, which is also her nickname. "So I disassembled my head. It turned out there is a radar, which receives and interprets inspiration and then emits it." After discovering the radar, she had to figure out how to do justice to the data with an effective translation. "I had no prior experience about label-making and didn't know where to have it produced," she says.

"The challenge was to understand which type of label would suit my purpose best and, of course, to find the right supplier—a time-consuming process."

The cards-cum-tags, which would be at home tucked inside a shirt collar, have layers of meaning as thick as Su's creativity itself. "The M indicates 'monkey,' not the size,' she says with a smile. And the "Made in Taiwan" legend is more than just an indicator of "Monkey's" home. "These three flags all relate to me," she notes. "I was born in Taiwan, received my master's degree in the UK, and am married to a German!"

1

www.panoramastock.com

Tiffany Wong 黃宇冬
Accounting Officer

PANORAMA
STOCK

27/F Catic Plaza
8 Causeway Road
Causeway Bay Hong Kong
D (852) 3187 7298
T (852) 2882 5286
F (852) 2882 5206
M (852) 6220 8732
tiffany@panoramastock.com

2

3

1 CREATIVE FIRM: **Blow - Hong Kong** CREATIVE TEAM: **Ken Lo - Creative Director, Designer** CLIENT: **Panorama Stock** 2 CREATIVE FIRM: **Robert Meyers Design - Pittsburgh, PA** CREATIVE TEAM: **Robert Meyers Design** CLIENT: **Robert Meyers Design** 3 CREATIVE FIRM: **Finished Art, Inc. - Atlanta, GA** CREATIVE TEAM: **Barbara Dorn, Luis Fernandez, Mary Jane Hasek, Kevin Ingalls, Cory Langner, Sutti Sahunalu - Designer/Illustrators** CLIENT: **Finished Art, Inc.**

1

Tim Langenberg
Creative Director

Devon Energy Corporation
20 North Broadway
Oklahoma City, OK 73102-8260

405 228 8727 Direct
405 248 7833 Mobile
405 552 7818 Fax
tim.langenberg@dvn.com

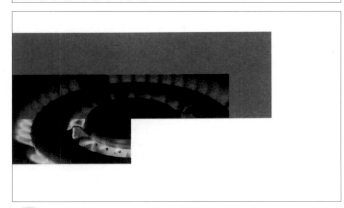

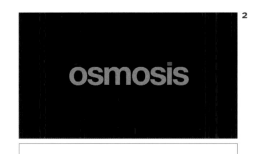

2

Shawn Thomson President

333 Hudson Street 10th Floor New York NY 10013
t 212 279 2680 x21 | f 212 279 2461
shawn@osmosis.net | osmosis.net

3

NEW SPACE FOR WOMEN'S HEALTH

CREATING A CENTER FOR
BIRTH AND WELLNESS

44° Lexington Avenue
19th Floor
New York, NY 10017

212.867.9646
www.newspacenyc.org

A PROJECT OF
FRIENDS OF THE BIRTH CENTER

I'm standing up
for women in
New York City. I'm
calling for change—
for you, for me,
for our daughters.
I'm standing in
the doorway of
the **NEW SPACE**.

Rebecca Hankin Benghiat
EXECUTIVE DIRECTOR

TALK BACK
becca@newspacenyc.org

Leadership: it's an
opportunity to shape
the future. It's a
chance to build a
NEW SPACE for
women and change
the landscape of New
York City. Leadership
is my privilege.

Alexandra Lally Peters
PRESIDENT, BOARD OF DIRECTORS

TALK BACK
alexandra@newspacenyc.org

Imagine the
NEW SPACE...Safe.
Healthy. Inclusive.
Sustainable. A new
paradigm in health
care for women and
families. We say it's
time for a change.

The New Space
for Women's Health

TALK BACK
info@newspacenyc.org

1 CREATIVE FIRM: Landor Associates - Cincinnati, OH CREATIVE TEAM: Christopher Lehmann - Creative Director; Ken Frederick - Designer CLIENT: Devon Energy 2 CREATIVE FIRM: Osmosis - New York, NY CREATIVE TEAM: Shawn Thomson - President; Simone Davidson - Art Director/Designer CLIENT: Osmosis 3 CREATIVE FIRM: Leibowitz Communications - New York, NY CREATIVE TEAM: Rick Bargmann - Creative Director; Courtney Dolloff - Sr. Art Director/Designer CLIENT: New Space for Women's Health

PLATINUM Ⓟ

CREATIVE FIRM: **Julia Tam Design - Palos Verdes Estates, CA**
CREATIVE TEAM: **Julia Tam - Designer**
CLIENT: **Julia Tam Design**

Year of mouse card

According to Chinese astrology, people born in the Year of the Rat (or Mouse) are creative and cheerful, so it only follows that Julia Tam of California's Julia Tam Design embraced her inner mouse when designing her annual zodiac card, completing the cycle of twelve collectible designs she's created over the past dozen years.

"Instead of a regular Chinese card, I made it a fusion of western and Chinese design," she says, citing "bold and colorful colors to be more visible and attractive and whimsical," including mice on the inside hiding behind a large piece of cheese on the front. "Instead of one mouse, I put in lots of mice—not only in different positions but different poses, so it's not redundant," she says, adding that the multiple mice "symbolize abundance and prosperity. The cute little white mice [are] lovable instead of [the image of] ugly, fearful, unlikable rats."

The small-is-beautiful theme extends to the card's size itself. "It's a small enough card that is easy and cheaper to mail," she says. "Plus, the probability of people displaying it on table or counter is high because of the size of the card. It's easy to handle and play with." Designed with interactivity in mind, Tam used diecuts and different folding techniques to create a multilevel look. "The interlocking closure," she says, "encourages interactive participation of the reader." Creative and cheerful, indeed.

PLATINUM P

CREATIVE FIRM: **Zuan Club - Tokyo, Japan**

CREATIVE TEAM: **Akihiko Tsukamoto - Design, Art Direction; Nobuko Kubota, Hiroshi Nagano - Creative Direction; Takao Nakamura - Photography; Kyoko Dan - Japanese Calligraphy**

CLIENT: **Riso Kagaku Corporation**

Wedding Invitation "Celebride"

Designing an elegant and unique wedding invitation became a marriage of East and West for Tokyo-based design firm Zuan Club. "[Our directions were] Japanese traditional beauty and the beauty of the Western world," they say of the Celebride line, the name of which plays upon the words celebration and bride. "The design [included] a balanced combination of Japan and the Western world and three themes: classical feeling, natural feeling and stylishness." On top of that, the designer permutated these three ideas into twelve different cards, all varied in paper quality and shape. "It's the biggest challenge to express the feature across twelve kinds of invitations," Zuan Club's designer reports. "I intended the simple design to convey beauty, gorgeousness, dignity, warmness, handmade and so on."

Still, despite Western influences, the aesthetic is definitely Japanese. "There are plum blossoms and the crane as traditional Japanese illustrations, kotobuki [congratulations], gold and silver color mizuhiki [paper cords] and the rose flower as the symbol of happiness... I selected the colors 'genuine and pure white' and 'delightful red' to express happiness."

The pleasure of the paper isn't limited to the bride and groom, either. "I [hope] this invitation will give joy and surprise to the recipient," the designer says, "and I put my wishes for a happy future in the whole invitation."

PLATINUM **P**

CREATIVE FIRM: **Lights!, LLC - Fairfield, CT**

CREATIVE TEAM: **Rick Shaefer - Creative Director; Paul Zalon, Steve Josephson**

CLIENT: **Lights!, LLC; Traffic Works, Inc.**

"City Lights" Light-up souvenir cards

Greeting card veterans Rick Shaefer and Paul Zalon creators of the PopShots line of three-dimensional cards pioneered paper engineering for the masses, and wanted to take it to a new and illuminating level after thirty years in the business. The duo, operating as Lights! LLC, came up with a new City of Lights line that features cards that actually light up when opened. Shaefer and Zalon explain: With our partner [and Traffic Works Inc. president] Steve Josephson, whom we had known for years and who specializes in high-end premium and promotional gift products, we decided to distribute this on the wholesale level, starting with New York, Los Angeles and Las Vegas.

Fitting the essence of these three cities into a card proved to be a challenge. Anyone who has tried to pack this much wiring, fibers, LEDs and circuitry between two pieces of paper for large production can attest to the difficulty of getting such an item produced, they report, adding that the development and patent process took several months to perfect. Along

with the cards, however, Lights! also produces light-up journals and picture frames, which have become hits in retail outlets ranging from museum shops to cruise ships and amusement parks. And it doesn't stop there, say the partners: Many new concepts [are] still in the development stages, so stay tuned.

1 CREATIVE FIRM: **Futura DDB d.o.o. - Ljubljana, Slovenia** CREATIVE TEAM: **Zare Kerin - Creative Director; Matjaz Zorc, Blaz Topolinjak - Designers** CLIENT: **Marjan Simcic** 2 CREATIVE FIRM: **Pareto - Toronto, ON, Canada** CREATIVE TEAM: **Egon Springer - Creative Director; Lori Honeycombe - Art Director, Copywriter; Jane Theodore - Studio Manager; Andre Van Vugt - Photographer** CLIENT: **Pareto** 3 CREATIVE FIRM: **Valentine Group New York - New York, NY** CREATIVE TEAM: **Robert Valentine - Art Director; Michael Myers - Designer** CLIENT: **Sarah & Steven O'Neil**

1

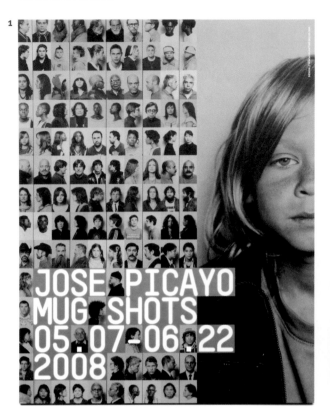

OPENING RECEPTION MAY 07 5:30 TO 8:30 PM
ROBIN RICE GALLERY | 325 W 11TH ST NYC 10014
212-366-6660 | WWW.ROBINRICEGALLERY.COM

JOSE PICAYO
MUG SHOTS
05.07-06.22
2008

ROBIN RICE GALLERY
FINE PHOTOGRAPHY

2

3

4

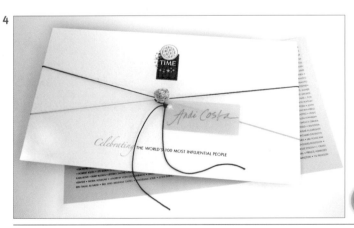

Celebrating THE WORLD'S 100 MOST INFLUENTIAL PEOPLE

1 CREATIVE FIRM: **Valentine Group New York - New York, NY** CREATIVE TEAM: **Robert Valentine - Art Director; Michael Myers - Designer** CLIENT: **Jose Picayo 2** CREATIVE FIRM: **Hornall Anderson - Seattle, WA** CREATIVE TEAM: **Mark Popich - Art Director; Hornall Anderson - Designers** CLIENT: **Hornall Anderson 3** CREATIVE FIRM: **MTV Networks - New York, NY** CREATIVE TEAM: **Aimee Heller - Copywriter; Nora Gaffney - Designer; Matt Lehman - Designer/Illustrator; Martha Rich - Illustrator; Jason Skinner - Creative Director/Art Director; James Hitchcock - Creative Director** CLIENT: **CMT
4** CREATIVE FIRM: **TIME - New York, NY** CREATIVE TEAM: **Andrea Costa - Art Director** CLIENT: **TIME**

creativity 38 annual awards

1

G

S

2
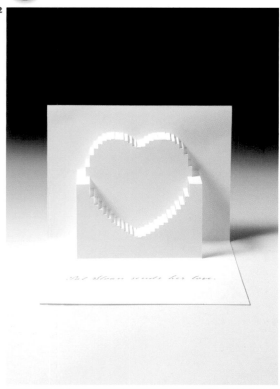

3

4

1 CREATIVE FIRM: **Hunter Public Relations - New York, NY** CREATIVE TEAM: **Louisa Caragan - Creative Director & Designer; David Cicirelli - Designer** CLIENT: **Diageo North America** 2 CREATIVE FIRM: **Pat Sloan Design - Fort Worth, TX** CREATIVE TEAM: **Pat Sloan Design** CLIENT: **Pat Sloan Design** 3 CREATIVE FIRM: **greenlight - Dallas, TX** CREATIVE TEAM: **Natalie Day - Graphic Designer; Erin Mason - Art Director; Olivia Cole - Account Services** CLIENT: **The MGHerring Group** 4 CREATIVE FIRM: **Design Nut - Kensington, MD** CREATIVE TEAM: **Brent Almond - Creative Director, Designer** CLIENT: **The Choral Arts Society of Washington**

1

S

Don Julio.
INVITES YOU TO KICK OFF SUMMER WITH
AN AFTERNOON OF TEQUILA COCKTAILS
& MUSIC AT THE BRAND NEW SURF LODGE
RESORT IN MONTAUK

SPECIAL ENTERTAINMENT BY DJ JAMES MURPHY (DFA/LCD SOUNDSYSTEM)

Saturday, June 3 2008
4:30 - 6:30 PM

THE SURF LODGE
183 EDGEMERE STREET
MONTAUK, LONG ISLAND, NY
Luxury coach transportation to/from Montauk is available, space is limited.

All guests must be 21 or older. This invite is non-transferable.
Kindly respond by Monday, June 2nd to TDJSurfLodge@hunterpr.com.

2

3

TEQUILA **DON JULIO**
MASTER DISTILLER
ENRIQUE DE COLSA
INVITES YOU TO AN INTIMATE PORTFOLIO TASTING
AND INNOVATIVE TEQUILA MIXOLOGY EXPERIENCE
WITH **DUGGAN MCDONNELL**

TUESDAY, JANUARY 29, 2008
6:30 - 9:00 PM
TEQUILA TASTING WILL BEGIN PROMPTLY AT 7 PM

NEW MUSEUM
SKY ROOM
235 BOWERY

SEATING IS LIMITED. KINDLY RESPOND BY FRIDAY, JANUARY 25TH TO
KAITLIN BITTING, KBITTING@HUNTERPR.COM OR 212-679-6600 EXT. 264.

MUST BE 21 YEARS OF AGE OR OLDER TO ATTEND.

TEQUILA **Don Julio.**

4

New location!

MELT DOWN 06
Saturday, September 16,

cockt...
di...

ShadyFide

MICHAEL E.
TAYLOR

Same great work!

S

EXCALIBUR
HOTEL · CASINO · LAS VEGAS

Mayoral Candidates Forum
Thursday, September 27, 2007

m
robert meyers design
communication
design and
planning

One Oxford Centre
301 Grant Street, Suite 825
Pittsburgh, Pennsylvania 15219

t 412 288 9933
f 412 288 9966
robertmeyersdesign.com

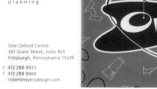
Orbit

1 CREATIVE FIRM: **Hunter Public Relations - New York, NY** CREATIVE TEAM: **Louisa Caragan - Creative Director & Designer; Laura Desilvio - Designer** CLIENT: **Diageo North America** 2 CREATIVE FIRM: **Choice Hotels International - Cambria Suites - Silver Spring, MD** CREATIVE TEAM: **Cathy Poinsett - Senior Director, Brand Management; Amanda Morgan - Director, Brand Management; Kourtnie Perry - Project Manager, Brand Management** CLIENT: **Cambria Suites** 3 CREATIVE FIRM: **Hunter Public Relations - New York, NY** CREATIVE TEAM: **Louisa Caragan - Creative Director & Designer** CLIENT: **Diageo North America** 4 CREATIVE FIRM: **Robert Meyers Design - Pittsburgh, PA** CREATIVE TEAM: **Robert Meyers Design** CLIENT: **Robert Meyers Design**

1 CREATIVE FIRM: **Splash Productions Pte Ltd - Singapore** CREATIVE TEAM: **Norman Lai - Art Director, Illustrator; Daphne Chan - Illustrator; Terry Lee - Copywriter** CLIENT: **Norman & Daphne**
2 CREATIVE FIRM: **greenlight - Dallas, TX** CREATIVE TEAM: **Erin Mason - Art Director; Natalie Day - Graphic Designer** CLIENT: **Galleria Dallas** 3 CREATIVE FIRM: **Levine & Associates - Washington, D.C.**
CREATIVE TEAM: **Greg Sitzmann - Designer** CLIENT: **Verizon Center**

PLATINUM P

CREATIVE FIRM: **Fayda - Istanbul, Turkey**
CREATIVE TEAM: **Ilyas Bassoy - Creative Director; Zeynep Kisacik, Mükremin Secim, Ozlem Ozdemir - Art Directors; Umit Alan - Copywriter; Blagoy Toprakidis - Photographer**
CLIENT: **Fikri Visual Arts Company**

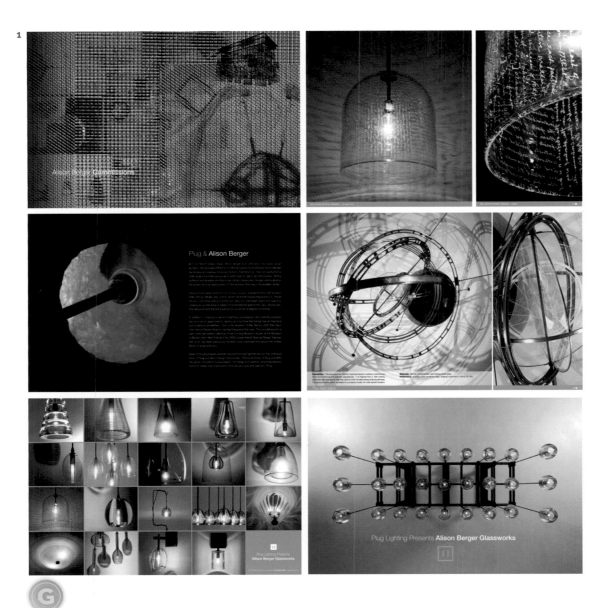

1 CREATIVE FIRM: Dustin W Design - Los Angeles, CA CREATIVE TEAM: Dustin Woehrmann - Creative Director, Concept; Lori Bush, Pia DeLeon - Clients - Plug Lighting; River Bohanna - Senior Designer; Derek Billings, Leslie Pollock - Project Management CLIENT: PLUG Lighting 2 CREATIVE FIRM: Besanopoli - Milan, Italy CREATIVE TEAM: Davide Besana - Creative Direction; Roberto Marino - Creative Direction and Art Director; Vincenzo Baratta - Graphic Design CLIENT: Baleri Italia

PLATINUM

COLE HAAN

CREATIVE FIRM: **Valentine Group New York - New York, NY**

CREATIVE TEAM: **Robert Valentine - Art Director**

CLIENT: **Cole Haan**

Two names, Cole Haan and Nike, may seem disparate: One is a designer of high-end leather goods ranging from dog carriers to shoes you wouldn't want in the same room as Fido; the other, a manufacturer of casual and athletic shoes found on every playground in America. But when it fell upon Valentine Group New York to elevate Cole Haan's image and express their quality, craftsmanship and Nike Air technology, the union fit like, well, a leather glove. "We included details into the catalog's design that would further convey quality," Valentine says. "The cover is embossed with a CH pattern. We interpreted the logo in stitch form to connote the craftsmanship and detail of their products." At the heart of it all, the photos evoke a sophistication with the secret knowledge of Nike's innovation at the soul—or sole—of it all.

1

2

3

1

2

1 CREATIVE FIRM: **Twice Graphics - Sheung Wan, Hong Kong** CREATIVE TEAM: **Steve Lau - Design Director** CLIENT: **Franck Muller** 2 CREATIVE FIRM: **Center for Digital Imaging Arts at Boston University - Waltham, MA** CREATIVE TEAM: **Liz Abbate Hyman - Creative Director; Charice Kalis - Graphic Designer** CLIENT: **(CDIA) Center for Digital Imaging Arts**

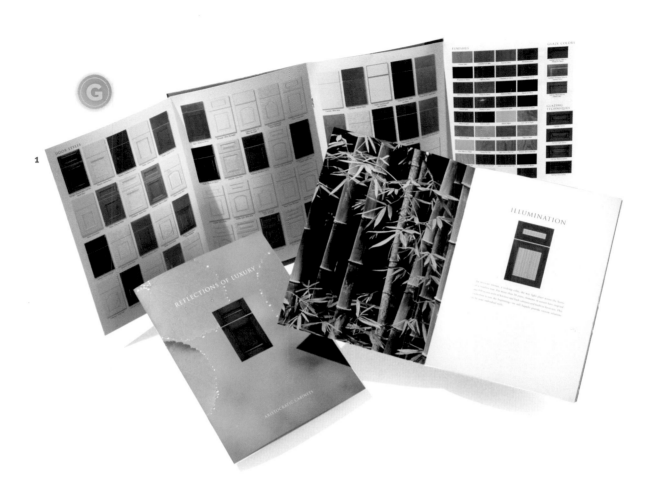

1 CREATIVE FIRM: **Phinney Bischoff Design House - Seattle, WA** CREATIVE TEAM: **Gina Tolentino - Designer; Alise Tarica - Production Manager; TJ Hatfield - Copywriter; Dean Hart - Creative Director** CLIENT: **Aristocratic Cabinets** 2 CREATIVE FIRM: **Zeeland Oy - Turku, Finland** CREATIVE TEAM: **Juuso Korpinen - Art Director; Mikko Vaija - Art Director/Production; Anna Korpi-Kyyny, Henri Alinen, Juuso Enala - Copywriters; Sari Lommerse - Editor** CLIENT: **Puustelli**

PLATINUM P

CREATIVE FIRM: **1919 Creative Studio - New York, NY**

CREATIVE TEAM: **Peter Klueger - Creative Direction,
Graphic Designer, Photographer; Nick Wollner - Copywriter**

CLIENT: **Sundance Reserve**

Sundance Preserve:
The nature of inspiration

Everyone knows *of* Sundance—the mere word conjures the image of the Wasatch Mountains and, of course, the Sundance Institute and Film Festival—but who really knows the *real* Sundance? New York's 1919 Creative Studio created a book to help people capture the truest possible image in their hearts. "We were engaged to refine the vision, mission and motivation for Sundance Preserve, the culmination of Robert Redford's thirty-five-year quest to make Sundance, Utah a self-sustaining retreat for artists, scientists and thoughtful citizens to share ideas and to inspire and implement meaningful change," the firm explains. "A better world starts here and is inspired by the more than five thousand acres of pristine American wilderness."

The primary objective 1919 had to meet, establishing the "place" called Sundance and its noble purpose, was not as simple as it sounded. "Sundance is so many things already but it is often not understood as a place, a retreat, a resort, a laboratory for creative explora-tion," they say. "Our deliverable was to be a complete identity... that could express the true spirit of Sundance and capture the imagination of donors and investors, the leaders of the various Sundance commercial enterprises and the existing Sundance community."

Wilderness and nature came together in the ensuing book and Web site, *A Place Set Apart*. "Sundance, Utah has a remarkable landscape and spirit which transforms and renews itself with each season," 1919 explains. The photography, as wide in scope and vision as the land itself—many of the panoramic photographs within were shot by 1919's creative director, Peter Klueger—is bound in classic picture-book style but oversized and printed on heavy paper stock. "The narrative focuses on Redford's passionate commitment to the combination of preservation, conservation and inspiration," the studio says. "The result is an experience that was nothing short of revelatory—even for those who thought they knew Sundance."

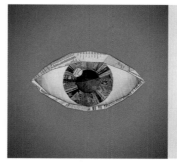

![PLATINUM P]

Wall Street Journal's Business SmartKit

CREATIVE FIRM: **Musto Kehoe - New York, NY**

CREATIVE TEAM: **Mark Musto - Creative Director/Copywriter/Art Director; Kevin Kehoe - Creative Director/Art Director/Copywriter; Steve Driggs - Creative Director; Peder Singleton - Design Director; David Habben - Illustrator; Tatyana Ayrapetova - Account Manager**

CLIENT: **The Wall Street Journal**

The Wall Street Journal's Business SmartKit is a comprehensive resource designed to elevate business thinking throughout an organization, and so New York design firm Musto Kehoe elevated their own creativity to reach a different kind of market—one with one eye on the economic market, the other on its own marketable future—with its brochure promoting the SmartKit's benefits.

"The Journal challenged us to create an organizing idea for the program that was big enough and flexible enough to live in a variety of media spaces, from print to digital to direct mail," says Musto Kehoe of the kit, which includes a variety of Journal resources aimed at collaboration and creative thinking among business stakeholders. Not only did they have to put this across in a promotional piece the space of sixteen sparse pages, they also had to capture the imagination of top executives who equate sophistication with a premium price—and are willing to pay for it.

Musto Kehoe created nine intricate collages made from actual Journal articles—simple, powerful iconic figures in the shape of a rocket, a coffeepot, even an insect (illustrating "buzz")—designed to convey the program's benefits on both the business and lifestyle fronts of the eminent newspaper. Beyond graphic elements, "The writing then had to live up to the intelligence and sophistication of the Journal's brand voice." This intelligence and sophistication, tempered with a touch of whimsy and wonder, is evident—on paper and beyond.

1

3

2

1 CREATIVE FIRM: **1919 Creative Studio - New York, NY** CREATIVE TEAM: Peter Klueger - Creative Direction, Graphic Designer, Photographer; Nick Wollner - Copywriter CLIENT: **Sundance Reserve**
2 CREATIVE FIRM: **Fitting Group - Pittsburgh, PA** CREATIVE TEAM: Travis Norris - Creative Director; Andrew Ellis - Designer; Alexander Denmarsh - Photographer CLIENT: **The College of William & Mary**
3 CREATIVE FIRM: **1919 Creative Studio - New York, NY** CREATIVE TEAM: Peter Klueger - Creative Direction, Graphic Designer, Photographer; Nick Wollner - Copywriter CLIENT: **Ritz– Carlton**

G

1

2

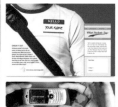

S

3

4

1 CREATIVE FIRM: **ERIC CAI DESIGN CO.** - Beijing, China CREATIVE TEAM: **Cai Shi Wei, Eric - Creative Director, Art Director; Tan Yan, Esther - Copywriter; Duan Lian - Designer** CLIENT: **WWF CHINA**
2 CREATIVE FIRM: **The College of Saint Rose** - Albany, NY CREATIVE TEAM: **Mark Hamilton - Art Director; Chris Parody - Graphic Designer; Lisa Haley Thomson - Copywriter** CLIENT: **The College of Saint Rose** 3 CREATIVE FIRM: **Design Objectives Pte Ltd** - Singapore CREATIVE TEAM: **Ronnie S. C. Tan - Creative Director** CLIENT: **Singapore Post Limited** 4 CREATIVE FIRM: **University of Akron/ design x nine** - Akron, OH CREATIVE TEAM: **Janice Troutman, John Morrison - Creative Directors; Dominic Caruso, Julia Hartman, Scott Rutan, Seth Trowbridge - Designers** CLIENT: **Sherry Simms and Sayumi Yokouchi**

PLATINUM P

CREATIVE FIRM: **Durso Design - Santa Monica, CA**

CREATIVE TEAM: **Rovane Durso - Chief Creative Officer; Susan Yu - Executive Creative Director; Eric Holman - Associate Creative Director**

CLIENT: **Wella Professionals**

Wella's Expressionism

Remember Wella Balsam? The haircare product, whose most famous face—and head of hair—was Farrah Fawcett, is still around, but with a whole new style. For Wella's 2008 spring collection, the company approached DursoDesign in Santa Monica in search of an eye-catching campaign that would inspire stylists and support salon owners in their business. "The creative brief brought to light a problem in the lack of collateral that clearly explained how trends in fashion and beauty come to life as services in the salon," the agency says. "Wella presented four trend looks of the season, challenging us to create a solution that would both complement and elevate the most important design element, the haircolor."

As with any print campaign, DursoDesign explored a variety of graphic and typographic treatments to define a unifying concept, but sought above all to inspire colorists with Wella's biannual Colors of the World program, to "introduce a link between fashion trends and services in the salon, promoting color in an easy and clear way to their client." The resulting campaign, dubbed Expressionism, "pays homage to the artistic passion of the stylists," the agency says about the use of dramatic photographs of daring colors and hairstyles, appointment cards and pigment mixing guides. As many of the photographs feature full-body shots, DursoDesign says, "Services in the salon now come to life maintaining relevance to current fashion and beauty trends."

1

2

3

4

1 CREATIVE FIRM: Graham Hanson Design LLC - New York, NY CREATIVE TEAM: Graham Hanson - Creative Director; Elizabeth Ward - Designer CLIENT: American Institute of Architects/NY
2 CREATIVE FIRM: green.ight - Dallas, TX CREATIVE TEAM: Erin Mason - Art Director CLIENT: Polished 3 CREATIVE FIRM: Sayles Graphic Design - Des Moines, IA CREATIVE TEAM: John Sayles, Bridget Drendel CLIENT: The Iowa Wine Festival 4 CREATIVE FIRM: Foodmix - Westmont, IL CREATIVE TEAM: Foodmix - Creative & Production Team CLIENT: Insight Beverages

80

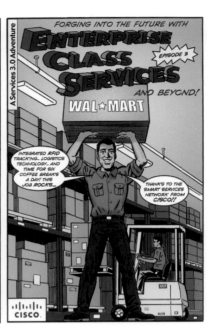

1 CREATIVE FIRM: Groove11 - San Rafael, CA CREATIVE TEAM: Pete McDonnell - Illustrator; Mike McGinty - Creative Director; Susan Clark - Producer; Rick Barsotti - Account Executive CLIENT: Cisco
2 CREATIVE FIRM: Karen Skunta & Company - Cleveland, OH CREATIVE TEAM: Karen Skunta - Creative Director; Jamie Finkelhor - Sr. Graphic Designer; Ellen Brown - Copywriter CLIENT: Whole Health Management Inc. 3 CREATIVE FIRM: Peterson Ray & Company - Dallas, TX CREATIVE TEAM: Dorit Suffness - Art Director, Designer, Illustrator; Jim Dale - Copywriter CLIENT: XTO Energy

CREATIVE FIRM: **Simon & Goetz Design GmbH & Co. KG -**
Frankfurt, Germany

CREATIVE TEAM: **Bernd Vollmöller - Creative Direction,**
Art Direction

CLIENT: **Sal. Oppenheim jr. & Cie.**

1

1 CREATIVE FIRM: **KNOCK inc. - Minneapolis, MN** CREATIVE TEAM: **Todd Paulson - Creative Director; Sara Nelson - Design Director; Zachary Richter - Designer, Illustrator; Nick Marshall, Creighton King - Photographers** CLIENT: **KNOCK inc.** 2 CREATIVE FIRM: **Don Schaaf & Friends, Inc. - Washington, D.C.** CREATIVE TEAM: **ds+f Creative Team** CLIENT: **Kennametal, Inc.**

1

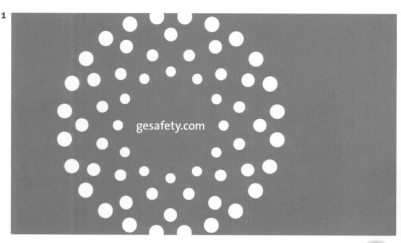

Guardian

EMERGENCY EYEWASH & SHOWER TECHNOLOGY

Carsten Birch
Vice President
cbirch@gesafety.com

Guardian Equipment
1140 N North Branch St
Chicago, IL 50642
312 447 8100 TELEPHONE
312 447 8101 FACSIMILE
312 543 5955 MOBILE

2

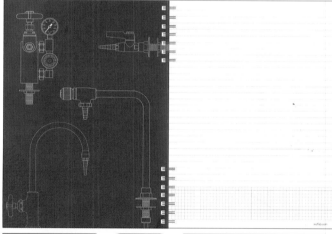

3

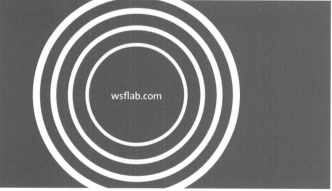

WaterSaver

INNOVATIVE PRODUCTS FOR RESEARCH

Steven A Kersten
President
skersten@wsflab.com

WaterSaver Faucet
701 W Erie St
Chicago, IL 60654
312 666 5500 TELEPHONE
312 666 5501 FACSIMILE

1 CREATIVE FIRM: **Paragraphs - Chicago, IL** CREATIVE TEAM: **Rachel Radtke - Senior Vice President; Carrie Ceresa - Senior Designer** CLIENT: **Guardian Eyewash & Shower Technology**
2 CREATIVE FIRM: **Primary Design, Inc. - Haverhill, MA** CREATIVE TEAM: **Allison Davis, Jules Epstein** CLIENT: **Abbott Development** 3 CREATIVE FIRM: **Paragraphs - Chicago, IL**
CREATIVE TEAM: **Rachel Radtke - Senior Vice President; Carrie Ceresa - Senior Designer** CLIENT: **WaterSaver Faucet**

1

Limelight Networks
2220 W. 14th Street, Tempe AZ, 85281

Limelight NETWORKS

2

³ LOVENIA

scrumptious DINING

1 CREATIVE FIRM: **Wirestone San Diego Office - San Diego, CA** CREATIVE TEAM: **Molly O'Shea - Creative Services Manager; Lee Scott - Designer** CLIENT: **Limelight Networks** 2 CREATIVE FIRM: **SKAGGS - New York, NY** CREATIVE TEAM: **Jonina Skaggs - Creative Director; Kim-Van Dang - Executive Brand Consultant; Joseph Guzman - Designer** CLIENT: **Scrumptious NYC** 3 CREATIVE FIRM: **SKAGGS - New York, NY** CREATIVE TEAM: **Jonina Skaggs - Creative Director; Samantha Edwards - Senior Designer; Joseph Guzman - Designer; Kim-Van Dang - Executive Brand Consultant** CLIENT: **Lovenia**

1

a Shadow

Identity Management

Beyond a Shadow of a Doubt℠

TRUSTED IDENTITIES: INTEGRATING TECHNOLOGY WITH POLICY AND PROCESS

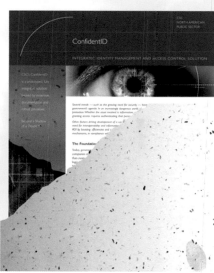

2

dulce
BY VISIONARI

1 CREATIVE FIRM: CSC's P2 Communications Services - Falls Church, VA CREATIVE TEAM: Terry Wilson - Creative Director; Mark Richards - Designer, Billboard and Brochure; Aaron Kobilis - Designer, Screensaver; Tom Hennessy - Account Manager; Jennifer Voltaggio - Art Director; Lalitha Sundaram - Copywriter CLIENT: CSC Corporate 2 CREATIVE FIRM: John Wingard Design - Honolulu, HI CREATIVE TEAM: John Wingard - Creative Director; Ted Saihara - Web/Flash Developer CLIENT: Visionari/Dulce

1

2

3

1 CREATIVE FIRM: **The Monogram Group - Chicago, IL** CREATIVE TEAM: **Harold Woodridge - Creative Director; Chip Balch - Art Director; Brett Hawthorne - Designer; Phil Schneider - Writer** CLIENT: **LiftFitness**
2 CREATIVE FIRM: **Neoscape, Inc. - Boston, MA** CREATIVE TEAM: **Travis Blake - Senior Graphic Designer; Leila Mitchell - Art Director** CLIENT: **The Blackstone Group** 3 CREATIVE FIRM: **Neoscape, Inc. - Boston, MA** CREATIVE TEAM: **Danne Dzenawagis - Graphic Designer; Leila Mitchell - Art Director** CLIENT: **The Blackstone Group**

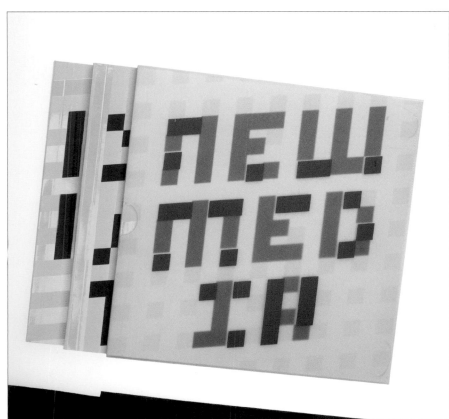

PLATINUM P

Bernstein & Andriulli Volume 16

CREATIVE FIRM: Bernstein & Andriulli - New York, NY

CREATIVE TEAM: Karlssonwilker - Designers; Pamela Esposito - Production Manager; Monika Maniecki - Production Assistant; Louisa St. Pierre - Art Consultant

CLIENT: Self Promotion

URL: www.ba-reps.com

For their sixteenth agency catalog, New York's Bernstein & Andriulli wanted something different, so they collaborated with KarlssonWilker—and in doing so focused on a more conceptual and interactive art piece than just a beautiful image.

Focusing on the agencies' versatility, KarlssonWilker chose to design a slipcase that, when interchanged with the three books, spells out the three main divisions of the client agency—Photography, Illustration and New Media—each featuring work from its respective division. "The brief was wide open, which allowed for the creative minds of KarlssonWilker to run wild, with few limitations," Bernstein & Andriulli says, "the only one being their trademark size and square shape."

And run wild KarlssonWilker did: "The playful design of the book requires immediate interaction as you take each book out and reveal the next message underneath," the client says. And, to complement this complex design, Karls-

sonWilker created a stop-motion, silent film-style video showcasing how the books "work."

1

2

3

4

1 CREATIVE FIRM: **Krug Creative - Asheville, NC** CREATIVE TEAM: **Emily Krug - Design, Copywriting; Brooke Thomas - Photography** CLIENT: **Krug Creative 2** CREATIVE FIRM: **Mauseth Design, LLC -
Hoboken, NJ** CREATIVE TEAM: **Ted Mauseth - Designer; Darren Farrell - Copywriter; Studio on Fire - Letterpress Printer** CLIENT: **Mauseth Design, LLC** URL: **www.mausethdesign.com 3** CREATIVE FIRM:
Rosebud Inc. - Vienna, Austria CREATIVE TEAM: **Ralf Herms - Creative Director, Art Director; Lukas Müllner - Designer; Bernd Preiml - Photographer** CLIENT: **Ute Ploier 4** CREATIVE FIRM: **19Blossom -
Singapore** CREATIVE TEAM: **Norman Leong, Shawn Yeo - Art Directors; Stan Wong - Photographer** CLIENT: **19Blossom**

1

There we are. Every morning. First in line for our daily fill of deadly diseases and debilitating conditions. Not that we're gluttons for punishment.

we wake up to a different blend

It's just that we've got a taste for a special brew of human drama and scientific achievement—a rich and potent blend that drives us in a way that caffeine will never be able to. It's not everyone's cup of tea, but we would never [have it any other way].

cancer

ckd ✓

dyslipidemia ✓

ed

diabetes type

never | generic

cdm

2

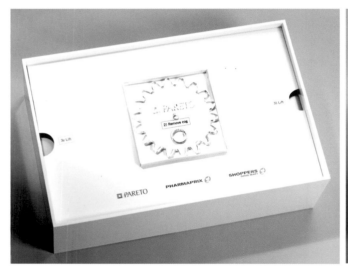

3

RED vs WHITE

F3ASTS

1 CREATIVE FIRM: Cline Davis and Mann LLC - New York, NY CREATIVE TEAM: Cline Davis and Mann LLC CLIENT: CDM 2 CREATIVE FIRM: Pareto - Toronto, ON, Canada CREATIVE TEAM: Egon Springer - Creative Director, Designer; Lori Honeycombe - Art Director; Jane Theodore - Studio Manager; Carrie Grand - Account Director CLIENT: Pareto 3 CREATIVE FIRM: Rule29 - Geneva, IL CREATIVE TEAM: Justin Ahrens - Art Director CLIENT: Self-Promotion

1

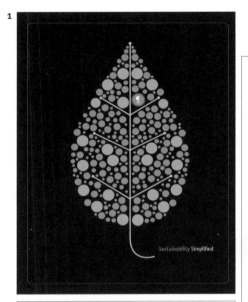

Peace is Disarming™

TAJIMAcreative

A New Kind
Did you know th
simply by donating r
helped to dismantle a w
Disarmament Fund: Then
from that weapon. We took so
We hope you'll wear it in peace.

For more information, visit tajimacrea

2

1 CREATIVE FIRM: **Paragraphs - Chicago, IL** CREATIVE TEAM: **Robin Zvonek - President; Rachel Radtke, Cary Martin - Senior Vice Presidents; Meow Vatanatumrak - Senior Designer** CLIENT: **Paragraphs**
2 CREATIVE FIRM: **Tajima Creative - Menlo Park, CA** CREATIVE TEAM: **Tajima Creative** CLIENT: **Tajima Creative** URL: **www.tajimacreative.com**

"¡Vaya grupo! inteligentes, creativos, inventivos, profesionales, detallistas, saben mantener la calma bajo presión y han sido ganadores de VARIOS reconocimientos... son muy divertidos."

Alfredo Fernandez, Director of Investor Relations
Coca-Cola FEMSA, Mexico City, Mexico

1 CREATIVE FIRM: 19Blossom - Singapore CREATIVE TEAM: Norman Leong, Shawn Yeo - Art Directors; Stan Wong - Photographer CLIENT: 19Blossom 2 CREATIVE FIRM: Paragraphs - Chicago, IL CREATIVE TEAM: Robin Zvonek - President; Rachel Radtke, Cary Martin - Senior Vice Presidents CLIENT: Paragraphs 3 CREATIVE FIRM: Sasges Inc. - Calgary, AB, Canada CREATIVE TEAM: Rita Sasges - Designer CLIENT: Nichole Sloan Photography URL: www.sasgesinc.com

1

2

1 CREATIVE FIRM: **People Design Inc** - Grand Rapids, MI CREATIVE TEAM: **Kevin Budelmann, Yang Kim** - Creative Directors; **Michele Brautnick** - Designer; **SVH/MPS** - Printer CLIENT: **People Design Inc**
2 CREATIVE FIRM: **School of Visual Arts** - New York, NY CREATIVE TEAM: **Genevieve Williams** - Creative Director CLIENT: **School of Visual Arts**

Wallace Church Thanksgiving Wine

CREATIVE FIRM: **Wallace Church, Inc. - New York, NY**

CREATIVE TEAM: **Stan Church - Creative Director; Bird Tubkam, Chung-Tao Tubkam - Designers; Akira Yasuda - Photographer**

CLIENT: **Wallace Church, Inc**

URL: **www.wallacechurch.com**

What kind of wine goes best with turkey? New York's Wallace Church makes sure any vintage is memorable with its annual wine bottle promotion for clients and friends. In its latest version, the label features a classic fork with a literal twist: One tine, bent to suggest a head and neck, turns the fork itself into a silver turkey figure. The "simple and elegant" design, says the branding agency, "suggests all things Thanksgiving: a turkey feast with a good wine."

While Wallace Church attempted to create something that no one had ever seen before, at the same time they stuck with a theme that fit within a series of design directions produced over the years with a black and white color scheme—including a silhouetted wishbone and pop-up turkey timer on the bottles themselves.

1

2

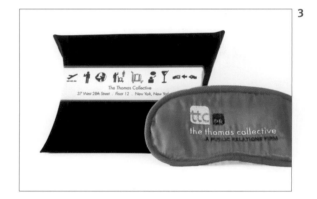

3

4

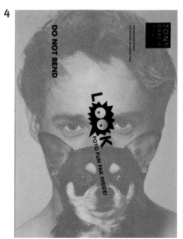

1 CREATIVE FIRM: **Valentine Group New York - New York, NY** CREATIVE TEAM: **Robert Valentine - Art Director; Michael Myers - Designer; Dianna Edwards - Copywriter** CLIENT: **Valentine Group New York**
2 CREATIVE FIRM: **School of Visual Arts - New York, NY** CREATIVE TEAM: **Michael Ian Kaye - Art Director** CLIENT: **School of Visual Arts** 3 CREATIVE FIRM: **The Thomas Collective - New York, NY** CREATIVE
TEAM: **Kimberly Howard - Art Director** CLIENT: **The Thomas Collective** 4 CREATIVE FIRM: **Konnect Design** CREATIVE TEAM: **Karen Knecht - Designer** CLIENT: **Tony Garcia Photography Inc.**

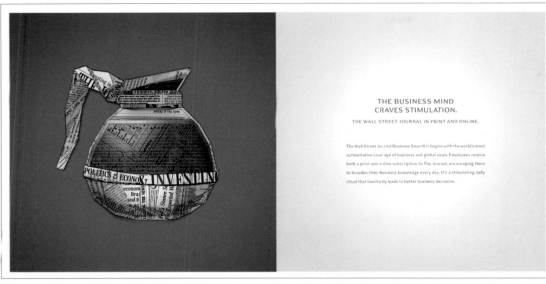

THE BUSINESS MIND
CRAVES STIMULATION.

THE WALL STREET JOURNAL IN PRINT AND ONLINE.

The Wall Street Journal Business SmartKit begins with the world's most authoritative coverage of business and global news. Employees receive both a print and online subscription to The Journal, encouraging them to broaden their business knowledge every day. It's a stimulating daily ritual that inevitably leads to better business decisions.

THE MISSION: BUSINESS MINDS
REACHING THEIR FULL POTENTIAL.

AN INTRODUCTION.

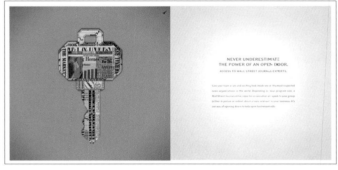

NEVER UNDERESTIMATE
THE POWER OF AN OPEN DOOR.

ACCESS TO WALL STREET JOURNAL EXPERTS.

PLATINUM P

CREATIVE FIRM: **Musto Kehoe** - New York, NY

CREATIVE TEAM: **Mark Musto, Kevin Kehoe** - Creative Director/ Copywriter/Art Directors; **Steve Driggs** - Creative Director; **Peder Singleton** - Design Director; **David Habben** - Illustrator; **Tatyana Ayrapetova** - Account Manager

CLIENT: **The Wall Street Journal**

Wall Street Journal Business SmartKit

The Wall Street Journal's Business SmartKit is a comprehensive resource designed to elevate business thinking throughout an organization, and so New York design firm Musto Kehoe elevated their own creativity to reach a different kind of market—one with one eye on the economic market, the other on its own marketable future—with its brochure promoting the SmartKit's benefits.

"The Journal challenged us to create an organizing idea for the program that was big enough and flexible enough to live in a variety of media spaces, from print to digital to direct mail," says Musto Kehoe of the kit, which includes a variety of Journal resources aimed at collaboration and creative thinking among business stakeholders. Not only did they have to put this across in a promotional piece the space of sixteen sparse pages, they also had to capture the imagination of top executives who equate sophistication with a premium price—and are willing to pay for it.

Musto Kehoe created nine intricate collages made from actual Journal articles—simple,

powerful iconic figures in the shape of a rocket, a coffeepot, even an insect (illustrating "buzz")—designed to convey the program's benefits on both the business and lifestyle fronts of the eminent newspaper. Beyond graphic elements, "The writing then had to live up to the intelligence and sophistication of the Journal's brand voice." This intelligence and sophistication, tempered with a touch of whimsy and wonder, is evident—on paper and beyond

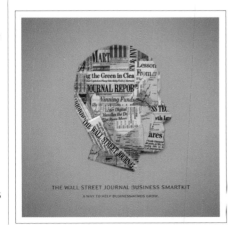

THE WALL STREET JOURNAL BUSINESS SMARTKIT

A WAY TO HELP BUSINESS MINDS GROW.

FOR A SAMPLE OF PERNOD ABSINTHE,
the creation inspired by the original absinthe
please contact Seine Kim at skim@ttc-pr.com

1

"When the member assambled the pieces he got this message."

Now also in slices. NEW!
li poli
Well done!
You've succeeded!
You've got a prize!

2

"This is what we sent to the members of Poli sausage club."

1 CREATIVE FIRM: **The Thomas Collective - New York, NY** CREATIVE TEAM: **Kimberly Howard, Seine Kim, Sara Bigelow, Amy Felmeister, Nancy Lee Russell** CLIENT: **Pernod** 2 CREATIVE FIRM: **Futura DDB d.o.o. - Ljubljana, Slovenia** CREATIVE TEAM: **Zoran Gabrijan, Bostjan Napotnik - Creative Directors; Miha Grobler - Art Director; Saso Petek - Copywriter; Marko Omahen - Designer** CLIENT: **Perutnina Ptuj**

1

2

1 CREATIVE FIRM: **KAA Design Group, Inc. - Brand Experience Studio - Los Angeles, CA** CREATIVE TEAM: **Melanie Robinson - Creative Director; Christina Cheng, Annette Lee, Alicia Nagel - Designer; Louis-Philippe Carretta - Production Manager** CLIENT: **KAA Design Group, Inc.** 2 CREATIVE FIRM: **G2 - New York, NY** CREATIVE TEAM: **Kurt Haiman - Founder** CLIENT: **Pantone**

1

MORE FIRE
MORE FORCE
MORE GRACE
MORE GRIT
MORE
soul

MORE GEOGRAPHIC

You know it when you see it. National Geographic images capture moments with unmistakable mastery, truth, feeling, power.
The world's best photographers can show you and move you like no one else. Rights managed and royalty-free available. **Expect more.**

NATIONALGEOGRAPHICSTOCK.COM

MORE GRIT
MORE AWE
MORE REAL
MORE CHILLS
MORE
guts

MORE GEOGRAPHIC

You know it when you see it. National Geographic images capture moments with unmistakable mastery, truth, feeling, power.
The world's best photographers can show you and move you like no one else. Rights managed and royalty-free available. **Expect more.**

NATIONALGEOGRAPHICSTOCK.COM

Only one National Geographic.
Only one source for it all.

For that unique quality that sets National Geographic photographs apart, come to the source:
www.nationalgeographicstock.com. No other site offers the entire breadth and depth of our
ever-expanding collection—more than 10 million stunning images. And no one knows each
photograph better than our experts, ready with free research help any time. Hundreds of thousands
of images are available in hi-res for immediate download, rights-managed and royalty-free.
So don't settle for a fraction of our shots—get the whole picture by coming here first.

NATIONAL
GEOGRAPHIC

NATIONALGEOGRAPHICSTOCK.COM

MORE WONDER
MORE TRUTH
MORE HEART
MORE POWER
MORE SOUL
MORE
heart

MORE GEOGRAPHIC

You know it when you see it. National Geographic images capture moments with unmistakable mastery, truth, feeling, power.
The world's best photographers can show you and move you like no one else. Rights managed and royalty-free available. **Expect more.**

NATIONALGEOGRAPHICSTOCK.COM

MORE SOUL
MORE REAL
MORE HEART
MORE THRILL
MORE
edge

MORE GEOGRAPHIC

You know it when you see it. National Geographic images capture moments with unmistakable mastery, truth, feeling, power.
The world's best photographers can show you and move you like no one else. Rights managed and royalty-free available. **Expect more.**

NATIONALGEOGRAPHICSTOCK.COM

2

The Facts

THE BLACK AND WHITE ON
NEW ENGLAND SCHOOL OF LAW
GRADUATES

NEW ENGLAND SCHOOL OF LAW
Career Services Office
(617) 422-7229
cso@admin.nesl.edu

Jeffrey
Escobar

Class of 2004
ASSOCIATE Mound Cotton Wollan &
Greengrass (NY)

POST-GRADUATE JUDICIAL CLERKSHIP
New York Supreme Court (Appellate Division)

CLERKSHIPS
United States Attorney's Office; Superfund Group
of the Office of Environmental Stewardship, U.S.
Environmental Protection Agency

Executive Managing Editor, *New England
Journal on Criminal and Civil Confinement*

You've seen the **black** and
white on New England School
of Law. Now, come check us out
in **full color.**

• Reserve an interview date – summer associate,
  associate attorney, part-time law clerk
• Schedule a resume collection
• Post a job for students or alumni

VISIT:
www.nesl.edu/cso/employerinfo.cfm

ON-CAMPUS INTERVIEW DATES:
September 2 – October 31
No cost to employers

WE'LL COLLECT STUDENT RESUMES FOR YOU.
On-campus interviews not a possibility?
We'll collect and forward students' resumes and
application materials by your deadline.

POST A JOB ONLINE.
Seeking a part-time law clerk or an experienced
attorney for a lateral hire? We can post your
job listing online. Current students and alumni
access our listings; employers manage their
postings at their convenience.

We welcome your recruitment questions and
look forward to your participation.

Thank you,

Mandie R. Araujo, Esq.
Director of Career Services
(617) 422-7229
cso@admin.nesl.edu

---

1 CREATIVE FIRM: Carol Cowie Design - Washington, D.C. CREATIVE TEAM: Carol Cowie - Designer; Susan Daugherty - Copywriter CLIENT: **National Geographic Stock 2 CREATIVE FIRM: kor group - Boston, MA CREATIVE TEAM: Justin Gonyea - Designer; MB Jarosik - Partner** CLIENT: **New England School of Law**

PLATINUM P

CREATIVE FIRM: Hornall Anderson - Seattle, WA
CREATIVE TEAM: Larry Anderson, Lisa Cerveny - Art Directors; Andrew Well, Jay Hilburn, Holly Craven - Designer
CLIENT: Cafe Yumm!

Cafe Yumm! Retail Graphics

World cuisines, even in a casual setting, taste even better when the restaurant itself is created from environmentally sustainable materials. Eugene, Oregon's Café Yumm! is a "fast casual" restaurant featuring "Mediterasian" style and its signature Yumm! sauce. "It's a unique sauce that's typically served with beans and rice to create a Yumm! bowl," explains Hornall Anderson, the Seattle agency tapped to help expand the brand. "The name was derived from customers' consistent reactions to the taste: 'Yumm! What is this?!'"

In designing a store prototype to help Café Yumm! develop a franchise model, Hornall Anderson had its work cut out for it: The restaurant's husband and wife team realized that they needed to create a brand framework to help manage their growth. But the work for the restaurant concept extends beyond the eye-pleasing aesthetics, which greet the visitor and help set the table for the restaurant's organic fare. "It's the canvas on which they're created," the agency says.

"Going green" may be the current trend, but Café Yumm! is already a couple of generations removed from the local diner. Hornall Anderson's branding strategy focused on linking healthy food concepts with an in-store dining experience that reinforces the progressive nature of the brand. "Café Yumm! tastefully points to what's next in environmentally responsible restaurant design," the agency asserts.

Warm wood panels sum up the restaurant's philosophies, including the evocative credo, "Yumm! is an act of passion: We love creating vital new flavors that fuel the soul." Soul, stomach, person, planet: "[There is] re-milled timber on which menu boards are printed [and] flooring made from recycled agriculture waste. Diners eat on tabletops manufactured from 50% post-consumer recycled paper, water-based phenolic resin with cashew nut shell binder and pigment, all while sitting under energy-efficient, low-wattage lighting," Hornall Anderson reports. "You won't find a trace of mercury anywhere at Café Yumm!"

1

2

3

1 CREATIVE FIRM: **Karen Skunta & Company - Cleveland, OH** CREATIVE TEAM: **Karen Skunta - Art Director; Dana Ross - Graphic Designer; Visual Marketing - Fabricator** CLIENT: **Whole Health Management Inc.** 2 CREATIVE FIRM: **G2 - New York, NY** CREATIVE TEAM: **Kurt Haiman - Founder** CLIENT: **Absolut** 3 CREATIVE FIRM: **JGA - Southfield, MI** CREATIVE TEAM: **Ken Nisch - Chairman; Kathi McWilliams - Creative Director** CLIENT: **Borders Group, Inc.**

1

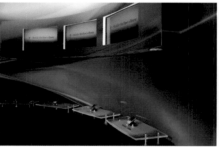

2

1 CREATIVE FIRM: Hornall Anderson - Seattle, WA CREATIVE TEAM: Jamie Monberg - Interactive Director; Halle Brunkella, Chris Monberg, Dana Kruse - Producers; Hayden Schoen, Rachel Blakely - Interactive Designers CLIENT: T-Mobile 2 CREATIVE FIRM: Karen Skunta & Company - Cleveland, OH CREATIVE TEAM: Karen Skunta - Creative Director; Jamie Finkelhor - Sr. Graphic Designer, Exhibits; Felix Lee - Sr. Graphic Designer, Interactive; Jen Maxwell, Kristal Ernst - Graphic Designers; Martin Spicuzza - Interior Designer CLIENT: Parker Hannifin Corporation

1

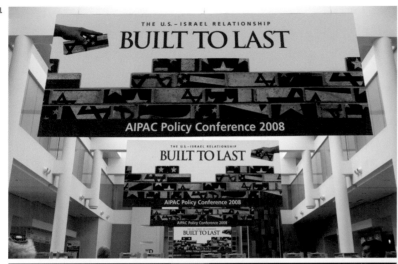

2

1 CREATIVE FIRM: **Beth Singer Design - Arlington, VA** CREATIVE TEAM: **Beth Singer, Howard Smith - Principals; Dennis Turbeville, Kapil Grover - Graphic Designer** CLIENT: **American Israel Public Affairs Committee (AIPAC) 2** CREATIVE FIRM: **Karen Skunta & Company - Cleveland, OH** CREATIVE TEAM: **Karen Skunta - Creative Director; Jamie Finkelhor - Sr. Graphic Designer, Exhibits; Felix Lee - Sr. Graphic Designer, Interactive; Jen Maxwell, Kristal Ernst - Graphic Designers; Martin Spicuzza - Interior Designer** CLIENT: **Parker Hannifin Corporation**

1

2

3

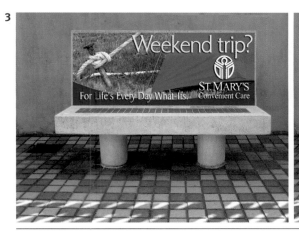

1 CREATIVE FIRM: Hornall Anderson Design Works - Seattle, WA CREATIVE TEAM: Jack Anderson, Kathy Saito - Art Directors; Elmer DelaCruz, Hayden Schoen - Designers CLIENT: CitationShares
2 CREATIVE FIRM: Karen Skunta & Company - Cleveland, OH CREATIVE TEAM: Karen Skunta - Creative Director; Jamie Finkelhor - Sr. Graphic Designer, Exhibits; Felix Lee - Sr. Graphic Designer, Interactive; Jen Maxwell, Kristal Ernst - Graphic Designers; Martin Spicuzza - Interior Designer CLIENT: Parker Hannifin Corporation 3 CREATIVE FIRM: Keller Crescent Company - Evansville, IN CREATIVE TEAM: Randy Rohn - Executive Creative Director; Naiyana Hardy - Art Director; Nancy Kirkpatrick - Copywriter CLIENT: St Marys Hospital

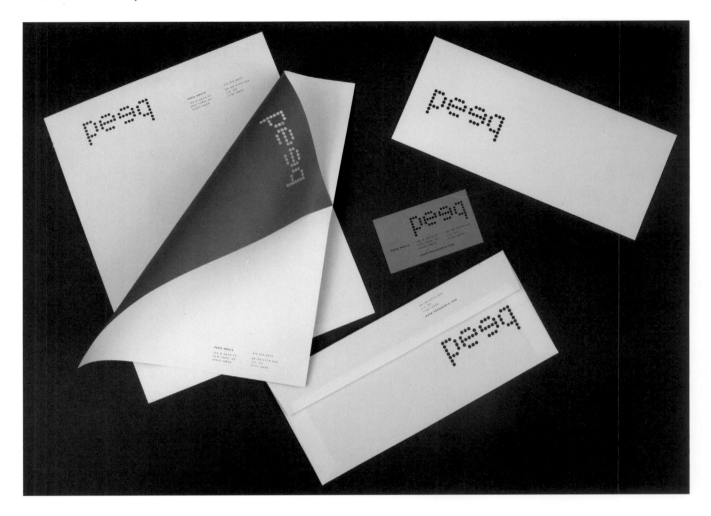

Peeq Media Corporate Stationery

CREATIVE FIRM: oLo Brand Group - New York, NY
CREATIVE TEAM: Peter Lord - Executive Creative Director
CLIENT: Peeq Media

A company formed by the merger of two printing houses needed a suitable identity, including a new name to convey its commitment to "Technology for the Creative Mind." New York's oLo Brand Group understood the market well, as it was their own. "Because the majority of our target audience is in the creative community, it was crucial that each deliverable produced had to stand out, look different and support the idea that Peeq looks at— and does—things differently," oLo says. "The objective was to develop a brand that helped to define and position this new company as the leading resource through which designers and marketers [could] accelerate their workflow with technology-based services."

Creating collateral for a technologically advanced printer demanded a contemporary look, and yet required traditional means for execution. "When a die cut is intrinsic to your design language, it takes a certain commitment level from the client," oLo says, referring to increased costs and development time required.

"Peeq's leadership embraced and supported the concept without [too much] concern." And the concept itself? It was a natural: "The design of the logotype grew directly from the letterforms within the name. By flopping the *E*, we were able to achieve a symmetrical logotype, and exploit that through die cutting, so the logo reads correctly from both sides." This symmetrical image, says oLo, exemplifies the idea of looking for, examining and implementing technology, processes and systems."

1

2

1 CREATIVE FIRM: Intelligent Fish Studio - Woodbuy, MN CREATIVE TEAM: Brian Danaher - Art Director, Designer, Illustrator CLIENT: Clutter Bear Records 2 CREATIVE FIRM: UNIT design collective - San Francisco, CA CREATIVE TEAM: Ann Jordan, Shardul Kiri - Creative Directors CLIENT: Approved Appraisers

1

Hello, I'm **Yang Kim**, Creative Director and owner.
I make sure our work is impactful and elegant.
In other words, I teach our people to push and pull
and work hard and play until it's right. Email me
at yang@peopledesign.com

People Design helps people make good experiences for other
people. We believe that good design makes better things and
makes things better. We work at 648 Monroe Avenue NW, Suite
212, Grand Rapids, Michigan, 49503. Call us at 616 459 4444.

peopledesign.com/yang

From **People Design Inc.** 648 Monroe Avenue NW, Suite 212, Grand Rapids, Michigan, 49503. 616 459 4444. peopledesign.com

2

3

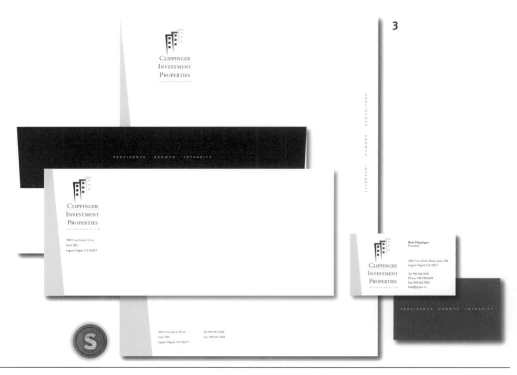

---

1 CREATIVE FIRM: **People Design Inc - Grand Rapids, MI** CREATIVE TEAM: **Kevin Budelmann - Creative Director; Yang Kim - Creative Director/Writer; Michele Brautnick, Tim Calkins - Designers; Julie Ridl - Writer** CLIENT: **People Design Inc** 2 CREATIVE FIRM: **Sayles Graphic Design - Des Moines, IA** CREATIVE TEAM: **John Sayles, Bridget Drendel** CLIENT: **Integrated Wellness** 3 CREATIVE FIRM: **Vince Rini Design - Huntington Beach, CA** CREATIVE TEAM: **Vince Rini** CLIENT: **Clippinger Investment Properties**

1

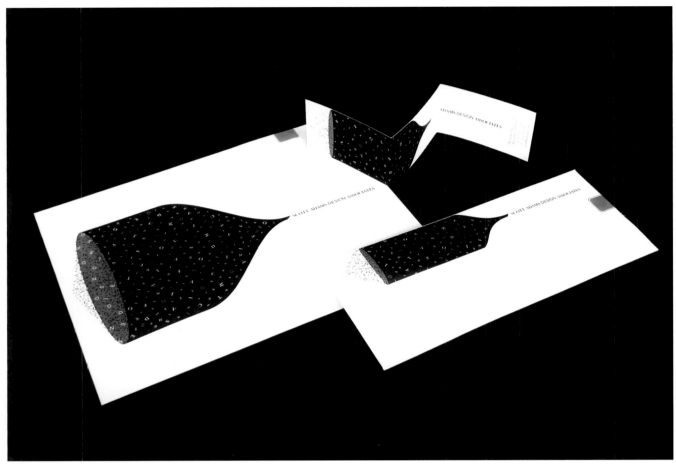

2

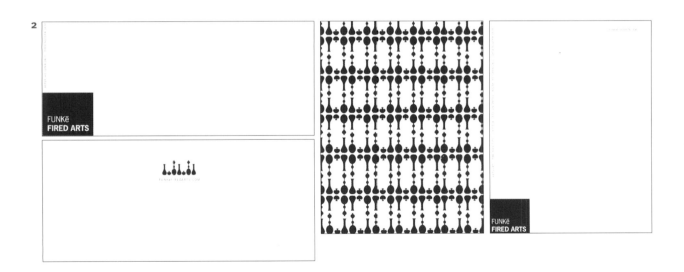

1 CREATIVE FIRM: **Scott Adams Design Associates - Minneapolis, MN** CREATIVE TEAM: **Scott Adams - Designer and Illustrator** CLIENT: **Scott Adams Design Associates** 2 CREATIVE FIRM: **Barefoot - Cincinnati, OH** CREATIVE TEAM: **Jodi Greene - Creative Director, Designer; Doug Worple - Executive Creative Director** CLIENT: **Funke Fired Arts**

mypetspace.com Logo

If people have their own social networks, why not their best friends? Liska + Associates created a whimsical logo for Mypetspace.com, "a social networking Web site for and by pet owners." Incorporating elements of various pets—a rabbit's ear, fish's body, bird's wing and dog or cat's mouth—the logo is a colorful, appealing amalgam of all that animal lovers hold dear. "The logo needed to convey the idea of multiple pets," the agency says. "The shapes and color convey the playfulness between pets and their owners."

CREATIVE FIRM: **Liska + Associates - Chicago, IL**
CREATIVE TEAM: **Katie Schweitzer - Designer; Steve Liska - Creative Director**
CLIENT: **Mypetspace.com LLC**

LIFe In AbunDANCe.

INTERNATIONAL

HUMANE SOCIETY
INTERNATIONAL

1 CREATIVE FIRM: **Rule29 - Geneva, IL** CREATIVE TEAM: **Justin Ahrens - Art Director; Kerri Liu - Designer** CLIENT: **Life In Abundance** 2 CREATIVE FIRM: **UNIT design collective - San Francisco, CA** CREATIVE
TEAM: **Ann Jordan, Shardul Kiri - Creative Directors** CLIENT: **Approved Appraisers** 3 CREATIVE FIRM: **Black & White - Louisville, KY** CREATIVE TEAM: **Phillip Means - Director of Design** CLIENT: **Farm
Credit Services** 4 CREATIVE FIRM: **Kevin Hall Design - Milford, CT** CREATIVE TEAM: **Kevin Hall Design** CLIENT: **Splash, LTD.** 5 CREATIVE FIRM: **The Humane Society of the United States - Washington,
D.C.** CREATIVE TEAM: **Paula Jaworski - Creative Director** CLIENT: **Humane Society International** 6 CREATIVE FIRM: **Planet 3 - Venice, CA** CREATIVE TEAM: **Michele Castagnetti - Art Director/Designer**
CLIENT: **Planet 3**

1 CREATIVE FIRM: **Nickelodeon Preschool Brand Creative - New York, NY** CREATIVE TEAM: **Jennifer Cast - Art Director, Nickelodeon Preschool Brand Creative; Matthew Duntemann - VP, Design: Nickel-odeon Preschool Brand Creative; Jennifer Cast - Illustrator/Designer, Nickelodeon Preschool Brand** CLIENT: **Nick Jr.** 2 CREATIVE FIRM: **Peterson Ray & Company - Dallas, TX** CREATIVE TEAM: **Scott Ray, Dorit Suffness - Art Directors; Scott Ray - Designer; Nham Pham - Illustrator** CLIENT: **Dallas Pottery Invitational** 3 CREATIVE FIRM: **Hornall Anderson - Seattle, WA** CREATIVE TEAM: **Jack Anderson, Kathy Saito - Art Directors; Leo Raymundo, Hayden Shoen, Chang Ling Wu, Yuri Schvets - Designers** CLIENT: **CitationShares** 4 CREATIVE FIRM: **Hornall Anderson - Seattle, WA** CREATIVE TEAM: **Lisa Cerveny, Julie Lock - Art Directors; Vu Nguyen, Don Stayner, Elmer DelaCruz, Katie Phipps - Designers** CLIENT: **Holland America** 5 CREATIVE FIRM: **mad studios - Hong Kong** CREATIVE TEAM: **Brian Lau - Principal Designer** CLIENT: **the art gallery** 6 CREATIVE FIRM: **UNIT design collective - San Francisco, CA** CREATIVE TEAM: **Ann Jordan, Shardul Kiri - Creative Directors** CLIENT: **Olatherapy**

1

KAMMERKÓR NORÐURLANDS

2

3

stratford
Shakespeare
festival

4

K A M M E R K Ó R   A K R A N E S S

5

BRICK BY BRICK
The campaign to rebuild Glen Cedar park

6

zereoué

7

OK R Á Ð G J Ö F

8

---

1 CREATIVE FIRM: **ISROR ehf - Hafnarfjordur, Iceland** CREATIVE TEAM: **Holmfridur Valdimarsdottir, Frida - Design** CLIENT: **Chamber Choir in north part of Iceland** 2 CREATIVE FIRM: **id29 - Troy, NY** CREATIVE TEAM: **Doug Bartow - Art Director; Bryan Kahrs - Senior Designer** CLIENT: **Ryan-Biggs Associates, P.C.** 3 CREATIVE FIRM: **Karacters Design Group DDB Canada - Vancouver, BC, Canada** CREATIVE TEAM: **John Furneaux - Executive Creative Director; Erick Nielsen - Creative Director, Designer; Marsha Larkin - Designer; Ivan Angelic - Illustrator** CLIENT: **Stratford Shakespeare Festival** 4 CREATIVE FIRM: **ISROR ehf - Hafnarfjordur, Iceland** CREATIVE TEAM: **Holmfridur Valdimarsdottir, Frida - Design** CLIENT: **Chamber Choir in Akranes** 5 CREATIVE FIRM: **LEBOW - Toronto, ON, Canada** CREATIVE TEAM: **Ronnie Lebow** CLIENT: **The Glen Cedar Park Committee** 6 CREATIVE FIRM: **G2 - New York, NY** CREATIVE TEAM: **Kurt Haiman - Founder** CLIENT: **Zereoue** 7 CREATIVE FIRM: **ISROR ehf - Hafnarfjordur, Iceland** CREATIVE TEAM: **Holmfridur Valdimarsdottir - Design** CLIENT: **Ok Advisory** 8 CREATIVE FIRM: **TFI Envision, Inc. - Norwalk, CT** CREATIVE TEAM: **Elizabeth P. Ball - Creative Director, Art Director, Designer and Illustrator** CLIENT: **Graphics 3, Inc.**

creativity 38 annual awards

SOUNDBRIDGE

colormunki™
DESIGN

CitationShares

colormunki™
PHOTO

Mammoth
RESORT

CLIPPINGER
INVESTMENT
PROPERTIES
INCORPORATED

bernard katz glass

1 CREATIVE FIRM: RainCastle Communications - Newton, MA CREATIVE TEAM: Paul Regensburg - Principal & Creative Director; Tony Catlin - Sr. Art Director; Steve Boris - Sr. Designer CLIENT: Sound-Bridge 2 CREATIVE FIRM: G2 - New York, NY CREATIVE TEAM: Kurt Haiman - Founder CLIENT: Pantone 3 CREATIVE FIRM: Hornall Anderson Design Works - Seattle, WA CREATIVE TEAM: Jack Anderson, Kathy Saito - Art Directors; Henry Yiu, Sonja Max, Elmer DelaCruz, Hayden Schoen - Designers CLIENT: Citation Shares 4 CREATIVE FIRM: Hornall Anderson - Seattle, WA CREATIVE TEAM: Jack Anderson, David Bates - Art Directors; Javas Lehn, Julie Lock - Designers CLIENT: Mammoth Mountain Ski Area 5 CREATIVE FIRM: Vince Rini Design - Huntington Beach, CA CREATIVE TEAM: Vince Rini CLIENT: Clippinger Investment Properties 6 CREATIVE FIRM: bliss & white - Swedesboro, NJ CREATIVE TEAM: Lisa May, Christine Fajardo - Owner/Designers CLIENT: Bernard Katz Glass

1

MARK RICHEY
woodworking

2

3

4

5

1 CREATIVE FIRM: **RainCastle Communications - Newton, MA** CREATIVE TEAM: **Paul Regensburg - Principal & Creative Director; Rotem Meller - Art Director & Designer** CLIENT: **Mark Richey Woodworking**
2 CREATIVE FIRM: **mad studios - Hong Kong** CREATIVE TEAM: **Brian Lau - Principal Designer; Lilian Chan - Designer** CLIENT: **babyfirst** 3 CREATIVE FIRM: **Fitting Group - Pittsburgh, PA** CREATIVE TEAM:
Travis Norris - Creative Director; Andrew Ellis - Designer CLIENT: **WDUQ 90.5 FM** 4 CREATIVE FIRM: **G2 - New York, NY** CREATIVE TEAM: **Kurt Haiman - Founder** CLIENT: **Trinity Wall Street** 5 CREATIVE FIRM:
Intelligent Fish Studio - Woodbuy, MN CREATIVE TEAM: **Brian Danaher - Art Director, Designer, Illustrator** CLIENT: **Clutter Bear Records**

  1

 3

devon

2

woodland

SPRING LODGE

4

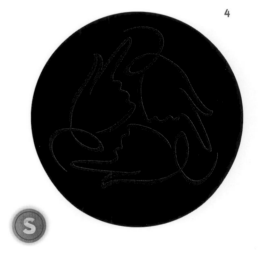

5

6

1 CREATIVE FIRM: **LEBOW - Toronto, ON, Canada** CREATIVE TEAM: **Ronnie Lebow** CLIENT: **Seeslim Sportswear** 2 CREATIVE FIRM: **Paradowski Creative - St. Louis, MO** CREATIVE TEAM: **Matthew Evans - Senior Designer; Steve Cox - Creative Director; Thomas Finan - Account Manager** CLIENT: **Boys & Girls Town of Missouri** 3 CREATIVE FIRM: **Landor Associates - Cincinnati, OH** CREATIVE TEAM: **Christopher Lehmann - Creative Director; Ken Frederick - Designer; Bob Kersten - Strategy Director** CLIENT: **Devon Energy** 4 CREATIVE FIRM: **Design Source Creative, Inc. - Aptos, CA** CREATIVE TEAM: **Stacey Boscoe - Lead Designer; Cari Class - Creative Director** CLIENT: **Monterey Bay Wine Company** 5 CREATIVE FIRM: **Devon Energy - Oklahoma City, OK** CREATIVE TEAM: **Tim Langenberg - Creative Director** CLIENT: **Devon Energy** 6 CREATIVE FIRM: **kellum McClain Inc. - New York, NY** CREATIVE TEAM: **kellum McClain Inc.** CLIENT: **The Moto-Gators**

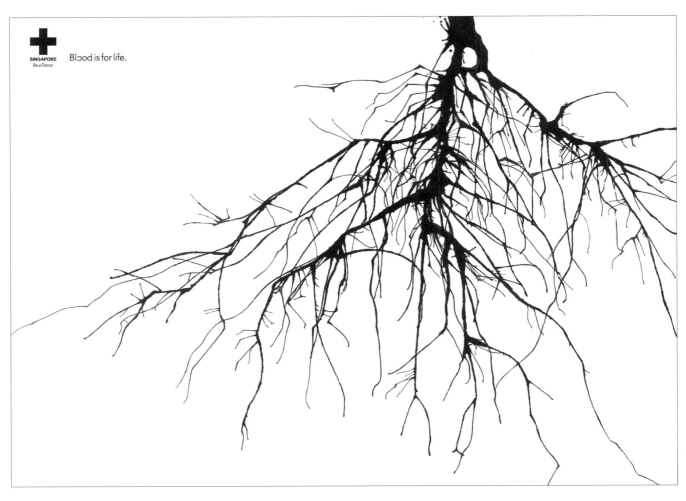

PLATINUM P

CREATIVE FIRM: **Ad P anet Group - Singapore**

CREATIVE TEAM: **Teck Chong Leo - Executive Creative Director; Alfred Teo - Associate Creative Director; Leong Lee Tan - Senior Art Director**

CLIENT: **Red Cross**

Blood is for Life

Like most blood banks, the Singapore Red Cross is constantly in need of donors to maintain sufficient amounts in its supply. Although this is widely known issue, the Singapore Red Cross took a new and refreshing approach to communicate this need. Singapore's Ad Planet Group created an advertisement that cast the "Blood is for life" message in a new light, with a stark red-on-white image of branches that could be from a plant—or a network of human veins. "The challenge in creating this design was to ensure that the artificially created 'dribbles' of blood looked authentic enough to resemble the shape of roots growing down into the earth," the agency says. "This 'organic' feel required an eye for detail and a concise understanding of natural branching patterns."

Thematic Poster of Humanity

CREATIVE FIRM: **Ameba Design Ltd. - Hong Kong**

CREATIVE TEAM: **Gideon, Wai Kwan Lai - Creative Director**

CLIENT: **Taiwan Int. Poster Design Award**

Hong Kong's Ameba Design Ltd. took a wider worldview when designing a simple-looking poster for Taiwan's International Poster Design Awards 07, titled "We're One" and representing a truly international theme: humanity. But, says designer Lai Wai Kwan, there's more to the poster than meets the eye. "We're one!" Lai says. "Human lives as a whole need humanity, love, freedom and respect, and they also need to help each other to survive." The poster conveys this message on multiple levels. "In this poster, the road (*humanity road*, or 人道) is created by lots of humans, or the Chinese character 人," Lai says. "They are helping each other and getting balance. If someone gets hurt, the road will be blocked. [So] it also affects others."

But, as the Chinese alphabet has thousands of characters, the graphic holds even deeper meaning. "The whole graphic looks like the word *prisoner*, or 囚," Lai explains. "If there is no humanity, it's just like living in a prison. Every day, people get hurt, and [no one cares]."

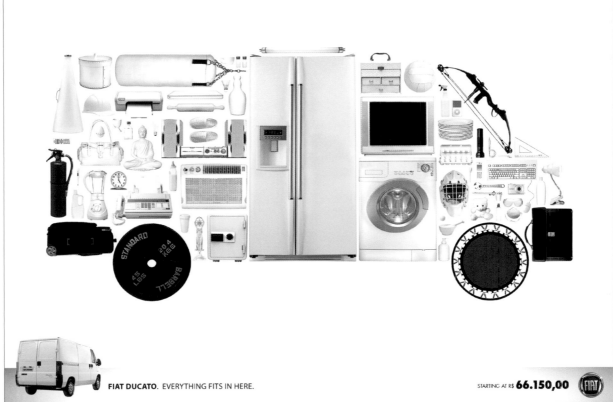

FIAT DUCATO. EVERYTHING FITS IN HERE.

STARTING AT R$ **66.150,00**

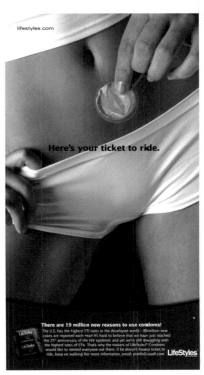

lifestyles.com

Here's your ticket to ride.

There are 19 million new reasons to use condoms!

1 CREATIVE FIRM: **GIOVANNI+DRAFTFCB - São Paolo, Brazil** CREATIVE TEAM: **Adilson Xavier - President/Nacional Creative Director; Cristina Amorim, Fernando Barcellos - Creative Directors; Felipe Gomes - Art Director; Ricardo Câmara - Copywriter** CLIENT: **Fiat** 2 CREATIVE FIRM: **GIOVANNI+DRAFTFCB - São Paolo, Brazil** CREATIVE TEAM: **Adilson Xavier - President/Nacional Creative Director; Cristina Amorim, Ferrando Barcellos - Creative Directors; Fábio Penedo - Copywriter; Marcus Saulnier, Cidney Neto - Art Directors** CLIENT: **S.C.Johnson** 3 CREATIVE FIRM: **SGW Integrated Marketing Communications - Montville, NJ** CREATIVE TEAM: **Niles Wolfson - Chief Creative Officer; Chez Pari - Creative Director** CLIENT: **Lifestyles**

1

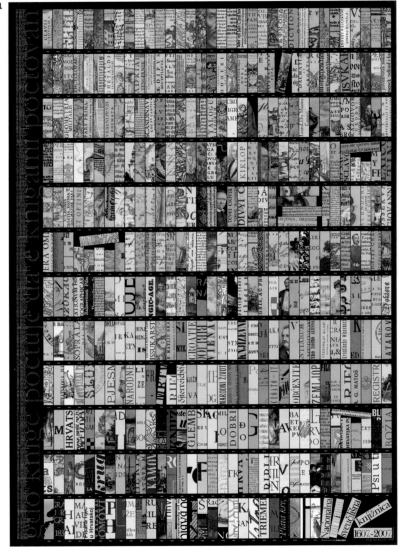

2

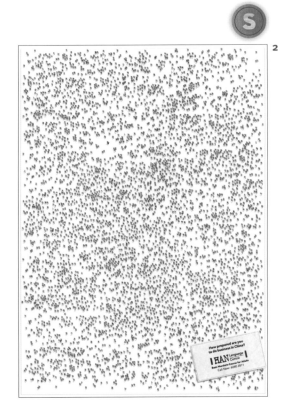

3

1 CREATIVE FIRM: **STUDIO INTERNATIONAL** - Zagreb, Croatia CREATIVE TEAM: **Boris Ljubicic - Designer** CLIENT: **National and University Library** 2 CREATIVE FIRM: **Ad Planet Group - Singapore** CREATIVE TEAM: **Teck Chong Leo - Executive Creative Director; Alfred Teo - Associate Creative Director; Jean Low - Creative Designer** CLIENT: **Han Language Centre** 3 CREATIVE FIRM: **Atomic Design - Crowley, TX** CREATIVE TEAM: **Lewis Glaser - Designer/Art Director; Leslie Scott - Photographer** CLIENT: **TCU School of Classical & Contemporary Dance**

1

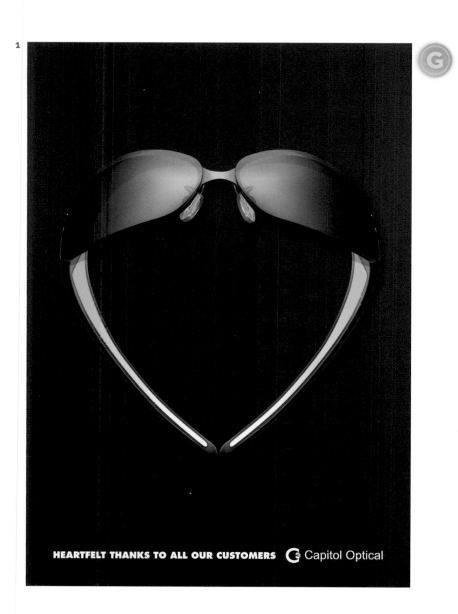

2

1 CREATIVE FIRM: Planet Ads & Design P/L - Singapore CREATIVE TEAM: Hal Suzuki - Executive Creative Director; Eran Husni Amir Husni - Art Director; Rachel Lee - Senior Account Executive; Suzanne Lauridsen - Senior Copywriter; Takahiro Kiyota - Photographer; Jolene Goh - Retoucher CLIENT: Capitol Optical 2 CREATIVE FIRM: GIOVANNI+DRAFTFCB - São Paolo, Brazil CREATIVE TEAM: Adilson Xavier - President/Nacional Creative Director; Cristina Amorim, Fernando Barcellos - Creative Directors; Rafael Pitanguy - Copywriter; Marcelo Lobo, Gabriel Lamartine - Art Directors CLIENT: S.C. Johnson

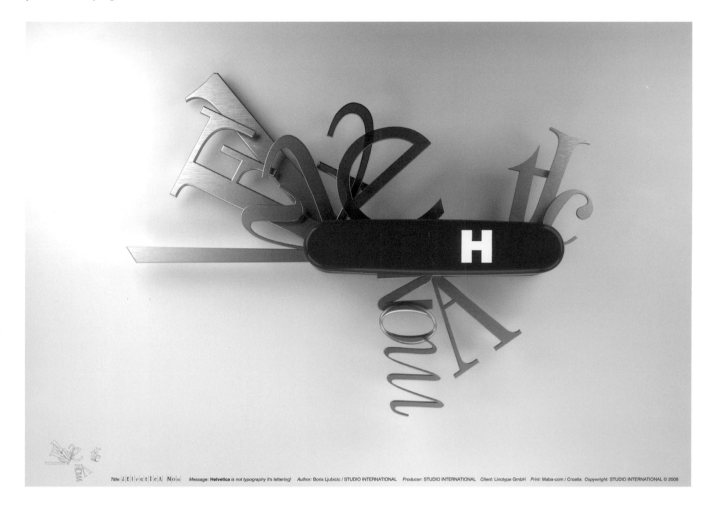

Title: Helvetica Now Message: **Helvetica** is not typography it's lettering! Author: Boris Ljubicic / STUDIO INTERNATIONAL Producer: STUDIO INTERNATIONAL Client: Linotype GmbH Print: Maba-com / Croatia Copyright: STUDIO INTERNATIONAL © 2008

PLATINUM (P)

CREATIVE FIRM: **STUDIO INTERNATIONAL - Zagreb, Croatia**
CREATIVE TEAM: **Boris Ljubicic - Designer; Igor Ljubicic - Illustrator**
CLIENT: **STUDIO INTERNATIONAL/Linotype**

1

2

3

1 CREATIVE FIRM: **Yan-Ting Chen - Keelung City, Taiwan** CREATIVE TEAM: **YanTing Chen, TzuLun Huang - Designers** CLIENT: **Musicut** 2 CREATIVE FIRM: **Davis Design Partners - Holland, OH** CREATIVE TEAM: **Matt Davis, Karen Davis - Designer & Illustrators; Various Stock Agencies - Photographer** CLIENT: **Purdue Theatre (Purdue University)** 3 CREATIVE FIRM: **Campbell-Ewald - Warren, MI** CREATIVE TEAM: **Bill Ludwig - Vice Chairman, Chief Creative Officer; Mark Simon - Executive Creative Director; Dan Ames, Eric Olis - SVP, Associate Creative Directors; Al Majewski, Jason Fetterman - Art Directors; Jeff Warner, Mike O'Connell - Writers** CLIENT: **United States Navy**

1

HOPE.

DON'T TRASH IT.

If you have unused HIV meds that you're going to throw away, give them to us. We'll make sure they get into the right hands.

In Africa, millions of HIV victims go untreated every year, while here in the US, millions of unused HIV medications go into the garbage. With your help, Viral Hope can make a difference. Viral Hope is an outreach program sponsored by The Starfish Project, an organization dedicated to making sure that patients with HIV/AIDS in Africa, and their communities, get the medicines they desperately need.

For more information visit www.thestarfishproject.org or call Marcio Maeda at 212-746-3890.

VIRALHOPE
Share the health.

EXTEND HOPE.

VIRALHOPE
Share the health.

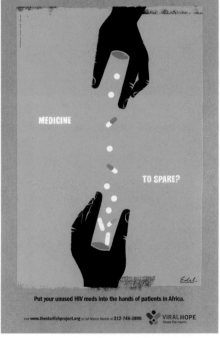

MEDICINE TO SPARE?

Put your unused HIV meds into the hands of patients in Africa.

VIRALHOPE
Share the health.

2

Want variety?
STUDLEY STORE

Stomach growling?
STUDLEY STORE

Hungry?
STUDLEY STORE

1 CREATIVE FIRM: **Cline Davis and Mann LLC - New York, NY** CREATIVE TEAM: **Cline Davis and Mann LLC** CLIENT: **Starfish Foundation** 2 CREATIVE FIRM: **KreativeDept - Studley, VA** CREATIVE TEAM: **Kenny Sink - Writer, Art Director, Creative Director** CLIENT: **Studley Store**

1

2

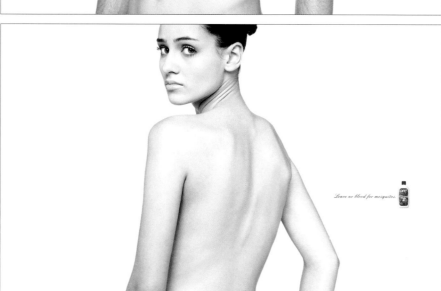

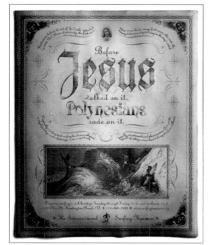

1 CREATIVE FIRM: **GIOVANNI+DRAFTFCB** - **São Paolo, Brazil** CREATIVE TEAM: **Adilson Xavier** - President/Nacional Creative Director; **Sidney Araújo, Ricardo John** - Creative Directors; **Fábio Penedo** - Copywriter; **Marcus Saulnier, Luiz Kanadani** - Art Directors CLIENT: **S.C. Johnson** 2 CREATIVE FIRM: **Draftfcb** - **Chicago, IL** CREATIVE TEAM: **Christopher Gyorgy** - Art Director and Creative Director; **Dave Horton** - Writer CLIENT: **International Surfing Museum**

1

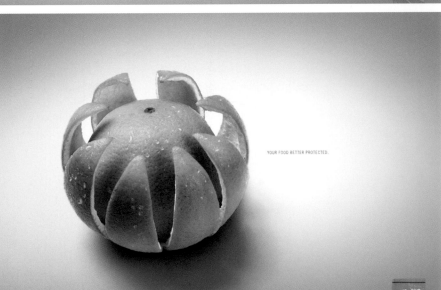

2

3

1 CREATIVE FIRM: **GIOVANNI+DRAFTFCB** - São Paolo, Brazil CREATIVE TEAM: **Adilson Xavier - President/Nacional Creative Director; Cristina Amorim, Fernando Barcellos - Creative Directors; Leonardo Bartoli - Copywriter; Felipe Gomes - Art Director** CLIENT: **S.C. Johnson** 2 CREATIVE FIRM: **PLANET 3** - Venice, CA CREATIVE TEAM: **Michele Castagnetti - Art Director/Designer; Dylan Gerber, Stefan Gerber - Creative Director/Copywriters** CLIENT: **TMZ** 3 CREATIVE FIRM: **GIOVANNI+DRAFTFCB** - São Paolo, Brazil CREATIVE TEAM: **Adilson Xavier - President/Nacional Creative Director; Cristina Amorim, Fernando Barcellos - Creative Directors; Cláudio Gatão - Copywriter, Art Director** CLIENT: **Eye Fit**

Dangerous curves ahead.

Check out our complete line of women's apparel designed to handle any curve.

Christmas Ham on the table. Christmas Hog in the garage.

Check out all our bikes this holiday season.

On Softail®, on Dyna®, on Sportster®, on Fatboy®...

Time for a new sled?

Check out our great selection of bikes this holiday season.

A GRAND ARRIVAL

ESCALA

1 CREATIVE FIRM: **Hafer brack Marketing - Dayton, OH** CREATIVE TEAM: **Jon Brooks - Creative Director; Derick Myers - Photoshop** CLIENT: **F&S Harley-Davidson 2** CREATIVE FIRM: **Phinney Bischoff Design House - Seattle, WA** CREATIVE TEAM: **Dean Hart - Senior Designer; Leslie Phinney - Creative Director; Lorie Ransom - Designer** CLIENT: **Realogics**

1

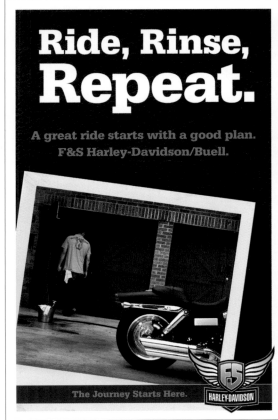

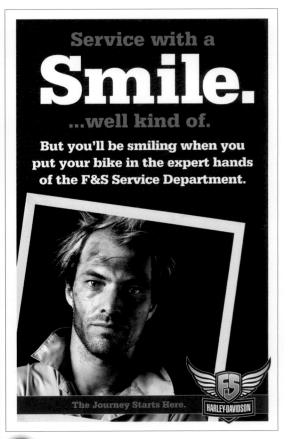

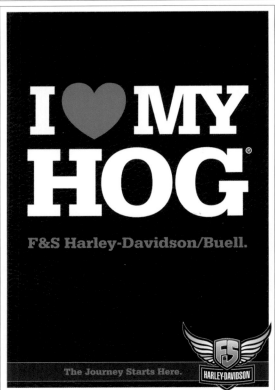

2

1 CREATIVE FIRM: **Hafenbrack Marketing - Dayton, OH** CREATIVE TEAM: **Jon Brooks - Creative Director; Derick Myers - Photoshop** CLIENT: **F&S Harley-Davidson** 2 CREATIVE FIRM: **Hafenbrack Marketing - Dayton, OH** CREATIVE TEAM: **Jon Brooks - Creative Director; Derick Myers - Photoshop** CLIENT: **F&S Harley-Davidson**

1

2

1 CREATIVE FIRM: **EP&M International - Albany, NY** CREATIVE TEAM: **Colleen McClaine - Project Manager; Lily Wei - Designer** CLIENT: **GE Energy** 2 CREATIVE FIRM: **EP&M International - Albany, NY** CREATIVE TEAM: **Colleen McClaine - Project Manager; Lily Wei - Designer** CLIENT: **GE Energy**

1

2

3

4

5

1 CREATIVE FIRM: **Mattel, Inc. - El Segundo, CA** CREATIVE TEAM: **Richard Dickson - Sr V.P., Worldwide Media, Marketing, Entertainment; Lisa McKnight - V.P. Creative & Marketing Communications; Herve Grison - Director, Photography; Kristina Gould - Sr Manager, Brand Design; Heather Lazarus - Sr Manager, Account Management; Armena Jehanian - Sr Manager, Design Services** CLIENT: **Mattel, Inc.** 2 CREATIVE FIRM: **Mattel, Inc. - El Segundo, CA** CREATIVE TEAM: **Richard Dickson - Sr V.P., Worldwide Media, Marketing, Entertainment; Lisa McKnight - V.P. Creative & Marketing Communications; Herve Grison - Director, Photography; Kristina Gould - Sr Manager, Brand Design; Heather Lazarus - Sr Manager, Account Management; Armena Jehanian - Sr Manager, Design Services** CLIENT: **Mattel, Inc.** 3 CREATIVE FIRM: **EP&M International - Albany, NY** CREATIVE TEAM: **Tiffeny Cantu - Project Manager; Lily Wei - Designer** CLIENT: **GE Energy** 4 CREATIVE FIRM: **George P. Johnson - North Easton, MA** CREATIVE TEAM: **Charles Bajnai - Creative Director; Jeff Rohlfing - Senior Project Designer; Chris Lusk - Multimedia Designer** CLIENT: **Motorola** 5 CREATIVE FIRM: **George P. Johnson - North Easton, MA** CREATIVE TEAM: **Tanja Richter, Larissa Carpenter, Garrett Clum - Graphic Designers** CLIENT: **Toyota**

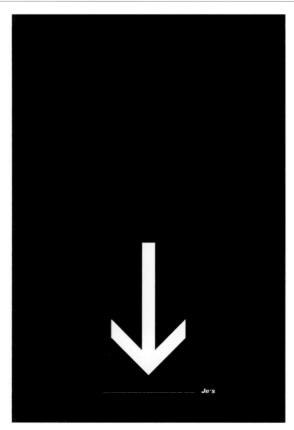

COPY:
At this moment, your bum is completely exposed. If it were in a sexy pair of jeans, it would attract attention all the time!

PLATINUM P

Bum

CREATIVE FIRM: **BRUKETA&ZINIC OM - Zagreb, Croatia**
CREATIVE TEAM: **Moe Minkara - Creative Director; Martina Marinic, Krunoslav Franetic - Art Directors; Daniel Vukovic - Copywriter**
CLIENT: **Jegerstar**

If your store sells what you consider to be world's sexiest jeans, what's the best way to show them off? "[Retailer] Je*s wanted us to communicate how, in their jeans, every bum looks very attractive," explain the creative team at Zagreb, Croatia-based Bruketa&žinić om of the motivation behind their innovative bus shelter poster. "The intention was to create an experience of having your bum exposed," they say of the white arrow against a stark black background, inviting passers-by to look closer at the fine copy below. "We designed it to have an arrow pointing to very small text at the bottom making people bend down and expose their bums in order to read the text." And what does it say? *"In this moment your bum is completely exposed. If you were in a sexy pair of jeans, it would attract attention all the time!"* Mission accomplished.

1 CREATIVE FIRM: LekasMiller Design - Walnut Creek, CA CREATIVE TEAM: Lana Ip - Graphic Designer; Chantal Reynoso, Keanna Riley - Slogan Competition Winners CLIENT: Kaiser Permanente 2 CREATIVE FIRM: Yellow Shoes Creative - Anaheim, CA CREATIVE TEAM: Scott Starkey - Art Director; Wes Clark - Copywriter; Marty Muller - Sr. VP Global Creative, Walt Disney Parks & Resort; Joe Schneider - VP Global Creative; Jacquelyn L. Moe - Director of Creative CLIENT: Disneyland Resort

1

BILL HAS THREE WIVES
AND FAMILY VALUES.
Series returns June 15

NOW IT'S ALL OUT IN THE OPEN.

BIGLOVE

BIGLOVE

BIGLOVE

BIGLOVE

BIGLOVE

BIGLOVE

HBO

BIGLOVE
Series returns June 15
HBO

2

BIG LOVE
THREE WIVES. ONE BIG HAPPY FAMILY.
Series returns June 15
HBO

3

CREATE. INNOVATE. DOMINATE

CREATE. INNOVATE. DOMINATE

4

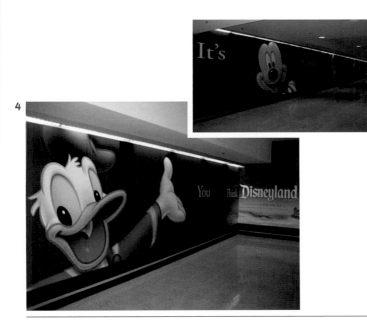

It's

You Think Disneyland

---

1 CREATIVE FIRM: **John Sposato Design & Illustration - Piermont, NY** CREATIVE TEAM: **John Sposato - Design, Photography, Illustration; Chris Spadaccini - Creative Director, Copywriter** CLIENT: **HBO**
2 CREATIVE FIRM: **Levine & Associates - Washington, D.C.** CREATIVE TEAM: **Maggie Soldano - Art Director; David Sharpe - Photographer** CLIENT: **Verizon Center 3** CREATIVE FIRM: **MTV Networks - New York, NY** CREATIVE TEAM: **Nigel Cox-Hagan - Creative Director: EVP Creative & Marketing, VH1; Phil Delbourgo - SVP Brand & Design, VH1; Nancy Mazzei - Art Director; Julie Ruiz - Designer; Traci Terrill - Editorial Director; Beth Wawerna - Writer; Allison Sierra - Producer; Pascal Duval - Illustrator** CLIENT: **VH1 4** CREATIVE FIRM: **Yellow Shoes Creative - Anaheim, CA** CREATIVE TEAM: **Scott Starkey - Art Director; Wes Clark - Copywriter; Marty Muller - Sr. VP Global Creative, Walt Disney Parks & Resort; Joe Schneider - VP Global Creative; Jacquelyn L. Moe - Director of Creative** CLIENT: **Disneyland Resort**

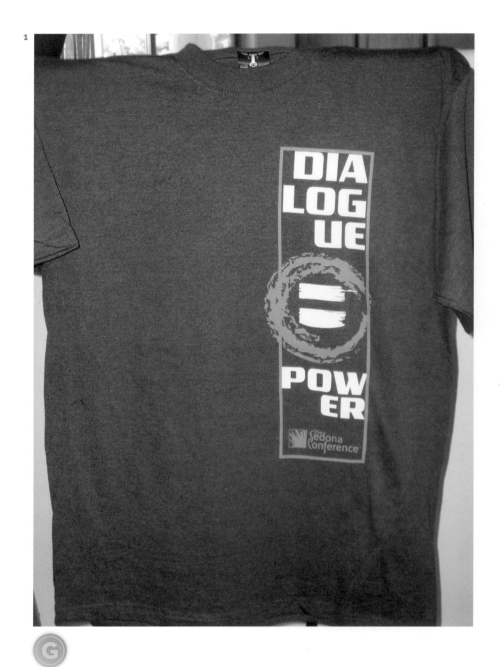

1 CREATIVE FIRM: Studio D - Sedona, AZ CREATIVE TEAM: Margo Braman - Graphic Communicator CLIENT: The Sedona Conference URL: www.thestudiod.com

PLATINUM ⓟ

CREATIVE FIRM: Auto Events.org - New Albany, IN

CREATIVE TEAM: Gerry Durnell - Editor & Publisher; Dan Bulleit - Art Director; Tracy Powell - Managing Editor

CLIENT: Automobile Quarterly Magazine

The AQ Flyer

The word *bookmobile* evokes a fusty image of a run-down bus teeming with dog-eared volumes of oft-lent books, but on the road today is a different kind of book-mobile for a whole new audience and generation. It's the AQ Flyer—a converted Bluebird bus designed to showcase the wares of publisher *Automobile Quarterly*. Serving as both a traveling billboard and storefront for *AQ*, the bus visits destinations such as vintage car shows, and representatives sell books and sideline items transported inside.

Publisher Gerry Durnell chose his vehicle carefully. "In a former life, the AQ Flyer was a stalwart friend of airline travelers commuting from an Avis rental car parking lot back and forth to the airport," he says. "A dependable Cummins turbo diesel engine hooked to an Allison AT-545 four-speed transmission all contained in a Bluebird bus configuration made for a safe, highly reliable, easy-to-drive vehicle that proved to be an excellent choice for a conversion." After turning the vehicle into a cargo workhorse to hold the company's

published wares as the sales team traveled from its home base to the particular car event of choice, *AQ* art director Dan Bulleit designed a scale model and attendant graphics for the thirty-foot vehicle. Bulleit took a truly novel approach, combining the looks of a sporty classic convertible against the background of an elegant English library complete with imaginative book titles.

The titles are as whimsical as the Flyer itself, and even nonreaders are bound to be intrigued. "At first glance, the shelves of the faux library that adorns the sides of the AQ Flyer are filled with familiar literary classics," he says. "On closer inspection, however, one discovers that substantial license has been taken and the titles have morphed into an automotive theme. For example, [we changed] *A Tale of Two Cities, To Kill a Mockingbird* and *Gone With the Wind* to *A Tale of Two Chevys, To Kill a Thunderbird* and *Gone With the Winnebago*."

1

2

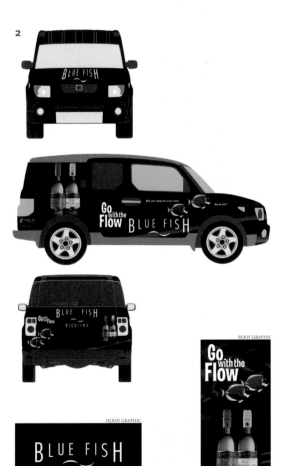

ROOF GRAPHIC

HOOD GRAPHIC

3

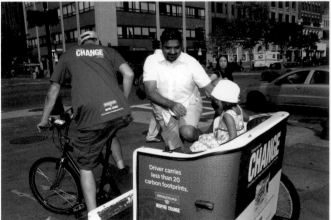

1 CREATIVE FIRM: **NBC Universal Global Networks Italia - Rome, Italy** CREATIVE TEAM: **M. Theresia Braun - Marketing & On Air Director; Emanuele Pulvirenti - Art Director; Antonio Giannone - Copy-writer** CLIENT: **Studio Universal** 2 CREATIVE FIRM: **REVOLUCION - New York, NY** | CREATIVE TEAM: **Alberto Rodriguez - Chief Creative Officer; Roberto Alcazar - Executive Creative Director; Henry Alvarez - Art Director** CLIENT: **Palm Bay International** 3 CREATIVE FIRM: **Alcone Marketing - Irvine, CA** CREATIVE TEAM: **Shivonne Miller - Art Director; Carlos Musquez - Creative Director; Luis Camano - SVP, Creative Director; Cameron Young - Copywriter** CLIENT: **Seeds of Change**

PACKAGING

   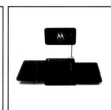 

PLATINUM ℗

CREATIVE FIRM: Ogilvy Brasil - Sâo Paolo, Brazil
CREATIVE TEAM: Marco Antonio Almeida, Reinaldo César Junior - Creative Directors; Milene Azevedo - Art Director; Claudia Pimenta - Copywriter
CLIENT: Motorola

Motorola Modular Display

Ogilvy Brasil in São Paulo faced a tough challenge when designing a point-of-sale (POP) display for Motorola: maintaining the identity of the Motorola brand while allowing scalability across product lines and physical retail areas. "Points-of-sale vary widely in terms of the space they provide," the agency says. "As an object of fierce competition among brands, their dimensions and design can range from intricate displays suitable for larger-sized facilities to compact solutions required by tiny stores."

To this end, Ogilvy hit upon the theme of modularity. "We developed independent components that, by connecting to each other, provide a number of display designs in multiple combinations," they explain. "This flexibility allows each point-of-sale to customize its own display according to the area available." And the displays aren't your typical flimsy cardboard, either: The choice of acrylic as the POP's primary material "ensured durability and sophistication to the project, giving Motorola a distinctive identity over competitors and highlighting the design—a strong feature of the brand." For color, the agency chose black and orange— colors already in the Motorola brand identity palette—to lend elegance and visibility to the displays. Vendors loved the "powerful, consolidated image of the brand among clients visiting its points-of-sale."

creativity 38 annual awards

142

1 CREATIVE FIRM: **The UXB - Beverly Hills, CA** CREATIVE TEAM: **NJ Goldston - CEO and Founder** CLIENT: **Cleatskins** 2 CREATIVE FIRM: **TFI Envision, Inc. - Norwalk, CT** CREATIVE TEAM: **Elizabeth P. Ball - Creative Director, Art Director, Designer; Phillip Doherty - Designer** CLIENT: **Unilever Home and Personal Care USA**

1 CREATIVE FIRM: **G2 - New York, NY** CREATIVE TEAM: **Kurt Haiman - Founder** CLIENT: **Absolut** 2 CREATIVE FIRM: **Ogilvy Brasil - São Paolo, Brazil** CREATIVE TEAM: **Marco Antonio Almeida, Reinaldo César Júnior - Creative Directors; Milene Azevedo - Art Director; Cláudia Pimenta - Copywriter** CLIENT: **Motorola** 3 CREATIVE FIRM: **Ogilvy Brasil - São Paolo, Brazil** CREATIVE TEAM: **Marco Antonio Almeida, Reinaldo César Júnior - Creative Directors; Mariana Ferrari - Art Director; Cláudia Pimenta - Copywriter** CLIENT: **Motorola**

PLATINUM

CREATIVE FIRM: **Loomis Group - San Francisco, CA**

CREATIVE TEAM: **George Steeley - Creative Director/Copywriter; Lee Queza - Art Director; Jen Campbell, Jeff Tanhueco - Designers**

CLIENT: **Fabrik**

Black Cherry Mini

Everyone knows how food packaging, even opaque designs, can make the contents downright mouthwatering. But what about inedibles? The Loomis Group created a delectable wrapper for the Fabrik Black Cherry Mini, a cherry-red USB drive with "320 juicy drippin' gigabytes."

"This tiny morsel of a drive began as an effort to reach a broader audience beyond the professional user," says the San Francisco design firm, citing "people amassing loads of images, like digital moms, and self-expressionists, who communicate their personalities through their belongings." With these recreational consumers in mind, Loomis realized that they were "not only asking them to show off their style and attitude with these drives, but we were also looking for new ways for them to relate to the hard drive category."

The agency's breakthrough came as they began to view the drives as personal accessories, and what could be more personal than exploration through the senses? "Eventually, we turned these bite-size drives into a delicious and sumptuous expression of our consumer's personal style," Loomis says. "By using flavors to define colors, we were able to imbue the drives with not only a hue but also with an attitude, an emotion or a memory, evoking the same senses as our favorite foods do time and again."

The proverbial cherry atop the Mini lay in the outer wrapper—concealing a durable utilitarianism. "We knew the custom transparent enclosure and subtle use of spot varnishes would add a high-end, jewel-like quality to the presentation that both highlighted the sleek lines of the product design while keeping the drive securely in place," the agency says.

1

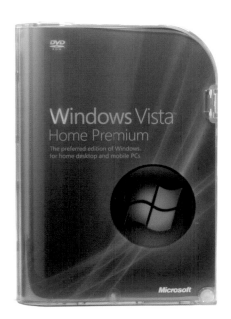

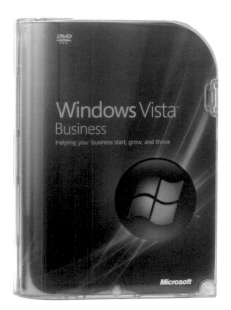

creativity 38 annual awards

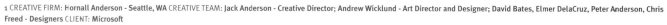

1 CREATIVE FIRM: Hornall Anderson - Seattle, WA CREATIVE TEAM: Jack Anderson - Creative Director; Andrew Wicklund - Art Director and Designer; David Bates, Elmer DelaCruz, Peter Anderson, Chris Freed - Designers CLIENT: Microsoft

PLATINUM Ⓟ

CREATIVE FIRM: **Crabtree + Company - Falls Church, VA**

CREATIVE TEAM: **Susan Angrisani - Creative Director, Illustrator; Lisa Suchy - Production Manager; Billy Weinheimer - Production Artist**

CLIENT: **Solomons Island Winery**

Rosé Of Merlot

Trends come and go, but the allure of the grape—and the human body that enjoys it—remains a perennial favorite. Still, says Falls Church, Virginia's Crabtree + Company, "Solomons Island Winery decided to reposition one of its wines to appeal to a new demographic." Playing on the current upsurge in rosé wines' popularity, the agency was asked to repackage a white merlot to target women in their mid-twenties to early forties, while at the same time retaining its broad base of male consumers.

"Our client's goal, first and foremost, was to capture a specific consumer segment who had a newfound interest in rosé wines," the firm says. "In the past, rosé had been popular with an older cohort, but in recent years it has taken root with a younger, more affluent audience, fond of enjoying wine socially. C+C created imagery that evoked sensuality in a stylish way, perfectly engaging the target audience and helping relaunch our client's Rosé of Merlot brand."

To make this particular blend stand out, C+C developed artwork as unique—and familiar—as the flavors themselves. The labels "convey a classic, master's style, echoing Degas, while adding a twist of the contemporary in the wholly unexpected tattoo," they explain. "Employing a nude figure, it was important to balance sophistication and broad appeal without appearing off-putting." Why the focus on the body, complete with floral tattoo? "The language of wine has always had a connection to things of beauty, including both flowers and the human form," C+C maintains. "We speak of wine as being floral and having a rich bouquet. We describe wine as full-bodied, and having both legs and a nose. The label makes these connections more apparent and the wine itself, as a sommelier might say, a little more approachable."

1

2

3

4

5

1 CREATIVE FIRM: **Anthem New York - New York, NY** CREATIVE TEAM: **Walter Perlowski - Creative Director; Kathleen Bertini - Sr. Designer** CLIENT: **Unilever** 2 CREATIVE FIRM: **Sabingrafik, Inc. - Carlsbad, CA** CREATIVE TEAM: **Tracy Sabin - Illustrator/Designer; Bridget Sabin - Art Director** CLIENT: **Seafarer Baking Company** 3 CREATIVE FIRM: **Pearlfisher - London, England** CREATIVE TEAM: **Lisa Simpson - Creative Director & Designer; Serge Bloch - Illustration** CLIENT: **Hershey** 4 CREATIVE FIRM: **Futura DDB d.o.o. - Ljubljana, Slovenia** CREATIVE TEAM: **Zare Kerin - Creative Director** CLIENT: **Istenic** 5 CREATIVE FIRM: **Futura DDB d.o.o. - Ljubljana, Slovenia** CREATIVE TEAM: **Zare Kerin - Creative Director; Bojan Jablanovec - Copywriter; Blaz Topolinjak - Designer** CLIENT: **Ljubljanske mlekarne**

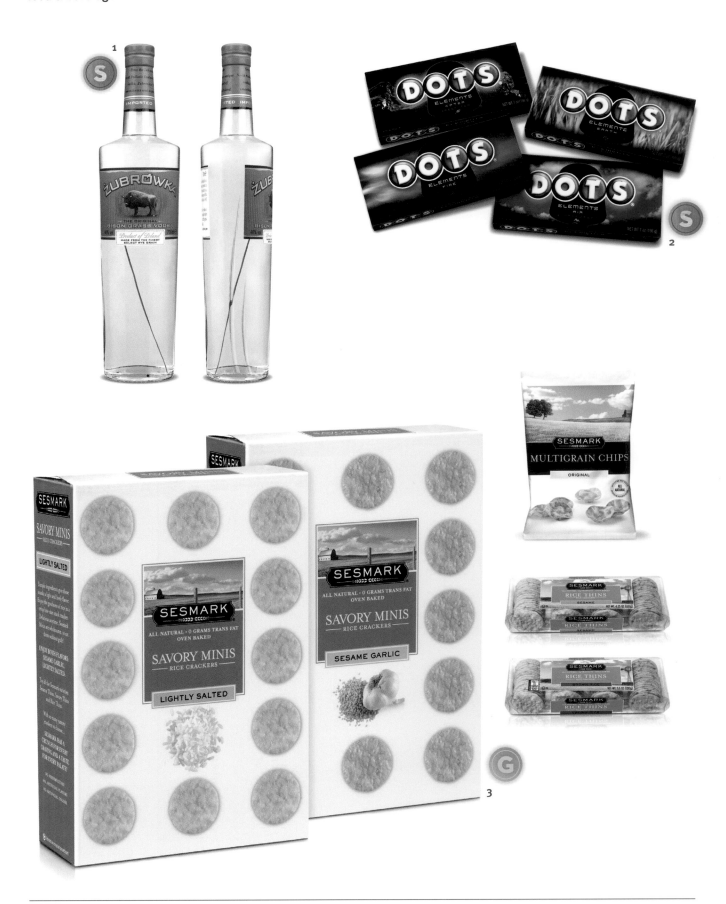

1 CREATIVE FIRM: Pearlfisher - London, England CREATIVE TEAM: Lisa Simpson - Creative Director & Designer; Sarah Butler - Designer; Simon Critchley - Illustration CLIENT: Polmos Bialystok
2 CREATIVE FIRM: Design Resource Center - Naperville, IL CREATIVE TEAM: John Norman - Creative Director; Eric Timm - Designer CLIENT: Tootsie Roll Industries LLC URL: www.drcchicago.com
3 CREATIVE FIRM: Wallace Church, Inc. - New York, NY CREATIVE TEAM: Stan Church - Creative Director; Marco Escalante - Design Director; Maritess Manaluz - Designer CLIENT: PANOS brands

1 CREATIVE FIRM: Biz-R - Totnes, UK CREATIVE TEAM: Blair Thomson - Creative Director / Designer; Paul Warren - Designer CLIENT: Clives Organic Bakery 2 CREATIVE FIRM: Mark Oliver, Inc. - Solvang, CA CREATIVE TEAM: Mark Oliver - Creative Director; Patty Driskel - Art Director; Chris Wiltse - Illustration CLIENT: Full of Life Foods 3 CREATIVE FIRM: Mark Oliver, Inc. - Solvang, CA CREATIVE TEAM: Mark Oliver - Creative Director; Patty Driskel - Art Director; Deborah Denker - Photography CLIENT: Original Rangoon

1

2

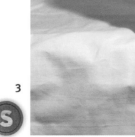

3

1 CREATIVE FIRM: **Pure Equator - Nottingham, UK** CREATIVE TEAM: **David Rogers - Creative Director; Tamara Johnson - Designer** CLIENT: **Winterbotham Darby** 2 CREATIVE FIRM: **Cornerstone Strategic Branding - New York, NY** CREATIVE TEAM: **Cornerstone Strategic Branding** CLIENT: **Silver Brands, Inc.** 3 CREATIVE FIRM: **Shea, Inc. - Minneapolis, MN** CREATIVE TEAM: **Susan Donahue - Artistic Director; Amy Barthel - Graphic Designer; Rebecca Bradley - Illustrator** CLIENT: **Macy's**

1 CREATIVE FIRM: **Zunda Group, LLC - South Norwalk, CT** CREATIVE TEAM: **Charles Zunda, Todd Nickel** CLIENT: **World Finer Foods, Inc.** 2 CREATIVE FIRM: **Shikatani Lacroix Design - Toronto, ON, Canada** CREATIVE TEAM: **Christopher Woo - Graphic Designer, Creative Director; Kim Yokota - Creative Director; Mark Willard - Photographer** CLIENT: **Labatt Breweries** 3 CREATIVE FIRM: **Shikatani Lacroix Design - Toronto, ON, Canada** CREATIVE TEAM: **Ocean McCrindle - Graphic Designer; Kim Yokota - Creative Director; Mark Willard, Doug Bradshaw - Photographers** CLIENT: **Gourmantra Foods** 4 CREATIVE FIRM: **TRIDVAJEDAN - Zagreb, Croatia** CREATIVE TEAM: **Ms. Jelena Gvozdanovic - Creative Director; Ms. Izvorka Juric - Creative Director, Art Director, Designer** CLIENT: **Brachia p.z.**

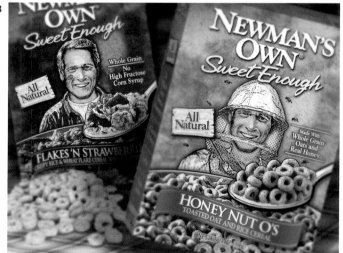

1 CREATIVE FIRM: **Sterling Cross Creative - Sonoma, CA** CREATIVE TEAM: **Jerome Maureze - Designer; Mike Gray - Illustrator** CLIENT: **Diageo** 2 CREATIVE FIRM: **Sterling Cross Creative - Sonoma, CA** CREATIVE TEAM: **Peggy Cross - Creative Director; Rico Peng - Designer** CLIENT: **Trinchero** 3 CREATIVE FIRM: **Zunda Group, LLC - South Norwalk, CT** CREATIVE TEAM: **Charles Zunda, Maija Riekstins-Rutens** CLIENT: **Newman's Own, Inc.** 4 CREATIVE FIRM: **Launch Creative Marketing - Chicago, IL** CREATIVE TEAM: **Liz Schwartz - Sr. Art Director; Bruce Butcher - Creative Director** CLIENT: **Sara Lee Food & Beverage**

1 CREATIVE FIRM: it∋m:grafika - Cracow, Poland CREATIVE TEAM: Igor Banaszewski - Graphic Designer, Art Director CLIENT: Alma Market S.A. 2 CREATIVE FIRM: FactorTres Comunicacion - Mexico CREATIVE TEAM: Rodrigo Cordova - Design Director / Designer; Edgar Medina - Designer CLIENT: Panni Foods 3 CREATIVE FIRM: Sterling Cross Creative - Sonoma, CA CREATIVE TEAM: Peggy Cross - Creative Director CLIENT: Wente Vineyards

food & beverage

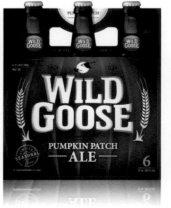

1 CREATIVE FIRM: **Optima Soulsight - Highland Park, IL** CREATIVE TEAM: **Leslie Park - Designer** CLIENT: **Coffee Masters** 2 CREATIVE FIRM: **Optima Soulsight - Highland Park, IL** CREATIVE TEAM: **Optima Soulsight** CLIENT: **Lake Champlain Chocolates** 3 CREATIVE FIRM: **Object 9 - Baton Rouge, LA** CREATIVE TEAM: **Object 9** CLIENT: **Wild Goose Brewery**

S
1

2

G
3

S
4

1 CREATIVE FIRM: Optima Soulsight - Highland Park, IL CREATIVE TEAM: Adam Ferguson CLIENT: Miller Brewing Co. 2 CREATIVE FIRM: The Biondo Group - Stamford, CT CREATIVE TEAM: Charles Biondo - Creative Director; The Biondo Group - Creative Team; Peter Pioppo - American Beverage Corp CLIENT: American Beverage Corporation 3 CREATIVE FIRM: Optima Soulsight - Highland Park, IL CREATIVE TEAM: Aaron Funke - Sr. Designer CLIENT: Duke, Red 7 & Wellington 4 CREATIVE FIRM: Hornall Anderson - Seattle, WA CREATIVE TEAM: Larry Anderson - Art Director and Designer; Jay Hilburn, Vu Nguyen, Elmer DelaCruz - Designers CLIENT: Widmer Brewing Company

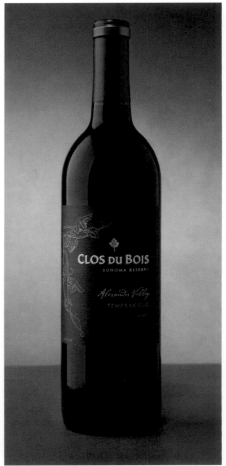

1 CREATIVE FIRM: Keller Crescent Company - Evansville, IN CREATIVE TEAM: Randy Rohn - Executive Creative Director; Bill Shuman - Creative Director CLIENT: Heaven Hill 2 CREATIVE FIRM: Sterling Cross Creative - Sonoma, CA CREATIVE TEAM: Peggy Cross - Creative Director; Julie Butts - Designer CLIENT: Beam Wine Estate 3 CREATIVE FIRM: Object 9 - Baton Rouge, LA CREATIVE TEAM: Object 9 CLIENT: Fire & Flavor Grilling Company

1 CREATIVE FIRM: Sterling Cross Creative - Sonoma, CA CREATIVE TEAM: Jerome Maureze - Designer CLIENT: Diageo 2 CREATIVE FIRM: Keller Crescent Company - Evansville, IN CREATIVE TEAM: Randy Rohn - Executive Creative Director CLIENT: Heaven Hill 3 CREATIVE FIRM: Sterling Cross Creative - Sonoma, CA CREATIVE TEAM: Julie Butts - Designer CLIENT: Diageo 4 CREATIVE FIRM: Optima Soulsight - Highland Park, IL CREATIVE TEAM: Mindy Kyung CLIENT: Unilever

1 CREATIVE FIRM: **Object 9 - Baton Rouge, LA** CREATIVE TEAM: **Object 9** CLIENT: **Flying Dog Brewery** 2 CREATIVE FIRM: **Object 9 - Baton Rouge, LA** CREATIVE TEAM: **Object 9** CLIENT: **Caffe Bom Dia**
3 CREATIVE FIRM: **Object 9 - Baton Rouge, LA** CREATIVE TEAM: **Object 9** CLIENT: **Reily Foods Company**

creativity 38 annual awards

PLATINUM P

Boxes Create Buzz

CREATIVE FIRM: narrow house - Madrid, Spain
CREATIVE TEAM: narrow house
CLIENT: pasión for fashion

Madrid-area design firm Narrow House loves its clients—especially their very first one, Pasión for Fashion, an online boutique. Narrow House designed their brand identity, including Web site design. "At that time they had just started their business and their budget was particularly small, in fact we accepted bags, shoes and jewelry as payment," they explain.

Given creative license to develop this identity, Narrow House took a chance and created a range of limited-edition packaging, starting with three special-edition boxes the first year. "They proved to be an enormous success, creating a buzz and gaining free publicity in many newspapers and fashion magazines," the firm says.

Today Narrow House continues to design up to ten different boxes annually for Pasión for Fashion, and the pasión endures: "We base the designs for each box on the fashion/beauty theme, but they can easily go off on a tangent, often

becoming quite abstract. They are great fun to design and we are lucky that our client loves what we do and gives us freedom to do it."

PLATINUM P

CREATIVE FIRM: **NICOSIA CREATIVE EXPRESSO (NiCE LTD.) -
New York, NY**

CREATIVE TEAM: **Davide NICOSIA - Creative Director; Ian CARN-
DUFF - 3D Design Director; Ian SWANSON - 3Product Designer**

CLIENT: **Procter&Gamble**

1

2

3

1 CREATIVE FIRM: **NICOSIA CREATIVE EXPRESSO (NiCE LTD.)** - New York, NY CREATIVE TEAM: Davide NICOSIA - Creative Director; Ian CARNDUFF - 3D Design Director C_IENT: Procter&Gamble 2 CRE-
ATIVE FIRM: **Design Resource Center** - Naperville, IL CREATIVE TEAM: John Norman - Creative Director; Traci Milner - Designer CLIENT: Noni Biotech International URL: www.drcchicago.com 3 CREATIVE
FIRM: **Pearlfisher** - London, England CREATIVE TEAM: Sarah Butler - Creative Director & Designer; Sarah Carr - Designer; Darren Foley - Realisation Director; Henry Preston - Digital Artworker; Kerry
Plummer - Account Director; Sarah Picgeon - Designer CLIENT: **Nude Skincare**

1 CREATIVE FIRM: **Webb Scarlett deVlam - Chicago, IL** CREATIVE TEAM: **Webb Scarlett deVlam** CLIENT: **Proctor and Gamble** 2 CREATIVE FIRM: **The Weber Group, Inc. - Racine, WI** CREATIVE TEAM: **Anthony Weber - President; Scott Schreiber, Shad Smith - Senior Designers; Steve Westfall - Designer** CLIENT: **S.C. Johnson & Son, Inc.** 3 CREATIVE FIRM: **Webb Scarlett deVlam - Chicago, IL** CREATIVE TEAM: **Webb Scarlett deVlam** CLIENT: **Proctor and Gamble** 4 CREATIVE FIRM: **The Weber Group, Inc. - Racine, WI** CREATIVE TEAM: **Anthony Weber - President; Scott Schreiber, Shad Smith - Senior Designers; Steve Westfall - Designer** CLIENT: **S.C. Johnson & Son, Inc.**

1

PLATINUM P

Trader Vics Restaurant Menus

CREATIVE FIRM: **Jacob Tyler Creative Group - San Diego, CA**
CREATIVE TEAM: **Les Kollegian, Richard Truss - Creative Directors; Gordon Tsuji - Designer**
CLIENT: **Trader Vics**

Trader Vics invented the mai tai seventy-five years ago, and so when they hired San Diego's Jacob Tyler Creative Group to update their brand, they sought something similarly iconic and timeless, while at the same time contemporary and elegant for their restaurant and Ultra Bar launch in Las Vegas in the fall of 2007.

Jacob Tyler started with the calling card of any restaurant: the menu. "After reviewing interior design samples of the overall restaurant look and feel, we decided to use a menu made of wood that would contrast nicely with the silver and dark brown organic color palette chosen for furniture and accessories," the firm says. "As well, we had the logo and complimentary design etched and burned into the menu to compliment the Polynesian feel." To enhance the menu with minute, yet elegant details, Jacob Tyler decorated the covers with a small illustration representing the place setting of each meal portion.

A restaurant doesn't stay on top for three-quarters of a century without constant adaptation, and Jacob Tyler was aware of this. "The executive chef changes the dinner and wine menu often, thus the interior pages had to be easily reprinted and changed," they say. "This is why we opted to design an extremely high-end cover that could be bound internally for simple removal of pages rather than using multiple colors and high-end paper on the inside." The ease of use didn't affect the rich feel of the presentation; after rejecting a brushed steel backing for each cover, Jacob Tyler and Trader Vics settled on a less expensive leather back—which also fared well with the binding. "the menus look extremely expensive," says the firm, "but they were extremely well received by restaurant staff—and customers."

creativity 38 annual awards

1

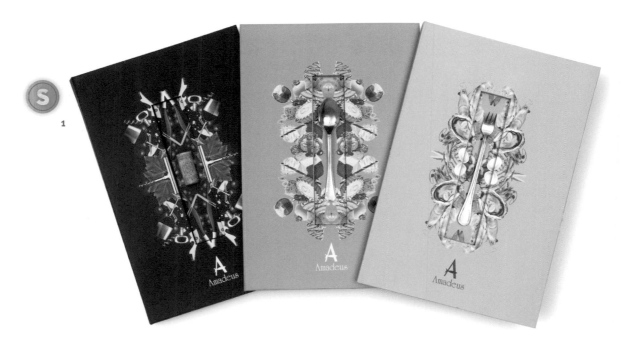

S

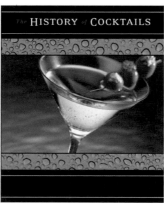

2

THE MARTINI
Bombay Sapphire Gin
or Level Vodka and
Cinzano Dry Vermouth.

NEGRONI
Beefeater Gin, Campari,
Cinzano Rosso
Vermouth and soda.

The HISTORY of COCKTAILS

« REMEMBERING QUALITY 1990s

A movement toward quality versus quantity started in this era, which
included micro brew beers, fine wines and boutique-quality spirits. The
popularity of wine coolers in the 1980s led to a new regard for
traditional wine.

PINOT GRIGIO
Francis Coppola
Bianco, California
00.00

Maso Canali, Italy
00.00

Santa Margherita,
Italy 00.00

CHARDONNAY
Beringer Founders'
Estate, California
00.00

Kendall-Jackson
Vintner's Reserve,
California 00.00

Chalone Monterey,
Monterey, California
00.00

Sonoma-Cutrer
"Russian River
Ranches," Sonoma
Coast, California 00.00

Frei Brothers
Reserve, Russian
River Valley,
California 00.00

« FUN AND FRUITY 1980s

A time when wine coolers adorned the hands of many and when
happy-hour traditions were made of peach schnapps and fuzzy navels.

**AMARETTO
SOUR**
Disaronno
Amaretto Liqueur
with sweet & sour
flavors.

MELON BALL
SKYY Vodka, Midori
Melon Liqueur and
orange juice.

POM TINI
Grey Goose Vodka,
PAMA Pomegranate
Liqueur, cranberry
and lime juices.

BLUE LAGOON
Pyrat Rum, DeKuyper
Blue Curacao and
pineapple juice.

**ORIGINAL
MOJITO**
BACARDI Rum and
soda muddled with
fresh mint and lime.

3

Grand Gold Bite

Dublin Apple

LATE NIGHT BITES

KILLIAN'S
IRISH RED.
PREMIUM LAGER

BEER

1 CREATIVE FIRM: **Ogilvy Brasil - São Paolo - Brazil** CREATIVE TEAM: **Marco Antonio Almeida, Reinaldo César Júnior - Creative Directors; Milene Azevedo - Art Director; Claúdia Pimenta - Copywriter** CLIENT: **Amadeus Restaurant 2** CREATIVE FIRM: **Patrick Henry Creative Promotions, Inc. - Stafford, TX** CREATIVE TEAM: **Christy Sevier - Assistant Director; Julia Austin Church - Art Director** CLIENT: **Inter-state Hotels & Resorts 3** CREATIVE FIRM: **Patrick Henry Creative Promotions, Inc. - Stafford, TX** CREATIVE TEAM: **Julia Austin Church - Art Director** CLIENT: **Hospitality USA**

PLATINUM ℗

Zunda Design Group Celebrates 25 years
1981-2006

CREATIVE FIRM: Zunda Group, LLC - South Norwalk, CT

CREATIVE TEAM: Charles Zunda, Todd Nickel, Maija Riekstins-Rutens, Dan Price, Lauren Millard, Siri Korasgren, Doug Pashley

CLIENT: Zunda Group, LLC

The Zunda Design Group likes to center its annual holiday promotions around creativity, individuality and the spirit of giving back—and its 2006 contribution was no exception. "[It is] an expression of gratitude and thanks to those with whom we have had the pleasure and privilege of working with over the past year," says the Connecticut agency. And they took the "spirit" part literally, choosing to communicate their warm wishes through the gift of wine: an Italian Moscato d'Asti, a light, festive sparkler suitable for an apéritif or as a dessert wine.

The team designed and critiqued the full creative concept, which included the labels and hangtags as a commemoration of the agency's twenty-fifth year of "creating brands that inspire." The entire design team contributed to the conceptual development, as they invited each member to create a variety of labels that visually communicated the themes of celebration and festivity through the use of color, shape and imagery—along with "essential graphic design elements hav-

ing an individual personality and appeal to the recipient," they note.

"The unique, customized design of the hangtag supported the theme with copy, such as 'Eight designs as unique as the individuals who created them' and 'We wish you health, happiness and inspiration throughout the upcoming year,'" cites the agency.

The limited run of five hundred bottles and hangtags with eight different labels, Zunda says, was "a labor of care and partnership, as each was applied to the bottle by hand, lending a more homespun, crafted appeal." Cheers.

1

2

3

1 CREATIVE FIRM: **Wallace Church, Inc. - New York, NY** CREATIVE TEAM: **Stan Church - Creative Director; Chung-Tao Tu - Designer** CLIENT: **Wallace Church, Inc** URL: **www.wallacechurch.com** 2 CREATIVE
FIRM: **Hershey|Cause - Santa Monica, CA** CREATIVE TEAM: **R. Christine Hershey - Creative Director; Joanna Lee - Design Director; Jerry Lazaro - Senior Designer** CLIENT: **Hershey|Cause** 3 CREATIVE
FIRM: **Hunter Public Relations - New York, NY** CREATIVE TEAM: **Louisa Caragan - Creative Director; Laura Desilvio - Designer** CLIENT: **Diageo North America**

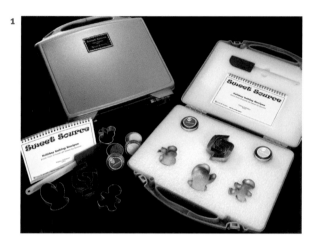

1 CREATIVE FIRM: Cases By Source, Inc. - Mahwah, NJ CREATIVE TEAM: Matthew Adler - Art Director, Designer; Emily Adler - Designer; Gabrielle Simon - Producer 2 CREATIVE FIRM: Hunter Public Relations, LLC - New York, NY CREATIVE TEAM: Louisa Caragan - Creative Director & Designer CLIENT: Diageo North America 3 CREATIVE FIRM: HBO - New York, NY CREATIVE TEAM: Venus Dennison - Creative Director; Christian Martillo - Design Manager; Mary Tchorbajian - Art Director CLIENT: HBO

1

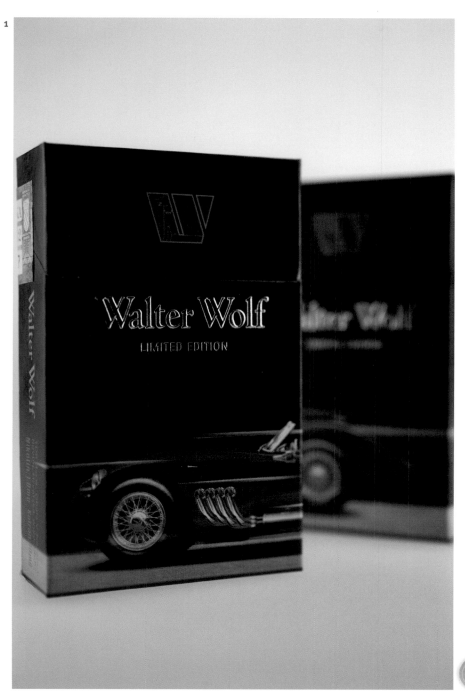

PLATINUM P

CREATIVE FIRM: **G2 - New York, NY**

CREATIVE TEAM: **Kurt Haiman - Founder**

CLIENT: **Pantone**

1 CREATIVE FIRM: **Valentine Group New York - New York, NY** CREATIVE TEAM: **Robert Valentine - Art Director & Designer** CLIENT: **InterfaceFLOR** 2 CREATIVE FIRM: **G2 - New York, NY** CREATIVE TEAM: **Kurt Haiman - Founder** CLIENT: **Pantone** 3 CREATIVE FIRM: **The UXB - Beverly Hills, CA** CREATIVE TEAM: **NJ Goldston - CEO and Founder** CLIENT: **Cleatskins** 4 CREATIVE FIRM: **G2 - New York, NY** CREATIVE TEAM: **Kurt Haiman - Founder** CLIENT: **Pantone** 5 CREATIVE FIRM: **Rosslyn Snitrak Design - Seattle, WA** CREATIVE TEAM: **Rosslyn Snitrak - Designer** CLIENT: **Rosy Rings**

1

2

3

1 CREATIVE FIRM: i_d Buero - Stuttgart, Germany CREATIVE TEAM: Oliver-A. Krimmel, Prof. Uli Cluss - Creative Directors; Anja Osterwalder, Pia Bardesono, Susanne Wagner, Martin Drozdowski - Art Directors CLIENT: Pro Bono 2 CREATIVE FIRM: Optima Soulsight - Highland Park, IL CREATIVE TEAM: Adam Ferguson - Creative Director CLIENT: Alonzo Savage 3 CREATIVE FIRM: Optima Soulsight - Highland Park, IL CREATIVE TEAM: Justin Berguland - Designer CLIENT: G-Men

ALTERNATIVE
MEDIA

1

creativity 38 annual awards

1 CREATIVE FIRM: Campbell-Ewald - Warren, MI CREATIVE TEAM: Bill Ludwig - Vice Chairman, Chief Creative Officer; Mark Simon, Jim Gorman - Executive Creative Directors; Marcia Levenson - SVP, Associate Creative Director; Kayu Tai - Art Director CLIENT: United States Postal Service

1

Concepto: La compañia de danza Elisa Montes está cerca de ti. Llegó a Dallas.

Idea: Usamos la imagen de una bailarina efectuando la "5ta. Posición" de ballet. Se manipuló la impresión y la colocación de los pósters de manera que la bailarina se veía en 3a. Dimensión.

Estrategia: Se elaboraron anuncios impresos con dimensiones de 20 X 30 pulgadas. El frente de la bailarina se imprimió en un lado del póster, mientras que la espalda se imprimió en el otro. El póster se pegó hasta la mitad dejando la espalda viendo hacia la calle. La parte superior del póster se dobló hacia el frente. De manera que lo que ve la gente es a una bailarina en 3a. Dimensión haciendo la 5ta. Posición de ballet. Los pósters se pegaron cerca del LCC que es donde se presentó la compañía de danza.

Find **your**
one in a million

1 CREATIVE FIRM: **Dieste Harmel & Partners - Dallas, TX** CREATIVE TEAM: **Alex Duplan - Creative Director; Ernesto Fernandez, Florencia Leibaschoff - Copywriters; Sarai Gomez, Ale Torres - Art Directors** CLIENT: **Latino Cultural Center 2** CREATIVE FIRM: **AKQA - London, England** CREATIVE TEAM: **James Capp, Colin Byrne - Creative Directors; Shahpour Abbasvand - Art Director; Claire Langler - Project Manager** CLIENT: **Yell Group**

PLATINUM P

CREATIVE FIRM: AKQA - London, England

CREATIVE TEAM: Daniel Bonner - Co-Chief Creative Officer; Masaya Nakade, Andrew Tuffs - Associate Creative Directors; Stefan Kostov - Designer; David Wiltshire - Creative Developer; Paul Anglin - Copywriter

CLIENT: Nike

NIKEiD London Studio - Nike
Shoppers create the ads

If you've ever thought that having one's design on an athletic shoe is the domain only of Michael Jordan and other stratospheric celebrities, let the NIKEiD customization studio in London's NikeTown blow that idea to pieces.

At the studio, any customer can spend time with a design consultant to create completely custom Nikes. "We wanted to open up this experience to a wider audience, letting sneaker heads and cool young Londoners in on the game," says AKQA, the agency that spearheaded the kickoff event. "We invited one hundred and fifty influential Londoners via personalized video messages on complimentary iPod Nanos." After making that splash, "We then made the shoe addicts who created their own designs the stars of the campaign. Once people had created their kicks, we displayed their photo, shoe and a line written by them against a kaleidoscopic background on giant video walls in NikeTown's windows."

Each "kaleidoscope," dynamically created out of components from every different customer's design, ensured the unique-

ness of every ad. The ads themselves didn't stay in the store; these one-off pieces appeared in near-real time in Nike-Town, via a live feed at NIKEiD.com and on cube installations on the streets of London. On top of that, AKQA reports, "the cubes took the ads to a wider audience, releasing fast-track studio appointments via Bluetooth, giving everyone the opportunity to get into the [NIKEiD] studio."

1

2 Name: Rave Wireless
Industry: Wireless Communications

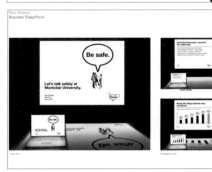

1 CREATIVE FIRM: **Ad Planet Group - Singapore** CREATIVE TEAM: **Teck Chong Leo - Executive Creative Director; Yi Long Chen, Joyce Lim - Art Directors; Alfred Teo - Associate Creative Director/Copy-writer; Joy Lee - Senior Copywriter** CLIENT: **Alteco Chemical 2** CREATIVE FIRM: **Siegel+Gale - New York, NY** CREATIVE TEAM: **Sven Seger - Worldwide Executive Creative Director; Howard Belk - Chief Creative Officer; Doug Sellers - Creative Director; Rob Saywitz - Senior Designer** CLIENT: **Rave**

creativity 38 annual awards

PLATINUM Ⓟ

CREATIVE FIRM: AKQA - London, England

CREATIVE TEAM: Nick Bailey - Associate Creative Director; Duan Evans - Creative Director; Davor Krvavac - Art Director; Paul Anglin - Copywriter; Stefan Kostov - Designer; Richard Leggatt - Associate Creative Development Director

CLIENT: Nike

Nike 1/1

A new Turner Prize for street art

Nike's iconic Dunks, introduced in 1985, have been everything from a basketball shoe to an icon of skateboard culture—but until now, no one had used the celebrated sneaker to represent street art and its ensuing manifestations as its own design. "Our initial brief was to celebrate Nike Dunks as a canvas for creativity," explains London's AKQA, the design hired to get the word out. "We flipped this around to use Nike Dunks as a platform for celebrating the creativity of Europe's street-inspired artists." The ensuing project, Nike 1/1, presented an opportunity for upcoming street artists to create an original piece of art to exhibit at Art Basel in Switzerland—and to serve as the inspiration for a completely original Nike Dunk design.

AKQA recruited street artists through online creative communities and invited them to submit their responses to the brief, entitled Art of Football. "The work could be graffiti, video, installation—it just had to be original," the agency says. Getting the ball rolling, however, involved an exercise in viral nuance. "We knew launching via conventional channels would kill our credibility, so we kicked off 1/1 with our own piece of art, a short video clip that announced 1/1 to our core audience," AKQA says. "The film was seeded across Europe's creative communities and we watched the buzz build."

After over two thousand individual pieces rolled in over the course of four weeks, the judging began. Finalists exhibited their work at Art Basel, coinciding with the International Art Fair and the first weekend of soccer's Euro 2008 competition. The eventual winner had his work immortalized on a unique pair of Nike Dunks: the ultimate limited edition.

1

2

3

1 CREATIVE FIRM: **AKQA - London, England** CREATIVE TEAM: **Daniel Bonner - Co-Chief Creative Officer; Duan Evans - Creative Director; Nick Bailey - Associate Creative Director; Rodrigo Sobral - Art Director; Rick Williams - Associate Creative Development Director; Alex Wills - Motion Graphics Director** CLIENT: **Nike** URL: **www.akqa.com** 2 CREATIVE FIRM: **MTV Networks Creative Services - New York, NY** CREATIVE TEAM: **Leslie Leventman - EVP/Creative Director; Carol Donovan - Executive Producer; Beth McCarthy - Executive Producer/Director; Vicki English, Lou Stellato - Producers; Cheryl Family - SVP, Editorial Director; Scott Wadler - SVP, Design; Matt Herron - Executive Producer/Director of Video; Nick Gamma - Design Director; Houman Pourmand, Anthony Carlucci, Shelly Fukushima, Joelle Mercado-Lau, Casey Stock, Arya Vilay - Designers; Ken Saji - Senior Copy Director; Tori Turner, David Lanfair, Chris Knight, Tory Mast - Copywriters; Will Deloney, Johnny Moreno - Producer/Editors; Elizabeth Boscoe - Associate Producer, Michael Boczon, Rhys Ernst - Editors; Oyku Cakar - Assistant Editor; Sarah Rabin, Kelly Wilson - Production Assistants; Hector Cardenas, Amanda Pecharsky, Cem Adiyaman, Jeffrey Welk, Anya Zavorina, Ashley Cromwell, Trevor Bowers, Marisol Baltierra, Ryan Hooks - Motion Graphics; Reggie Austin - Video Intern; Laura Calamari - Administrative Director; Barbara Crawford - Project Manager** CLIENT: **MTV Networks** 3 CREATIVE FIRM: **MTV Networks Creative Services - New York, NY** CREATIVE TEAM: **Leslie Leventman - EVP/Creative Director; Scott Wadler - SVP, Design; Joelle Mercado-Lau - Art Director/Designer; Red Giant Studio - Design/Production Company; Ken Saji - Senior Copy Director; Patrick O'Sullivan - Copy Director; Gil Arevalo, Chris Knight, Tory Mast - Copywriters; Matt Herron - Executive Producer/Director of Video; Hector Cardenas - Producer/Editor/Animation Artist; Elizabeth Boscoe - Associate Producer; Michael Boczon, Johnny Moreno - Editors; Oyku Cakar - Associate Editor; Sarah Rabin - Production Assistant; Marisol Baltierra - Animation Artist; Audrey Singer, Elizabeth Mundy - Account Directors** CLIENT: **MTV Networks**

1

2

1 CREATIVE FIRM: **AKQA - London, England** CREATIVE TEAM: **Daniel Bonner - Chief Creative Officer; Masaya Nakade, Andrew Tuffs - Associate Creative Directors; Stefan Kostov - Designer; David Wiltshire - Creative Developer; Paul Anglin - Copywriter** CLIENT: **Nike** URL: **www.akqa.com** 2 CREATIVE FIRM: **AKQA - London, England** CREATIVE TEAM: **Daniel Bonner - Co-Chief Creative Officer; Masaya Nakade, Nick Bailey - Associate Creative Directors; Paul Anglin - Copywriter; Emily Bull - Head of Production; Rodrigo Sobral - Art Director** CLIENT: **Nike** URL: **www.akqa.com**

1

Following the newest projects

You put me under your spell

From June 1st Studio Universal won't be available on SKY

and for you I overcame all obstacles

2

It's a new morning.

It's a new morning

3

4

1 CREATIVE FIRM: NBC Universal Global Networks Italia - Rome, Italy CREATIVE TEAM: NBC Universal Global Networks Italia CLIENT: Studio Universal URL: www.studiouniversal.it 2 CREATIVE FIRM: Primary Design, Inc. - Haverhill, MA CREATIVE TEAM: Mike Amaru, Sharyn Rogers, Jules Epstein CLIENT: Avalon Morningside Park 3 CREATIVE FIRM: MTV Networks - New York, NY CREATIVE TEAM: Nigel Cox-Hagan - Creative Director: EVP Creative & Marketing, VH1; Phil Delbourgo - SVP Brand & Design, VH1; Tony Maxwell - VP On-Air Promos, VH1; Nancy Mazzei - Art Director; Wendell Wooten - VP Creative Production, VH1; Traci Terrill - Editorial Director; Beth Wawerna, Evan Goldstein, Dan Tucker - Writers; Julie Ruiz - Designer; Shannon Horan, Allison Sierra - Producers; Pascal Duval - Illustrator; Adam Wilson - Senior Director On-Air Promotions; Micah Perta - Promo Writer/Producer; Fredgy Noel - Promo Junior Writer/Producer CLIENT: VH1 4 CREATIVE FIRM: MTV Networks Creative Services - New York, NY CREATIVE TEAM: Leslie Leventman - EVP/Creative Director; Scott Wadler - SVP, Design; Nick Gamma - Design Director; Joelle Mercado-Lau - Art Director/Designer; David Lanfair - Associate Copy Director; Gil Arevalo - Copywriter; Matt Herron - Executive Producer/Director/Editor; Marty Buccafusco - Producer; Tom Arnold - Director of Photography; Jon Zelenak - Editor; Elizabeth Boscoe - Associate Producer; Sarah Rabin - Production Assistant; Amanda Pecharsky, Min Soo Cho, Dimitri Luedemann, James Issacs, Natalie To - Motion Graphics CLIENT: MTV Networks

1

2

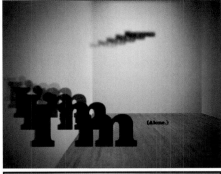

3

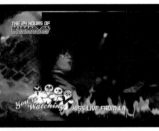

1 CREATIVE FIRM: **MTV Networks - New York, NY** CREATIVE TEAM: Nigel Cox-Hagan - Creative Director: EVP Creative & Marketing, VH1; Phil Delbourgo - SVP Brand & Design, VH1; Tony Maxwell - VP On-Air Promos, VH1; Wendell Wooten - VP Creative Production, VH1; Traci Terrill - Editorial Director; Jimmy Fingers, Jim Fitzgerald - Art Directors; Allison Sierra, Shannon Horan - Producers; Mammoth, We Are Royale - Designers; Adam Wilson - Senior Director On-Air Promotions; Corey Nealon - Promo Writer/Producer CLIENT: VH1 2 CREATIVE FIRM: **MTV Networks - New York, NY** CREATIVE TEAM: Stephen Friedman - General Manager; Ross Martin - Head of Programming; Eric Conte - Executive Producer; Paul Ricci - Supervising Producer; Sophia Cranshaw - Vice-President, Director, On-Air Promotions; Noopur Agarwal - Manager Public Affairs, mtvU Marketing; Chris McCarthy - VP mtvU Marketing and Strategic Development; Gina Esposito - Director, Music & Talent CLIENT: JED Foundation
3 CREATIVE FIRM: **MTV Networks - New York, NY** CREATIVE TEAM: Nigel Cox-Hagan - Creative Director: EVP Creative & Marketing, VH1; Phil Delbourgo - SVP Brand & Design, VH1; Wendell Wooten - VP Creative Production, VH1; Dave Perry - Producer; Gary Encarnacion - Graphics Producer; Daniela Patre - Manager Promotional Graphics Production; Georgina Martinez - Manager Promotional Graphics Scheduling; Tim Harrington - Designer; Lucas Ajemian - Bug Coordinator CLIENT: VH1

1

2

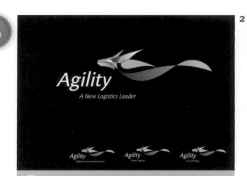

3

4

1 CREATIVE FIRM: **AKQA - London, England** CREATIVE TEAM: **James Hilton - Co-Chief Creative Officer; Miles Unwin, Kevin Russell - Associate Creative Directors; Per Nielsen, Matt Longstaff - Copywriters; Richard Hedges - Client Partner** CLIENT: **Unilever** 2 CREATIVE FIRM: **Siegel+Gale - New York, NY** CREATIVE TEAM: **Sven Seger - Worldwide Executive Creative Director; Marcus Bartlett - Design Director; Monica Chai - Senior Designer; Inesa Figueroa - Senior Interactive Strategist; Holmfridur Hardardottir - Project Director; Howard Belk - Chief Creative Officer** CLIENT: **Agility** 3 CREATIVE FIRM: **Primary Design, Inc. - Haverhill, MA** CREATIVE TEAM: **Kristina Mikulencak, Kristen Lossman, Sharyn Rogers, Jules Epstein** CLIENT: **Avalon Bay** 4 CREATIVE FIRM: **Cunning Communications Inc. - New York, NY** CREATIVE TEAM: **Floyd Hayes - Creative Director; Mark Voysey - President; Paymon Parsia - Account Manager** CLIENT: **NYC & Company** URL: **www.cunning.com**

PLATINUM P

CREATIVE FIRM: MTV Networks - New York, NY

CREATIVE TEAM: Nigel Cox-Hagan - Creative Director: EVP Creative & Marketing, VH1; Nancy Mazzei - Art Director; Wendell Wooten - VP Creative Production, VH1; Nancy Ratner - Director Consumer Partnerships & Promotions; Jon Wallach - Producer; Julie Ruiz - Designer; Evan Goldstein - Writer

CLIENT: VH1

VH1- Flavor of Love Valentines Day Cards

Flavor Flav may be a founding member of one of hip hop's most influential groups, but being a pioneering Public Enemy doesn't mean there should be animosity on Valentine's Day. When his reality show, "Flavor of Love," entered its final season in February of 2008, MTV Networks—parent company of "Flavor of Love" network VH1—saw a perfect opportunity to publicize the show with branded Valentine's Day cards with, MTV says, "a 'Flavor Flav' sentiment."

One challenge in marketing the eye-catching, humorous and usable cards was relating an adult-themed show to the concept of Valentine's Day card sharing. "As the primary viewing audience is 18-34, an old-fashioned card aesthetic was chosen for the basic design," says MTV of the cards'—dare we say it?—nostalgic quality. The creative elements, foil-paper hearts and branded white and red envelopes, combined with comical copy, created cards that consumers, MTV says, could use "in the workplace among friends and coworkers." Like

traditional grade school cards, the Flavor Flav cards featured two sides: one sheet with Flavor Flav imagery and various copy "Flavisms," the other with simple "to:" and "from:" notations. With twenty-one thousand Flavor Flav cards in circulation, Valentine's Day proved to be truly sweet for VH1.

guerilla marketing • single unit

1

3

2

mobile device • graphics

4

1 CREATIVE FIRM: **SKAGGS - New York, NY** CREATIVE TEAM: **Jonina Skaggs, Bradley Skaggs - Creative Directors; Samantha Edwards - Art Director; Elspeth Maxwell, Joseph Guzman - Designers** CLIENT: **SKAGGS** URL: **www.skaggsdesign.com** 2 CREATIVE FIRM: **Luminus Creative - Zagreb, Croatia** CREATIVE TEAM: **Tonci Klaric - Copywriter; Mislav Vidovic - Designer; Andrej Rubesa - Project Manager** CLIENT: **Weightlifting Club Metalac** 3 CREATIVE FIRM: **Barefoot - Cincinnati, OH** CREATIVE TEAM: **Todd Jessee - Senior Art Director; Sarah Knott - Copywriter; Rob Sloan - Creative Director; Doug Worple - Executive Creative Director** CLIENT: **Know Theatre** 4 CREATIVE FIRM: **Kelsey Advertising & Design - LaGrange, GA** CREATIVE TEAM: **Brant Kelsey - Creative Director / Programmer; Niki Studdard - Designer; Brandon Eley - Programmer** CLIENT: **McDonald's Corporation**

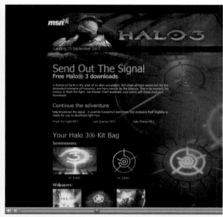

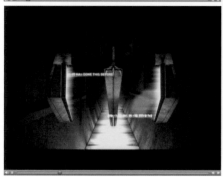

PLATINUM P

CREATIVE FIRM: **AKQA** - London, England

CREATIVE TEAM: **James Hilton** - Co-Chief Creative Officer; **Kevin Russell** - Associate Creative Director; **Michael Hobbs** - Senior Copywriter; **Alex Ajao** - Account Supervisor; **Andy Hood** - Creative Development Director

CLIENT: **Xbox**

Halo Sonic Vault

Microsoft's signature franchise, Halo 3, is more than a fun first-person shooter game—it's a gaming phenomenon. So expectations ran high in anticipation of the series' culmination in November of 2008, for established as well as brand-new casual gamers. To give the launch the cachet of a blockbuster movie, Microsoft hired London's AKQA.

Before the big launch, AKQA created a series of interactive puzzles that would reward the audience with exclusive Halo 3 material. "We wanted to play on the rich audio experience of the Halo trilogy and use mobile phone technology to reach the heart of our gamer audience," the agency says. Using this technology and inspired by keyless entry devices, AKQA used a Halo 3 mobile ringtone as a sonic key to activate hidden online content. "It felt perfect," they report. "All we needed was some custom-built ground-breaking sound recognition technology. Fortunately, that's just the kind of challenge our technical teams love."

The result, dubbed "The Device," enabled the beats of the ringtone—developed with the cooperation of Samsung, which gave it away for free—to be picked up by PC microphones and interpreted as a passcode to launch a special "Sonic Vault" hidden on the Halo site. "Within a couple of hours of going live, our exclusive content was being unlocked," the agency says. "But most satisfying of all was the widespread appeal of the Sonic Vault—ultimately, hundreds of thousands of ringtones [were] downloaded."

1 CREATIVE FIRM: **AKQA** - London, England CREATIVE TEAM: **Daniel Bonner** - Co-Chief Creative Officer; **Duan Evans** - Creative Director; **Nick Bailey** - Associate Creative Director; **Davor Krvavac** - Art Director; **Greg Mullen** - Motion Graphics Director; **Emily Bull** - Head of Production CLIENT: **Nike**

PUBLICATIONS

Beautiful Meals

CREATIVE FIRM: **Futura DDB d.o.o. - Ljubljana, Slovenia**
CREATIVE TEAM: **Zare Kerin - Creative Director; Marjan Bozic - Designer**
CLIENT: **Janez Bratovz**

Food, however memorable, is gone after it's eaten—but in the case of chef Janez Bratovz's creations, beautiful meals are made to last. "The idea of writing a book occurred while the three masters— Janez Bratovz, photographer Janez Pukiè and creative director Zare Kerin—were talking to each other," explains Ljubljana, Slovenia-based agency Futura DDB d.o.o. "Zare wanted to catch the spirit of JB Restaurant and incorporate it into the book. It's contemporary, fresh, subtle, a cuisine with the feeling for innovative and new recipes... [with] comfortable décor, attentive service and a friendly atmosphere."

The book cover represents a tablecloth, and the artfully bent fork subtly represents Bratovz's initials. "In the book, Zare placed a great emphasis on photographs of the food, while the text part was subtly organized," the designer says. "It seems that the book has two functions: We can read it as a book with useful recipes, or we can just leaf through it and focus on its strong, beautiful images. In each case it makes the mouth water."

1

2

3

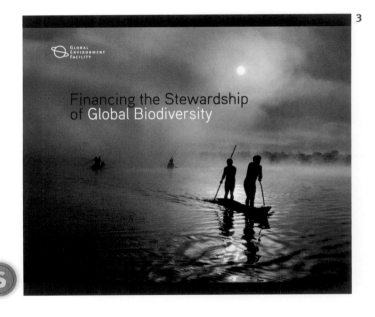

4

1 CREATIVE FIRM: **saturno press - Montgomery, AL** CREATIVE TEAM: **Anton Haardt - Author; Saturno Press - Publisher** CLIENT: **Anton Haardt** 2 CREATIVE FIRM: **Rick Shaefer Design - Fairfield, CT**
CREATIVE TEAM: **Rick Shaefer, Paul Zalon, Steve Josephson** CLIENT: **Lights! LLC and Traffic Works, Inc.** 3 CREATIVE FIRM: **Design Nut - Kensington, MD** CREATIVE TEAM: **Brent Almond - Creative Director;**
Brent Almond - Designer; Sabastião Salgado - Photographer; Mark Zimsky, Gustavo Fonseca - Copywriters CLIENT: **Global Environment Facility** 4 CREATIVE FIRM: **FactorTres Comunicacion - Mexico**
CREATIVE TEAM: **Rodrigo Cordova - Design Director/Designer** CLIENT: **Michelle Morales**

PLATINUM P

CREATIVE FIRM: **People Design Inc - Grand Rapids, MI**

CREATIVE TEAM: **Brian Hauch - Creative Director; Yang Kim, Kevin Budelmann - Designers; Julie Ridl - Editor; Jim Long, Jennifer Magnolfi - Writers**

CLIENT: **Herman Miller**

Always Building

In 1968, Herman Miller pioneered the office we know and love to hate—cubicles, modular furniture, partitions—with the publication of *The Office: A Facility Based on Change*. Forty years later, Miller is gone but his company glimpses the future with *Always Building: The Programmable Environment*. "It's a book that explores a future when commercial spaces might be programmed to suit their users," explains Brian Hauch, design director at Grand Rapids' People Design, in regard to Convia, a Herman Miller subsidiary that offers modular, programmable electrical infrastructures for buildings.

Convia found People Design to provide consulting and graphic design for the book. "As with their 1968 title," says Hauch, "Herman Miller wanted to reach an audience of change agents with *Always Building* and inspire them to adopt a new idea."

To inspire this audience, *Always Building* asks lots of "what if" questions. *What if buildings never became obsolete? What if information could be used as a design material? What if our buildings grew smarter the more we used them?* Hauch puts it this way: "So many hypothetical [questions], so many opportunities to help readers visualize how a bold idea not yet in common practice might soon impact their industries and their lives... This is a conceptual book, so the design had to communicate abstract, aspirational concepts in an intelligent and accessible manner."

People Design's approach resulted in a book that is easy to understand, yet still presents considerable depth for study. Hauch cites the style of the illustrations on the cover and throughout the book as the key to this facility of use. "The programmable environment is not yet fully formed, but still [is] being sketched out," he says. "The hand-drawn quality of the illustrations humanizes a topic that *could* feel cold and technical."

And if you think you've seen everything there is to see in the offices of yesterday and today, tomorrow brings something new. "The overall variety of imagery adds an element of surprise to the book," says Hauch, "challenging readers to envision how the programmable environment could improve many types of commercial spaces."

1 CREATIVE FIRM: **Bleached Whale Design - Chicago, IL** CREATIVE TEAM: **Zach Dodson - Author and Designer** CLIENT: **featherproof books** 2 CREATIVE FIRM: **Q - Wiesbaden, Germany** CREATIVE TEAM:
Matthias Frey, Laurenz Nielbock CLIENT: **m-real Zanders**

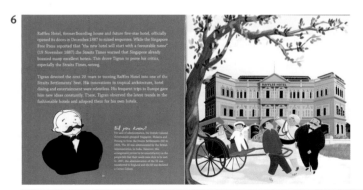

1 CREATIVE FIRM: **Design Boutique - Alameda, CA** CREATIVE TEAM: **Michele Copen - Photographer** CLIENT: **Design Boutique** 2 CREATIVE FIRM: **Rule29 - Geneva, IL** CREATIVE TEAM: **Justin Ahrens - Art Director** CLIENT: **Self-Promotion** 3 CREATIVE FIRM: **Design Nut - Kensington, MD** CREATIVE TEAM: **Brent Almond - Creative Director, Designer; Polina Pinchevsky - Designer; Susan Chenoweth - Production Artist; Mark Zimsky, Gustavo Fonseca - Copywriter** CLIENT: **Global Environment Facility** 4 CREATIVE FIRM: **saturno press - Montgomery, AL** CREATIVE TEAM: **Anton Haardt - Author; Saturno Press - Publisher** CLIENT: **Anton Haardt** 5 CREATIVE FIRM: **Interrobang Design Collaborative, Inc. - Richmond, VT** CREATIVE TEAM: **Mark Sylvester - Designer; Robert Packert - Photographer** CLIENT: **White-Packert Photography** 6 CREATIVE FIRM: **Splash Productions Pte Ltd - Singapore** CREATIVE TEAM: **Stanley Yap - Art Director, Siewlin Tee - Senior Designer, Serene See - Copywriter, Budi H Heru, Jia Jia Khoo - Illustrators** CLIENT: **National Heritage Board**

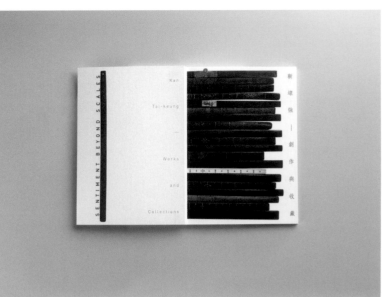

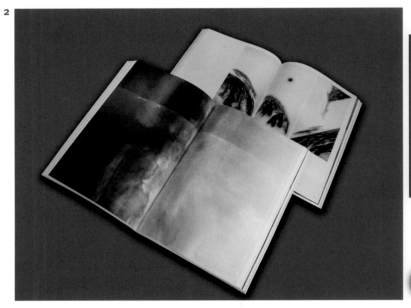

1 CREATIVE FIRM: **Kan & Lau Design Consultants - Kowloon Tong, Hong Kong** CREATIVE TEAM: **Kan Tai-Keung** CLIENT: **Hong Kong Design Centre** 2 CREATIVE FIRM: **Kan & Lau Design Consultants - Kowloon Tong, Hong Kong** CREATIVE TEAM: **Kan Tai-Keung, Justin Yu, Moby Ngan** CLIENT: **The University Museum & Art Gallery** 3 CREATIVE FIRM: **Besanopoli - Milan, Italy** CREATIVE TEAM: **Davide Besana, Valentina di Robilant - Creative Direction; Team Besanopoli - Graphic Design** CLIENT: **Lindt**

creativity 38 annual awards

PLATINUM Ⓟ

ArjoWiggins Calendar 2008

CREATIVE FIRM: Zuan Club - Tokyo, Japan

CREATIVE TEAM: Akihiko Tsukamoto - Design, Art Direction; Masami Ouchi - Creative Direction; Miyuki Ueda - Illustration

CLIENT: Arjowiggins K.K.

Companies may only buy paper a few times a year, but British paper supplier Arjowiggins wanted to make sure that their customers thought of them every day—so they had Tokyo's Zuan Club create something their clients could use, touch and enjoy all year long: a calendar.

The calendar's identity is evident in its very outline. "The shape is made with an *A*, the initial of Arjowiggins," Zuan Club says. Within that, though, the studio took good care to elegantly showcase the work of Miyuki Ueda—an illustrator whose flying, effortless lines bring to mind a kind of Japanese Chagall. "I expressed the beauty of space and stylishness as Japanese modern, [and] I asked Ueda to draw the illustrations with the material of a sense of the seasons," the agency says. "It's a very difficult work, [so we endeavored] to enhance her image with the greatest care."

The images themselves are carefully made, says Zuan Club. "Ms. Ueda is right-handed by nature but she uses the left hand intensively to draw the quaint lines," they explain. "The black and gold color is the best combination to express the Japanese world. It's happy—you will feel nobleness and gorgeousness."

1

2

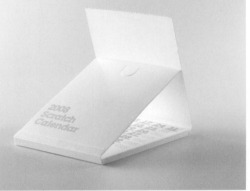

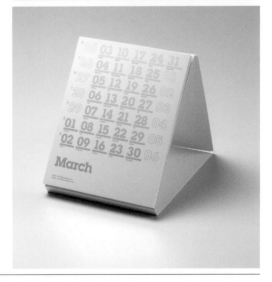

1 CREATIVE FIRM: **NBC Universal Global Networks Italia - Rome, Italy** CREATIVE TEAM: **M. Theresia Braun - Marketing & On Air Director** CLIENT: **Studio Universal** 2 CREATIVE FIRM: **Ink Copywriters - Bath, UK** CREATIVE TEAM: **Tom Chesher, Simon Jones - Joint Managing Directors; Alison Crocker - Account Manager; Sam Bowhay, James Wareham - Copywriters** CLIENT: **Ink copywriters**

1

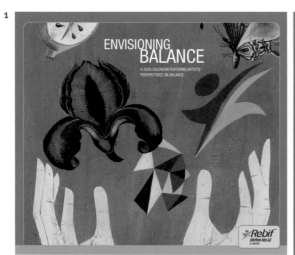

2

3

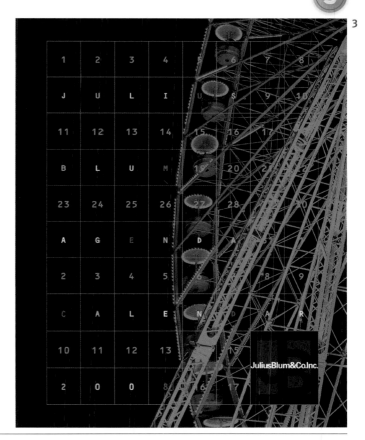

1 CREATIVE FIRM: **Cline Davis and Mann LLC - New York, NY** CREATIVE TEAM: **Cline Davis and Mann LLC** CLIENT: **Pfizer and Serono** 2 CREATIVE FIRM: **Cline Davis and Mann LLC - New York, NY** CREATIVE TEAM: **Cline Davis and Mann LLC** CLIENT: **Novartis** 3 CREATIVE FIRM: **Emerson Wajdowicz Studios Inc - New York, NY** CREATIVE TEAM: **Lisa LaRochelle - Art Director & Designer; Jurek Wajdowicz - Art Director, Designer, Photographer; Yoko Yoshida, Manuel Mendez - Designers** CLIENT: **Julius Blum & Co. Inc**

1

2

3

1 CREATIVE FIRM: **Missouri Botanical Garden - Brentwood, MO** CREATIVE TEAM: **Justin Visnesky - Designer; Elizabeth McNulty - Editor;** CLIENT: **Missouri Botanical Garden** URL: **www.finishedart.com**
2 CREATIVE FIRM: **Q - Wiebaden, Germany** CREATIVE TEAM: **Matthias Frey, Max Mollien, Laurenz Nielbock** CLIENT: **SOKA-BAU** 3 CREATIVE FIRM: **Ken-Tsai Lee Design Studio - Rego Park, NY** CREATIVE TEAM: **Ken-Tsai Lee, Yao-Feng Chou** CLIENT: **Fonso Enterprise Co., Ltd**

PLATINUM P

CREATIVE FIRM: Cahan & Associates - San Francisco, CA

CREATIVE TEAM: Bill Cahan - Creative Director, Art Director; Steve Frykholm - Art Director; Todd Richards - Art Director, Designer; Erik Adams - Designer (issue 6 only); Clare Rhinelander, Marlene Capotosto - Production Artists

CLIENT: Herman Miller

See: The Potential of Place

A magazine called *SEE* has a lot to say—especially if you subscribe to the old axiom that a picture is worth a thousand words. If the client is Herman Miller (of office furniture fame), each issue—written for "architects, designers and anyone interested in the power of the built environment to heighten human performance and creativity"—has to have an impact as solid as a building itself. Cahan & Associates got their inspiration from the source. "Herman Miller provided us with the most inspiring creative brief we have ever received, containing words like *spontaneous*, *eclectic*, *disruptive*, *personal expression*," the San Francisco firm says. "At the same time, they wanted the magazine to be in line with the Herman Miller brand dimensions of being spirited, purposeful and human."

To reinforce Herman Miller's image as a leader in purveying information necessary for the creation of great places and to affirm its connections with the architecture and design community, Cahan developed each issue of *SEE* around a theme. With longer essays and shorter takes on a single subject, the agency says that "each article is treated as its own vignette and it was intertional that every turn of the page [brings] a visual surprise. No two articles were to be alike, and [had] to be different from issue to issue." And, as with a large floor plan, the danger lay in too much freedom. "The biggest challenge with *SEE* is reacting to these wide open parameters and knowing when to refrain from going too far," they say.

To break up this environment into figurative rooms, the designers separated articles with color divider pages to show the reader a firm demarcation of where one article ends and another begins. And, lest anyone forget where it all comes from, the colors in *SEE* derive from the Herman Miller color swatch catalog—complete with color names on each divider spread.

1

1 CREATIVE FIRM: **BYU Publications & Graphics - Provo, UT** CREATIVE TEAM: **A.J. Rich - Designer/Art Director; LeGrand Richards - Writer; Mark Summers - Illustrator; David Eliason - Creative Director; Roxanna Johnson - Executive Editor; Karen Seely - Editor** CLIENT: **BYU School of Education** 2 CREATIVE FIRM: **Besanopoli - Milan, Italy** CREATIVE TEAM: **Davide Besana - Art Direction; Team Besanopoli - Graphic Design** CLIENT: **Sanpellegrino**

1

WAREHOUSING AND LOGISTICS

King Harald Blatand was a highly respected peacemaker in 10th century Scandinavia. A Danish Viking, Blatand is famous for uniting warring factions in areas of present-day Denmark, Norway, and Sweden.

In current times, however, the ruler is becoming better known for his very distinctive teeth. According to legend, Blatand adored blueberries and ate them to excess, thus tinting his smile a shocking—and permanent—shade of blue.

Wondering what oldstandard oral hygiene has to do with operations management? Well, in English, "Blatand" translates to "Bluetooth," and the king himself is the inspiration behind the technology's name. Indeed, many warehouse managers would argue that it's just as difficult to wirelessly connect headsets, scanners, and printers as it is to bring together whole countries.

Bluetooth basics

Bluetooth is an open standard for wireless, short-range radio technology. It transmits voice and data signals among various devices, including computers, printers, keyboards, scanners, mobile phones, headsets, and many more. The small Bluetooth chips initially were

Royal
BY ELIZABETH RENNIE
Blue

Will Bluetooth be crowned king of the warehouse?

1   September 2007 | APICS magazine

2

3

4

MAGIC MAN

CRISS ANGEL USED TO CRINGE AT THE SIGHT OF A SYRINGE IN THE DOCTOR'S OFFICE. THESE DAYS, THE MAGICIAN'S FEATS INCLUDE HANGING FROM FOUR LARGE FISHHOOKS BENEATH A HELICOPTER. TO PREPARE FOR SUCH DARING, ANGEL ADHERES TO A TOUGH FITNESS REGIMEN AND STRICT DIET. BUT NOTHING READIED ANGEL FOR HIS WORK OR HELPED HIM OVERCOME HIS FEARS MORE THAN HIS FATHER'S DETERMINATION TO FIGHT AN AGGRESSIVE CANCER.

BY ALLAN RICHTER

Thirteen years ago, Criss Angel's career as an illusionist and performance artist was climbing. Angel, then 28, was negotiating a contract to put on a show in Las Vegas when his father, John Sarantakos, called with the devastating news that he had been diagnosed with advanced stomach cancer. His father was told he would have three weeks of life left. Angel cut his career plans short, flew home to New York and spent the rest of his father's life close to him, through his last birthday at 60. That was three years after the diagnosis.

Angel has escaped from a double straightjacket. He has put himself on fire. He has been sandwiched between shards of glass and a moving steamroller. And he has appeared to levitate over the Luxor Hotel, his Las Vegas base where this summer he is to begin a 10-year run in a $100-million Cirque du Soleil show.

Nothing prepared Angel for any of those feats more than the determination with which he says his father fought and managed his cancer. "He really exemplified the power of the mind, body and spirit even in the

16   ENERGY TIMES   www.energytimes.com | ENERGY TIMES   27

1 CREATIVE FIRM: **Dever Designs - Laurel, MD** CREATIVE TEAM: **Jeffrey L. Dever - Art Director, Designer; Sara Tyson - Illustrator** CLIENT: **APICS magazine   2** CREATIVE FIRM: **Designagentur Wagner - Mainz, Germany** CREATIVE TEAM: **Oliver Wagner - solutions THE SCHOTT TECHNOLOGY MAGAZINE** CLIENT: **SCHOTT AG   3** CREATIVE FIRM: **Besanopoli - Milan, Italy** CREATIVE TEAM: **Valentina Di Robilant - Creative Direction; Davide Besana - Art Direction; Team Besanopoli - Graphic Design** CLIENT: **Sanpellegrino   4** CREATIVE FIRM: **Energy Times Magazine - Melville, NY** CREATIVE TEAM: **Donna Casola - Associate Publisher/Art Director** CLIENT: **Energy Times Magazine**

creativity 38 annual awards

1

2

3

1 CREATIVE FIRM: **Dieste Harmel & Partners - Dallas, TX** CREATIVE TEAM: **Miguel Moreno - Creative Director; Matias Sada - Senior Copywriter; Christian Hoyle - Art Director; Jaime Andrade - Executive Creative Director; Carlos Tourne - Chief Creative Officer** CLIENT: **Interstate Batteries** 2 CREATIVE FIRM: **Dieste Harmel & Partners - Dallas, TX** CREATIVE TEAM: **Miguel Moreno - Creative Director; Matias Sada - Senior Copywriter; Christian Hoyle - Art Director; Jaime Andrade - Executive Creative Director; Carlos Tourne - Chief Creative Officer** CLIENT: **Interstate Batteries** 3 CREATIVE FIRM: **Dieste Harmel & Partners - Dallas, TX** CREATIVE TEAM: **Miguel Moreno - Creative Director; Matias Sada - Senior Copywriter; Christian Hoyle - Art Director; Jaime Andrade - Executive Creative Director; Carlos Tourne - Chief Creative Officer** CLIENT: **Interstate Batteries**

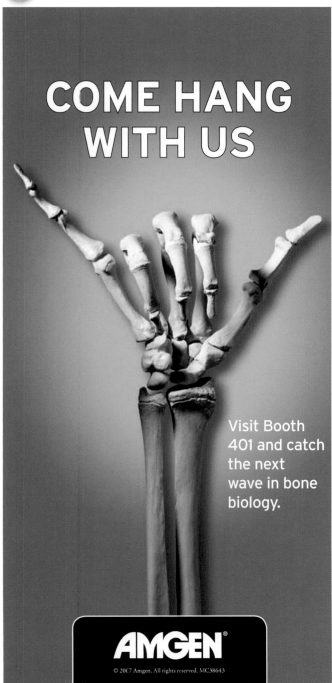

206

1 CREATIVE FIRM: **MTV Networks - New York, NY** CREATIVE TEAM: **Rolyn Barthelman - Art Director; Charles Hamilton - Designer** CLIENT: **Comedy Central** 2 CREATIVE FIRM: **Peak Seven Advertising - Deerfield Beach, FL** CREATIVE TEAM: **Brian Tipton - Art Director; Darren Seys - Creative Director** CLIENT: **Peak Seven Advertising (Self)** 3 CREATIVE FIRM: **Hitchcock Fleming & Associates Inc. - Akron, OH** CREATIVE TEAM: **Hitchcock Fleming & Associates Inc.** CLIENT: **Liquid Nails**

stay.
a modern dog hotel

CREATIVE FIRM: **Liska + Associates - Chicago, IL**

CREATIVE TEAM: **Kim Fry - Designer; Steve Liska - Creative Director**

CLIENT: **Stay**

The Place to "Stay"

Even our pets need a break, and so Liska + Associates created a logo for their client, Stay, to capture the essence of "a modern dog hotel" on Chicago's North Side. "Stay is an urban hotel for dogs that provides both boarding and daycare services for its clients," says the firm, "so the logo needed to convey that this is a contemporary premium facility." The simple logo transcends both human and canine language with its pleased pup figure. "A wagging tail communicates a happy dog, which is what it is all about."

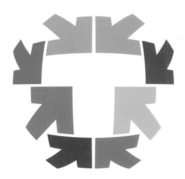

TURKU REGION

The growing, competent and innovative Turku region

CREATIVE FIRM: **Zeeland Oy - Turku, Finland**

CREATIVE TEAM: **Juuso Korpinen - Art Director; Ulla Jämä - Account Planner**

CLIENT: **Turku Region Development Centre**

Zeeland Oy designed a logo for its own home turf: the Turku Region of Finland, including the city of Turku front and center, surrounded by its municipalities. Not only that, the logo had to incorporate the various key stakeholders of Finland's oldest city, such as trade and industry, agriculture, growing entrepreneurship and the regional cooperation—without diminishing the importance of the surrounding municipalities.

"Our solution was plain and simple but fresh and dynamic," Zeeland Oy reports. Along with different colored arrows forming the letter *T* in negative space, the colors themselves illustrate the Baletic archepelago. "Earth, wind, fire and water reflect not only the different municipalities and branches of our industry but also our intellectual and historical roots and resources." And for those outside Finland, the logo carries a message: "Traditional industry and agriculture combined with high technology and education creates globally advanced innovations," they say.

"The main message of the logo is that the surroundings create completeness. The *T* has the key role but cannot be formed without its surroundings. In order to manage as a region, we have to connect and collaborate. All aiming at the same point makes us one. We have potential but achieving it depends on the innovative people of the Turku region."

CREATIVE FIRM: **Right Hat - South Boston, MA**

CREATIVE TEAM: **Charlyne Fabi - Creative Director; Dan Page - Illustrator**

CLIENT: **Berman & Simmons**

Berman & Simmons Advertising

Law firms largely are perceived as a flat and colorless bunch, but in order to appeal to fellow attorneys while making a positive impression, Right Hat added a bit of color in order to communicate to referral attorneys the benefit of using specialized trial counsel. "The design intent was to separate the firm from its competitors using color and illustration while communicating a dual message of strength and support," says the South Boston design agency. "Berman & Simmons is a law firm that receives the majority of their business from [general practice] attorneys who do not have extensive litigation or courtroom experience. They support these attorneys in their cases through the firm's breadth of trial experience and resources."

To this audience, the client endeavored to convey their position as a support resource in collaboration *with* them, not competition *against* them. "Berman & Simmons specializes in personal injury litigation and the majority of their business comes from individual lawyers or small law firms who need a more robust team to help them take a case to trial," Right Hat says. This message is conveyed in simple copy: "Our experience is your secret weapon." "Trial lawyers there when you need us." "Our experience is your safety net." The muted palette subtly highlights simple line drawings of figurative motifs of protection and safety. "Illustration was used because it was more suited to communicate the client's complex message using metaphor," the agency says. "The color bars were used to frame the illustration and provide a subtle message of coming together and working as a team. The bars were also a graphic device that was used to extend the Berman & Simmons brand to other materials where illustration could not be used."

But even where Right Hat used illustration to get the message across, they had to take great care to keep the pictures as serious as the subject matter—and economical as well. "The illustrations needed to be sophisticated and smart, since illustration is often considered by attorneys as 'cartoonish' and too playful," they say, adding that the limited budget played a role in the images' creation. "An illustrator needed to be found that could not only create original work, but would also be willing to customize existing stock illustration. It was necessary that the illustrator have a deep archive of stock imagery that could be repurposed for the client message." Case closed.

1

GO

BEYOND

Truer moments.
Fresher perspectives.
Deeper meaning.
Captured by the world's
best photographers.
Royalty-free available.

Stock that lives up to your best ideas.

NATIONAL GEOGRAPHIC   NATIONALGEOGRAPHICSTOCK.COM

2

TOBI. A powerful ally against
an ever-present CF threat.

TOBI
Tobramycin Inhalation Solution, USP

3

We reveal the insight within.

What IMS does for its clients is a revelation

If you think the IMS name just stands for data, think again. Lately we've also been making
quite a name for ourselves in Evidence-based Consulting℠ for the global healthcare market.

Now you can leverage the expertise of our specialized consultants - over 1400 worldwide -
who apply leading-edge analytics to shape information assets into valued business solutions.

Our unique combination of capabilities can support your decisions on commercial effectiveness,
product and portfolio strategy, and market access.

So the next time you're thinking, find out what we're thinking.

Contact our consulting team at 800-255-4110 or visit www.imshealth.com/insights.

ims   INTELLIGENCE.
APPLIED.

GO

BEYOND

We reveal the insight within.

What IMS does for its clients is a revelation

If you think the IMS name just stands for data, think again. Lately we've also been making
quite a name for ourselves in Evidence-based Consulting℠ for the global healthcare market.

Now you can leverage the expertise of our specialized consultants - over 1400 worldwide -
who apply leading-edge analytics to shape information assets into valued business solutions.

Our unique combination of capabilities can support your decisions on commercial effectiveness,
product and portfolio strategy, and market access.

So the next time you're thinking, find out what we're thinking.

Contact our consulting team at 800-255-4110 or visit www.imshealth.com/insights.

ims   INTELLIGENCE.
APPLIED.

1

entrances that create a buzz

environmentally responsible

watertight

2

Acrovyn faux wood and metal will defend themselves if attacked.

A new concept in wall protection has taken root.

PVC-Free Acrovyn 3000.

Acrovyn Wall Panels give you an infinite number of ways to protect walls.

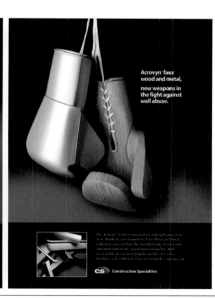

Acrovyn faux wood and metal, new weapons in the fight against wall abuse.

1 CREATIVE FIRM: **Brian J. Ganton & Associates** - Cedar Grove, NJ CREATIVE TEAM: **Brian Ganton Jr.** - Creative Director; **Mark Ganton** - Art Director/Copywriter; **Christopher Ganton** - Art Director/Photography; **Marc Milton, Pat Palmieri** - Designers CLIENT: **Oldcastle Glass** 2 CREATIVE FIRM: **Brian J. Ganton & Associates** - Cedar Grove, NJ CREATIVE TEAM: **Brian Ganton Jr.** - Creative Director; **Christopher Ganton** - Art Director/Photography; **Mark Ganton** - Art Director/Copywriter; **Pat Palmieri** - Designer CLIENT: **Construction Specialties**

1

PERSPECTIVE IS NOT JUST A MATTER OF
WHAT YOU SEE, BUT HOW YOU SEE IT.

FOLEY
HOAG LLP
Driving Business Advantage

IMMERSION IN YOUR BUSINESS AND
INDUSTRY IS THE KEY TO SUCCESS.

FOLEY
HOAG LLP
Driving Business Advantage

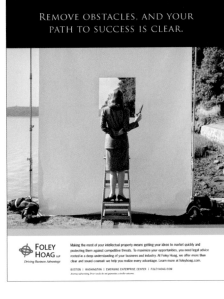

REMOVE OBSTACLES, AND YOUR
PATH TO SUCCESS IS CLEAR.

FOLEY
HOAG LLP
Driving Business Advantage

INNOVATE AND ACCELERATE.

FOLEY
HOAG LLP
Driving Business Advantage

2

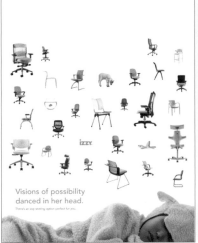

Visions of possibility
danced in her head.

Not your
grandmother's
classroom.

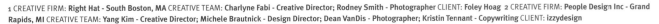

1 CREATIVE FIRM: **Right Hat - South Boston, MA** CREATIVE TEAM: **Charlyne Fabi - Creative Director; Rodney Smith - Photographer** CLIENT: **Foley Hoag** 2 CREATIVE FIRM: **People Design Inc - Grand Rapids, MI** CREATIVE TEAM: **Yang Kim - Creative Director; Michele Brautnick - Design Director; Dean VanDis - Photographer; Kristin Tennant - Copywriting** CLIENT: **izzydesign**

1

ReInterpreted   *Interface*FLOR*

2

Box me in?
Never.

Collaboration
rocks.

An izzy
favorite with
a twist
(and a tilt).

1 CREATIVE FIRM: **Valentine Group New York - New York, NY** CREATIVE TEAM: **Robert Valentine - Art Director & Designer** CLIENT: **InterfaceFLOR** 2 CREATIVE FIRM: **People Design Inc - Grand Rapids, MI**
CREATIVE TEAM: **Yang Kim - Creative Director; Michele Brautnick - Design Director; Mitch Ranger - Photographer; Mimi Ray - Stylist; Kristin Tennant - Copywriting** CLIENT: **izzydesign**

1

Both satisfy chocolate passions.
One is guilt-free.

KOZY SHACK
No Sugar Added

Indulge customers' tastes with Kozy Shack® No Sugar Added Puddings & Kozy Shack® GelTreats® Sugar Free.

KOZY SHACK

vantage.

To learn how our global law firm can help you achieve your key business objectives, visit www.klgates.com

K&L|GATES
1900 LAWYERS ON THREE CONTINENTS
www.klgates.com

2

illuminate.

To learn how our global law firm can help you achieve your key business objectives, visit www.klgates.com

K&L|GATES
1900 LAWYERS ON THREE CONTINENTS
www.klgates.com

intensity.

To learn how our global law firm can help you achieve your key business objectives, visit www.klgates.com

K&L|GATES
1900 LAWYERS ON THREE CONTINENTS
www.klgates.com

velocity.

To learn how our global law firm can help you achieve your key business objectives, visit www.klgates.com

K&L|GATES
1900 LAWYERS ON THREE CONTINENTS
www.klgates.com

All these treats are loved by kids.
Ours are applauded by parents.

KOZY SHACK
JAMMIN' GELS
FRUIT PUNCH FUSION

KOZY SHACK
POPPIN PUDDING
CRAZY CHOCOLATE

Kozy Shack Jammin' Gels® and Kozy Shack Poppin' Puddings® are good food and good fun.

With awesome flavors like Fruit Punch Fusion and Crazy Chocolate, Kozy Shack Jammin' Gels® and Kozy Shack Poppin' Pudding® have kids lining up. Kozy Shack Jammin' Gels® are made with real fruit juice and are bursting with fruity flavor. Made with low-fat milk, Kozy Shack Poppin' Puddings® are creamy and delicious, as well as a good source of calcium and fiber. Energize your reimbursable and à la carte meal programs with the great taste of Kozy Shack. Visit kozyshackfoodservice.com.

KOZY SHACK

---

1 CREATIVE FIRM: Foodmix - Westmont, IL CREATIVE TEAM: **Foodmix - Creative & Production Team** CLIENT: **Kozy Shack Foodservice 2** CREATIVE FIRM: **Right Hat - South Boston, MA** CREATIVE TEAM: **Charlyne Fabi - Creative Director** CLIENT: **K&L Gates**

PLATINUM P

CREATIVE FIRM: **Draftfcb - New York, NY**

CREATIVE TEAM: **Christoph Becker - Chief Creative Officer; Sandy Greenberg, Terri Meyer - Executive Creative Directors; Noah Davis - Creative Director; Henry Mathieu - Copywriter**

CLIENT: **Kraft Foods Inc.**

Mini Oreo "Creamer"

With Oreo long known as "milk's favorite cookie," how could an ad agency apply that equity to Oreo's little sibling, Mini Oreo, without causing trouble on the playground—er, plate? "The client certainly wanted to stay true to the Oreo look, feel and heritage," says New York's Draftfcb. Still, says the agency, the order was taller than a twelve-ounce glass of milk. "Living up to the creative burden was the biggest challenge—an assignment with a brief this great and a message this simple really had to become a great ad." Draftfcb took the Oreo-and-milk iconography and shrunk it down for the ad, but no one is complaining. "Clearly 'small' is a big part of any communication for a product called 'mini,'" Draftfcb says. "Keeping the image small, and letting it float in that sea of white is as much a part of the visual solution as the creamer cup is."

1

2

3

1 CREATIVE FIRM: **MTV Networks - New York, NY** CREATIVE TEAM: **James Hitchcock - Creative Director; Jason Skinner - Art Director; Nora Gaffney - Designer; James Wojcik - Photographer** CLIENT: **CMT**
2 CREATIVE FIRM: **NBC Universal Global Networks Italia - Rome, Italy** CREATIVE TEAM: **M. Theresia Braun - Marketing & On Air Director; Agostino Toscana, Guido Cornara - Creative Direction; Luca Pannese - Art Director; Luca Lorenzini - Copywriter** CLIENT: **Steel** 3 CREATIVE FIRM: **j.logan design - Seattle, WA** CREATIVE TEAM: **Lance Hood - Creative Director; Jack Oelschlager - Senior Graphic Designer; Kate Sawyer - Graphic Designer** CLIENT: **Kerry Food & Beverage**

1

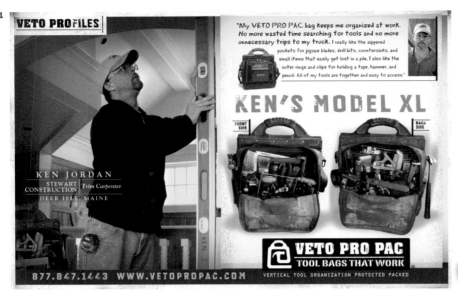

2

3

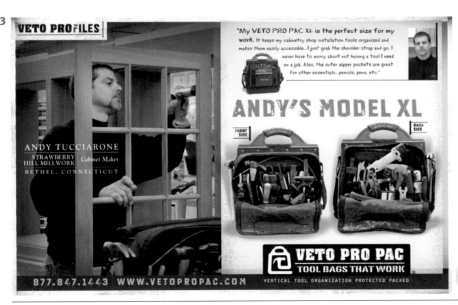

creativity 38 annual awards

1 CREATIVE FIRM: TFI Envision, Inc. - Norwalk, CT CREATIVE TEAM: Elizabeth P. Ball - Creative Director; Brien O'Reilly - Art Director, Designer, Illustrator CLIENT: Veto Pro Pac 2 CREATIVE FIRM: TFI Envision, Inc. - Norwalk, CT CREATIVE TEAM: Elizabeth P. Ball - Creative Director; Brien O'Reilly - Art Director, Designer, Illustrator CLIENT: Veto Pro Pac 3 CREATIVE FIRM: TFI Envision, Inc. - Norwalk, CT CREATIVE TEAM: Elizabeth P. Ball - Creative Director; Brien O'Reilly - Art Director, Designer, Illustrator CLIENT: Veto Pro Pac

A lost dog can't talk. But now he can text.

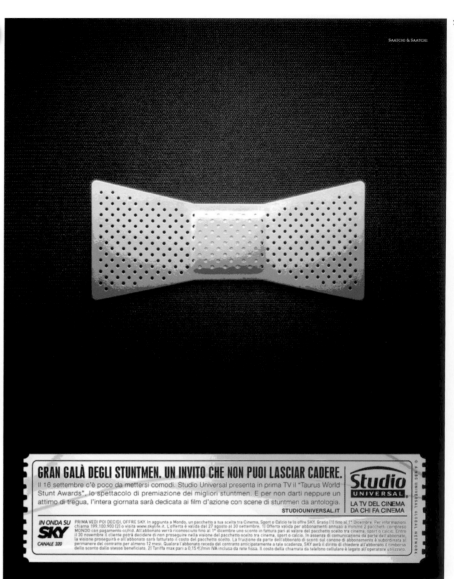

WE'RE GETTING ALL UP IN HIS GRILLZ

COMEDY CENTRAL
ROAST OF FLAVOR FLAV
Roastmaster KATT WILLIAMS
Sunday Aug 12 10/9c
COMEDYCENTRAL.COM

TWIN VINES
VINHO VERDE
CLASSIC, DRY VINHO VERDE
LIFE ON THE VINE

1 CREATIVE FIRM: **NBC Universal Global Networks Italia - Rome, Italy** CREATIVE TEAM: **M. Theresia Braun - Marketing & On Air Director; Laura Taddeo - Art Director; Alessandro Michetti - Copywriter** CLIENT: **Studio Universal** 2 CREATIVE FIRM: **Gotham Inc. - New York, NY** CREATIVE TEAM: **Gotham Inc.** CLIENT: **Zoombak** 3 CREATIVE FIRM: **MTV Networks - New York, NY** CREATIVE TEAM: **MTV Networks** CLIENT: **Comedy Central** 4 CREATIVE FIRM: **REVOLUCION - New York, NY** CREATIVE TEAM: **Alberto Rodriguez - Chief Creative Officer; Roberto Alcazar - Executive Creative Director; Henry Alvarez, Lorena Vasquez - Art Directors** CLIENT: **Palm Bay International**

1

YOUR PASSPORT
to a world of color.

2

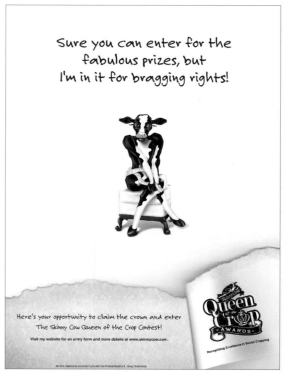

Sure you can enter for the
fabulous prizes, but
I'm in it for bragging rights!

Here's your opportunity to claim the crown and enter
The Skinny Cow Queen of the Crop Contest!

Visit my website for an entry form and more details at www.skinnycow.com.

Queen of the Crop AWARDS

Recognizing Excellence in Social Cropping

All other trademarks are owned by Société des Produits Nestlé S.A., Vevey, Switzerland.

creativity 38 annual awards

3

D MENTED

Demented (dĕ-mĕn'tĭd) *adj.* **1.** A state in which drivers might forget to eat, sleep or bathe, but they don't forget to wipe down their sidewalls after every drive. <That guy might be *demented*, but you have to admit, his Dunlop® Direzzas® always look good.>

Here's the deal – your car is who you are. End of story. Every centimeter of glass, steel, chrome and rubber tells the world exactly how you roll. Dunlop knows performance is about more than just grabbing the curves. It's about grabbing attention.

You've paid your dues; time to collect your respect. Because Drivers Know, this is more than a street; it's a statement.

GET IT RIGHT. GET DIREZZAS.

Learn more about Dunlop's hottest family of sport performance and racing tires. Get to www.dunloptires.com/etuner for more info. And while you're there, check out the Dunlop Driver's Seat for cool podcasts, free decals and a whole lot more!

DUNLOP TIRES | **DRIVERS KNOW.®**

PLATINUM P

The Ultimate Flash

CREATIVE FIRM: **Ad Planet Group - Singapore**

CREATIVE TEAM: **Teck Chong Leo - Executive Creative Director; Alfred Teo - Associate Creative Director; Leong Lee Tan, Meng Hau Khoo - Senior Art Directors; Feng Ling - Art Director; Michael Tai - Copywriter**

CLIENT: **Nikon Singapore**

The purpose of a camera flash is to illuminate a scene, and that's exactly what Singapore-based Ad Planet Group tried to do by positioning Nikon's "Ultimate Flash" into an already crowded market—even though most other flashes are nothing like the sun. "The client was open to using an approach that used visual humor," the agency says. "After all, this flash is used to produce eye-catching photographs, so what better way than to communicate its unique selling proposition with a series of eye-catching photographs too?" To create their memorable images, Ad Planet found three original photos that already captured the brilliance of the rising or setting sun—a farm, a village and a jetty—then digitally added a second, equally brilliant "sun." "This posed a new challenge in that the light from the flash had to also be crafted realistically enough to resemble the light of the sun, while still maintaining a certain difference so that they could be told apart."

1

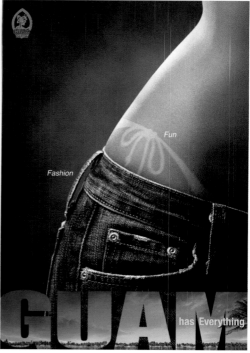

2

3

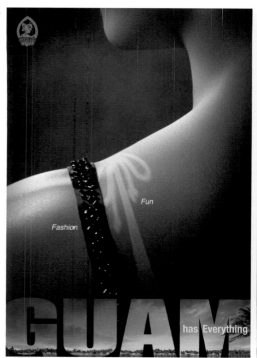

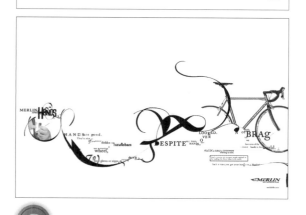

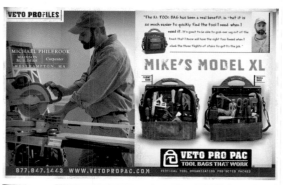

4

5

1 CREATIVE FIRM: Leo Burnett Korea - Seoul, South Korea CREATIVE TEAM: Jung-Tae Kim - Executive Creative Director; Soo-Hee Yang - Creative Director; Bong-Ho Jeon - Senior Copywriter; Yong-Jin Kim - Senior Art Director; Bae-Keun Nam - Senior Designer; Suk-Joon Jang - Photographer CLIENT: Guam Visitors Bureau Korea 2 CREATIVE FIRM: YARD - New York, NY CREATIVE TEAM: Stephen Niedzwiecki - Creative Director; Jennifer Carter-Campbell - Executive Producer; Ryan McGinley - Photographer; Alister Mackie - Stylist; Gio Campora - Hair Stylist; Pati Dubroff - Make Up Artist CLIENT: Converse by John Varvatos 3 CREATIVE FIRM: id29 - Troy, NY CREATIVE TEAM: Doug Bartow - Art Director; Bryan Kahrs - Senior Designer CLIENT: Merlin Metalworks 4 CREATIVE FIRM: TFI Envision, Inc. - Norwalk, CT CREATIVE TEAM: Elizabeth P. Ball - Creative Director; Brien O'Reilly - Art Director, Designer, Illustrator CLIENT: Veto Pro Pac 5 CREATIVE FIRM: YARD - New York, NY CREATIVE TEAM: Stephen Niedzwiecki - Creative Director; Jennifer Carter-Campbell - Executive Producer; Danny Clinch - Photographer; Heart - Hair Stylist; April Johnson - Make Up Artist CLIENT: John Varvatos

1

G

S

2
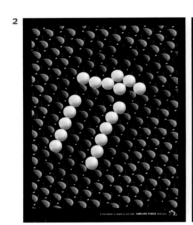

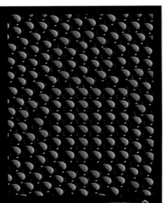

3

S

4

5

220

creativity 38 annual awards

1 CREATIVE FIRM: **STEELE+** - Alpharetta, GA CREATIVE TEAM: Chris Steele - Chief Executive Officer; Jim Fiscus - Creative Director/Photographer; Kelley Lear - Senior Art Director CLIENT: **BR-111** Exotic Hardwood Flooring 2 CREATIVE FIRM: **Draftfcb** - New York, NY CREATIVE TEAM: Christoph Becker - Chief Creative Officer; Sandy Greenberg, Terri Meyer - Executive Creative Directors; Rob Rooney - Creative Director; Claudio Lima - Senior Copywriter; Daniel Prado - Art Director CLIENT: Kraft Foods Inc. 3 CREATIVE FIRM: **YARD** - New York, NY CREATIVE TEAM: Stephen Niedzwiecki - Creative Director; Danny Clinch - Photographer; April Johnson - Stylist; Heart - Hair & Make Up Artist; Stephanie Morton - Photo Production CLIENT: John Varvatos 4 CREATIVE FIRM: **NBC Universal Global Networks Italia** - Rome, Italy CREATIVE TEAM: **M. Theresia Braun** - Marketing & On Air Director; Agostino Toscana, Guido Cornara - Creative Direction; Luca Pannese - Art Director; Luca Lorenzini - Copywriter CLIENT: **SCI FI** 5 CREATIVE FIRM: **YARD** - New York, NY CREATIVE TEAM: Stephen Niedzwiecki - Creative Director; Jennifer Carter-Campbell - Executive Producer; Tom Munro - Photographer; Alister Mackie - Stylist; WARD - Hair Stylist; Frank B - Make Up Artist CLIENT: Converse by John Varvatos 6 CREATIVE FIRM: **Cline Davis and Mann LLC** - New York, NY CREATIVE TEAM: Cline Davis and Mann LLC CLIENT: Novo Nordisk

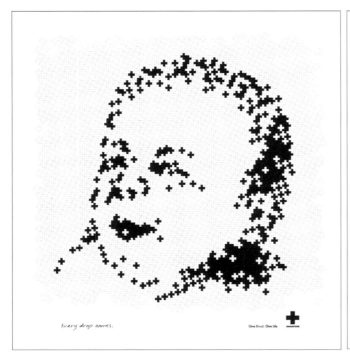

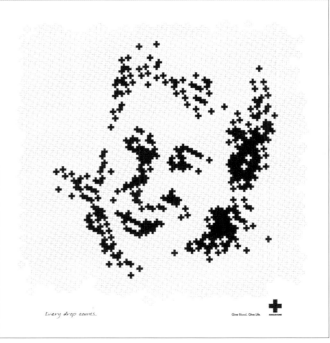

creativity 38 annual awards

PLATINUM P

CREATIVE FIRM: **Ad Planet Group - Singapore**

CREATIVE TEAM: **Teck Chong Leo - Executive Creative Director; Alfred Teo - Associate Creative Director; Yi Long Chen - Art Director; Joy Lee - Senior Copywriter**

CLIENT: **Red Cross**

Every Drop Counts

Ad Planet Group's client, the Singapore Red Cross, desperately wanted to recruit blood donors, but as funds are often as hard to come by as blood for the nonprofit organization, pricey pictures or original photography wasn't an option. "To overcome [this challenge], we created our own visuals," the agency says. "We used the Red Cross logo—which collectively resemble drops of blood from afar—to form images of people," including a man, a woman and a baby that represent—or could be—anyone. "The tagline, 'Every drop counts,' completes the message: Every drop of blood contributes to a life. So come forward to be a blood donor. No donation is insignificant."

1

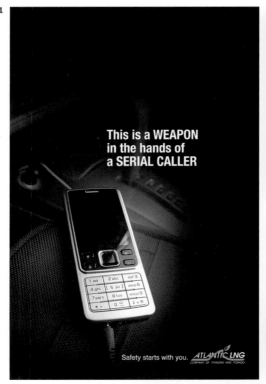

1 CREATIVE FIRM: **Inglefield, Ogilvy & Mather Caribbean Ltd. - Port of Spain, Trinidad & Tobago** CREATIVE TEAM: **David Gomez - Executive Creative Director; Gary Clarke - Creative Director; Glenn Forte - Art Director; Paula Obe - Senior Copywriter; Shane Lue Choy - Senior Account Executive** CLIENT: **Atlantic LNG**

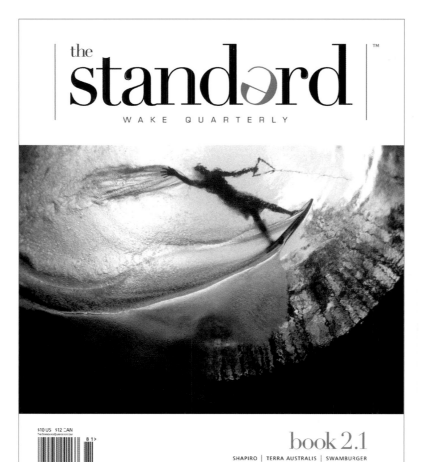

the
stand◑rd ™
WAKE QUARTERLY

$10 US $12 CAN
The Standerd Quarterly.com

8 1>

0 74470 24113 5

book 2.1
SHAPIRO | TERRA AUSTRALIS | SWAMBURGER

creativity 38 annual awards

PLATINUM Ⓟ

The Standerd Book 2.1

CREATIVE FIRM: The Standerd - Orlando, FL

CREATIVE TEAM: James Krawczyk - Editor/Art Direction; Joey Meddock, Josh Letchworth - Editor/Senior Photographers

CLIENT: The Standerd

The Standerd is an independently published quarterly photo journal that covers the action, lifestyle and beauty of wakeboarding and wakeskating.

Started by acclaimed photographers Joey Meddock and Josh Letchworth and art director James Krawczyk, The Standerd strives to define perfection in action sports publications.

Book 2.1 kicked off the publication's second year, so having a truly showstopping photo for the cover was a definite requirement. An underwater shot presents many challenges, which made it a perfect choice.

"For this shot we hiked back to a natural Florida spring, and set up right in the boil of the spring. After some distance and focus testing with a digital camera, I had the settings down and switched over to black-and-white film," senior photographer Letchworth said.

"I would go under the water and after all my bubbles cleared, the rider would get pulled across over my head. I could fire off about six frames as he passed."

The image made an ideal cover for The Standerd. It showcased the sport from a seldom-seen perspective and it was obscure enough to leave the reader intrigued. The left-to-right movement through the frame adds to the flow of opening the cover.

The challenges with water clarity and magnification were well worth it once the developed film came back. "The decision to put it on the cover was instantly unanimous," said senior photographer/editor Joey Meddock.

"The cover has one of the best photos in the history of the sport."

See more at www.StanderdOnline.com

CREATIVE FIRM: Valentine Group New York - New York, NY

CREATIVE TEAM: Robert Valentine - Art Director; Micheal Myers - Designer

CLIENT: **InterfaceFLOR**

Sexy, Sustainable Design

"Sustainable design practices" is a catchphrase that makes sense for the new century, and carpet company InterfaceFLOR wanted to take the lead, starting with its compendium, *Folio*. "*Folio* had multiple missions," explains Valentine Group New York, which designed the compendium. "To honor global eco-heroes such as the gentleman on its cover, [former New York party promoter] Scott Harrison, who became a media darling by turning his energies to digging wells for clean water in Africa."

Lest the unconventional cover subject— and style—not catch readers' attention, bigger names surely did. "We also used *Folio* to launch InterfaceFLOR's 2008 'Beautiful Revival' collection, the company's first fashion-inspired line," says Valentine. InterfaceFLOR's parent company Interface, a world leader in industrial ecology, used this vehicle to honor designers from Chanel and Diane von Furstenberg to Issey Miyake—thus turning the spotlight on themselves as well.

The compendium, which publishes twice a year, aims to tell an unexpectedly engaging story of sustainability to an ever-widening audience. Says Valentine: "With the launch of *Folio*, Interface is now poised to do for sustainability what Al Gore's Oscar win did for global warming: Make it sexy. And that is a unique and strategically ownable position."

1

usa PHILATELIC
THE OFFICIAL SOURCE FOR STAMP ENTHUSIASTS
Summer 2008 / Volume 13 / Number 2

CHARLES+RAY EAMES

2

the
standard

book 12

3

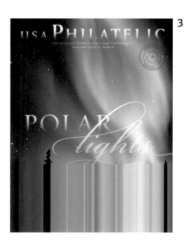

usa PHILATELIC
THE OFFICIAL SOURCE FOR STAMP ENTHUSIASTS

POLAR
lights

4

1 CREATIVE FIRM: United States Postal Service - Bethseda, MD CREATIVE TEAM: United States Postal Service CLIENT: United States Postal Service 2 CREATIVE FIRM: The Standerd - Orlando, FL CREATIVE TEAM: James Kraw-czyk - Editor/Art Direction; Joey Meddock, Josh Letchworth - Editor/Senior Photographers CLIENT: The Standerd 3 CREATIVE FIRM: United States Postal Service - Bethseda, MD CREATIVE TEAM: United States Postal Service CLIENT: United States Postal Service 4 CREATIVE FIRM: housemouse - Melbourne, Australia CREATIVE TEAM: Miguel Valenzuela - Creative Director; Andrea Taylor, Emily Harris - Graphic Designers CLIENT: housemouse

1

2

3

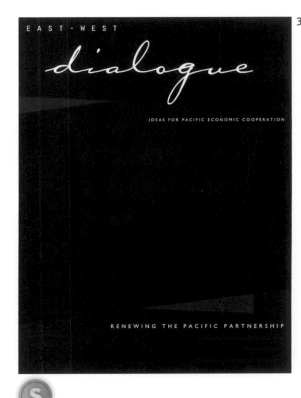

EAST · WEST

dialogue

IDEAS FOR PACIFIC ECONOMIC COOPERATION

RENEWING THE PACIFIC PARTNERSHIP

4

5

6

1 CREATIVE FIRM: **Mediascope Publicitas (I) Pvt Ltd - Mumbai, India** CREATIVE TEAM: **Peter Morgan - COO -Content; Jit Ray - Creative Art Director; Lakshmi Narayan - Asst Art Director** CLIENT: **The Oberoi Group** 2 CREATIVE FIRM: **Words&Pictures, Inc. - Homewood, IL** CREATIVE TEAM: **Words&Pictures, Inc.** CLIENT: **University of Chicago Biological Sciences Division** 3 CREATIVE FIRM: **Very Memorable Design - New York, NY** CREATIVE TEAM: **Michael Pinto - Art Director & Designer** CLIENT: **East-West Center** 4 CREATIVE FIRM: **HenryGill Advertising - Denver, CO** CREATIVE TEAM: **Mark Cohen - Creative Director; Leslie Bell - Art Director; Tim DeFrisco - Photographer** CLIENT: **Wild Blue Yonder Magazine** 5 CREATIVE FIRM: **Mediascope Publicitas (I) Pvt Ltd - Mumbai, India** CREATIVE TEAM: **Peter Morgan - Editor & COO -Content; Jit Ray - Creative Director; Lakshmi Narayan - Asst Art Director** CLIENT: **The Oberoi Group** 6 CREATIVE FIRM: **HenryGill Advertising - Denver, CO** CREATIVE TEAM: **Mark Cohen - Creative Director; Julie Von Gremp - Art Director; Tim DeFrisco - Photographer** CLIENT: **Wild Blue Yonder Magazine**

1

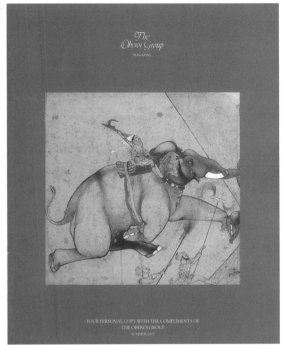

2

creativity 38 annual awards

3

4

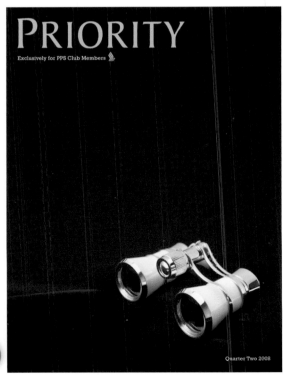

1 CREATIVE FIRM: **Mediascope Publicitas (I) Pvt Ltd - Mumbai, India** CREATIVE TEAM: **Peter Morgan - Editor & COO -Content; Jit Ray - Art Director; Lakshmi Narayan - Asst Art Director** CLIENT: **The Oberoi Group** 2 CREATIVE FIRM: **United States Postal Service - Bethseda, MD** CREATIVE TEAM: **United States Postal Service** CLIENT: **United States Postal Service** 3 CREATIVE FIRM: **HenryGill Advertising - Denver, CO** CREATIVE TEAM: **Mark Cohen - Creative Director; Leslie Ball - Art Director; Travis Commeau - Photo Retouching** CLIENT: **Wild Blue Yonder Magazine** 4 CREATIVE FIRM: **Emphasis Media Limited - North Point, Hong Kong** CREATIVE TEAM: **Percy Chung - Associate Creative Director; Eric Choon - Art Director; Eva Chan - Photo Editor** CLIENT: **Singapore Airlines**

218 plus • November 2007
ÖKONOMIE • Leadership
4

ES STÖRT MICH NICHT,
WAS MEINE MINISTER SAGEN,
SOLANGE SIE TUN,
WAS ICH IHNEN SAGE.

DIE AUTORITÄRE, KOMPROMISSLOSE
FÜHRUNGSPERSÖNLICHKEIT

Margaret Hilda Thatcher, Baroness Thatcher of Kesteven,
geboren am 13. Oktober 1925 in Grantham, Lincolnshire, England, war von 1979 bis 1990
Premierministerin des Vereinigten Königreichs.

218 plus • November 2007
ÖKONOMIE • Leadership
5

IN FÜHRUNG GEHEN

WIE ES MENSCHEN GELINGT,
ANDERE UND DIE WELT ZU BEWEGEN

Stellen Sie sich vor, jemand möchte ein Schiff bauen. Wie sollte er dabei am besten vorgehen? Leute zusammentrommeln, um Holz zu beschaffen, Planken zuzuschneiden und Aufgaben zu verteilen? Dann ist er sicherlich ein guter Vorarbeiter – aber bestimmt keine geniale Führungspersönlichkeit. „Wenn du ein Schiff bauen willst, dann lehre die Menschen die Sehnsucht nach dem weiten endlosen Meer", erkannte schon der französische Schriftsteller Antoine de Saint-Exupéry. Erfolgreiche Anführer haben die Gabe, andere Menschen zu begeistern, mitzureißen und zu Höchstleistungen anzuspornen. Denn sie sind beseelt von einer Idee, sie haben eine Mission. Und mit ihren Visionen revolutionieren sie Geschichte, Politik und Managementmethoden.

Wodurch zeichnet sich eine gute Führungspersönlichkeit sonst noch aus? Die renommierte Führungskräftevermittlung Heidrick & Struggles hat 2004 einmal untersucht, was Topmanager von denen abhebt, die es nicht bis ganz nach oben geschafft haben. Dafür legte sie 1 000 Manager „auf die Couch" und analysierte ihr Führungsverhalten und ihre Persönlichkeit. Das Ergebnis: Die Bosse sind keineswegs brillanter, kreativer oder gar intelligenter als Manager der zweiten Riege. Was Spitzenleute auszeichnet, ist vor allem eines: unerschütterliches Selbstvertrauen.

PLATINUM P

218 Plus

CREATIVE FIRM: **Simon & Goetz Design GmbH & Co. KG -
Frankfurt, Germany**
CREATIVE TEAM: **Christina Schirm, Gerrit Hinkelbein, Thomas
Tscherter - Art Direction**
CLIENT: **Sal. Oppenheim jr. & Cie. KGaA**

Top independent private bank Sal. Oppenheim jr. & Cie, prides itself on its asset management and investment services for its wealthy individual and corporate clients. To match its clients' sophistication and aspirational intents, the German bank turned to Simon & Goetz Design GmbH & Co. KG out of Frankfurt am Main to create a high-class, attention-grabbing magazine.

"Every issue has an overall topic: future, urban fascination and quality," says Simon & Goetz. "The design successfully communicates the traditional values, innovation, exclusiveness and independence of the private bank." In addition to features on economy, society and culture that reflective of Sal. Oppenheim's attitudes the design expresses the bank's open-mindedness to new industrial and economic developments, sensitivity to sociopolitical issues and personal commitment in many fields of art and culture.

1

Welcome to a brave new world of heroes: Heroic people, products, and initiatives dedicated to the art of change. Folio is a collaborative effort from InterfaceFLOR companies around the globe to celebrate people who are taking action to make their world – the world we all share – a little better, a little bit at a time. We are realists here at InterfaceFLOR. We have learned by doing that you don't have to know it all yourself, or do it all yourself, to effect change on a global level. It starts with changing what you can. And changing what you care about. In this issue, you'll meet "Five Heroes for Zero," people who are doing that right now. You'll also see the Just™ collection of products from the FairWorks initiative, which introduces the idea of Social Sustainability into the commercial lexicon. And as always with our work, this and every issue will gleam with inspiration to share with other readers. To begin, a tip of the hat to our No.1 cover hero, Scott Harrison, whose story for Charity: Water you'll find on page 24.

creativity 38 annual awards

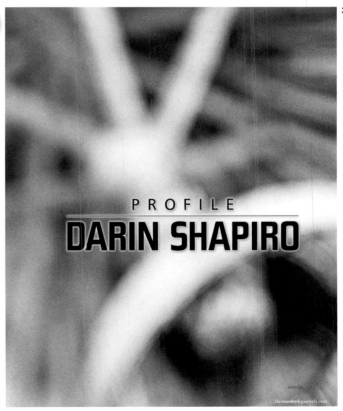

2

PROFILE
DARIN SHAPIRO

3

---

1 CREATIVE FIRM: **Valentine Group New York** - New York, NY CREATIVE TEAM: **Robert Valentine** - Art Director; **Michael Myers** - **Designer** CLIENT: **InterfaceFLOR** 2 CREATIVE FIRM: **The Standerd** - Orlando, FL CREATIVE TEAM: **James Krawczyk** - Editor/Art Direction; **Joey Meddock, Josh Letchworth** - Editor/Senior Photographers CLIENT: **The Standerd** 3 CREATIVE FIRM: **Zeeland Oy** - Turku, Finland CREATIVE TEAM: **Tiina Valve** - Art Director/Illustrator; **Mikko Vaija** - Art Director/Production; **Henri Alinen, Anna Korpi-Kyyny, Sari Lommerse, Paula Puikko** - Copywriters CLIENT: **VMP Group**

1

encounters

English designer Sir
Paul Smith's inspiration
has guided him to the very
pinnacle of the fashion
industry and his signature
collections are recognised
the world over. Here he
gives his impressions
on some suggested
sources of inspiration

英國設計師 Paul Smith 爵士
創意不絕，令他登上時裝界的殿堂
地位，他遍攜閣名的作品系列亦
在全球廣受推崇，這位設計大師
向本刊透露他的靈感之源

what
moves
you, **sir
paul**

英倫紳士
的繆思

2

encounters

keeping up with

中環倩影

claudia

Juggling a busy family life with a career in a high fashion house
is a tall order, but the beauty Claudia Shaw-d'Auriol
takes it all in her stride

澳洲行業足的款裝設計，主理葛細品的服裝兼同顧此工作，
相貌照人的葛細設計師在此輕設計的生活
事倩得對到過這

PORTRAITS BY PAUL HO

3

light

艷光流采

fantastic

STYLIST: RUTH DE CAEN FOR J BEAUTE CAREN / MODEL: CHRISTINA KRAGH

4

encounters

Thanks to one canny
collector, some of Scotland's
best landscapes can be
viewed in Central

有賴一位精明老練的收藏家，
令我們有機會在中環
欣賞奇麗的蘇格蘭山水畫

HK's
**bonny
wee
secret**

私密藝術空間

Scottish art collector
Alan G. Murray on
the main staircase
of The Hong Kong
Club, with two oils in
the background, one
depicting highland
cattle and the other an
Eastern Lothian tower
near his place of birth.

1 CREATIVE FIRM: **Emphasis Media Limited - North Point, Hong Kong** CREATIVE TEAM: **Percy Chung - Associate Creative Director; Eva Chan - Photo Editor** CLIENT: **Hongkong Land 2** CREATIVE FIRM: **Emphasis Media Limited - North Point, Hong Kong** CREATIVE TEAM: **Percy Chung - Associate Creative Director; Eva Chan - Photo Editor** CLIENT: **Hongkong Land 3** CREATIVE FIRM: **Emphasis Media Limited - North Point, Hong Kong** CREATIVE TEAM: **Percy Chung - Associate Creative Director; Eva Chan - Photo Editor** CLIENT: **Hongkong Land 4** CREATIVE FIRM: **Emphasis Media Limited - North Point, Hong Kong** CREATIVE TEAM: **Percy Chung - Associate Creative Director; Eva Chan - Photo Editor** CLIENT: **Hongkong Land**

1

MAY/JUN 2008

54

SILKWINDS

Animal House

For those of you accustomed to the familiar *Discovery Channel* or *National Geographic* footage of lions and zebras roaming the wide African savannah, or deer flitting through a dense forest undergrowth, or even cows and sheep grazing lazily on the old farm, this photo essay may come as a bit of a surprise. For her book, Animal House Photographer **Catherine Ledner** has taken an ark's quota of the animal world, plucked them from their natural habitat and plopped them in a house for a mugshot on the family carpet, complete with funky wallpaper background. Ledner admits she has quite an imagination, attributed to her formative years in her New Orleans family home filled with all kinds of critters, and this book certainly proves it. Alligators and armadillos sharing a shot on the shagpile? Good gracious! *Animal House*, published by Welcome Books, comes complete with cutesy witticisms on each animal to give your child a giggle – and perhaps even you, if you've a mind for the absurd.

No animals were harmed in the production of Ledner's book or this photo essay.

MAY/JUN 2008

55

SILKWINDS

2

A DIFFERENT KIND OF

OR

BY MEGAN SEERY

WHEN HE FACED A CORONARY BYPASS, JOE SISON NEVER IMAGINED THE SURGERY WOULD BE DONE BY A

ROBOT

But when a stress test revealed that one of his three stents was fully blocked, Sison balked at open heart surgery.

"There was no way I was getting my chest cracked open," Sison said. "I didn't want to be lying around [recuperating] for months."

Desperately seeking an alternative, the 60-year-old discovered a procedure that would allow him to get the bypass he urgently needed without having a surgeon saw through his sternum. All that would delve into his body would be the arms of a robot.

"It sounded good," he said. "I'd never heard of it before."

Many people haven't. Few doctors in the world are capable of using a robot to perform bypass surgery, and no one has performed as many as Sudhir Srivastava, MD.

"The work is to truly change the direction of cardiac surgery," said Srivastava, who joined the University of Chicago Medical Center in July 2007. "We want to create a phenomenon where surgeons will have to learn this technique."

Srivastava estimates that 97 percent of coronary bypasses are still performed conventionally, by opening the breastbone to access the chest. About 70 to 75 percent of those patients must have their blood routed to a heart-lung machine during the procedure. After operating, the surgeon wires the breastbone together.

Sison knew he needed a bypass for more than a year but was adamant about keeping his chest intact. Then he found Srivastava and da Vinci.

BENEFITS AND LIMITATIONS ● ● ● ●

The da Vinci robot—which is used for many kinds of procedures, like removing cancerous prostates or performing hysterectomies—is an improvement from earlier minimally invasive surgeries in which the surgeon uses specialized instruments, such as a grasper and scissors, that have limited dexterity. The doctor views his or her work on a two-dimensional monitor located next to the patient. About 2 to 3 percent of U.S. bypass surgeries are performed this way, Srivastava said.

SURGEON SARAH TEMKIN USES THE DA VINCI ROBOT FOR GYNECOLOGICAL PROCEDURES, INCLUDING ENDOMETRIAL CANCER RESECTIONS. PHOTO BY DAN DRY

24 University of Chicago Medicine on the Midway

Spring 2008 25

1 CREATIVE FIRM: **Emphasis Media Limited - North Point, Hong Kong** CREATIVE TEAM: **Percy Chung - Associate Creative Director; Teresita Khaw - Art Director; Davis Kwok - Senior Designer; Eva Chan - Photo Editor** CLIENT: **SilkAir 2** CREATIVE FIRM: **Words&Pictures, Inc. - Homewood, IL** CREATIVE TEAM: **Words&Pictures, Inc.** CLIENT: **University of Chicago Biological Sciences Division**

1

With reverence to Mother Earth and her bounty, New York City chefs are teaming up with local farmers—and cooking with ingredients so fresh they're practically still dewy.

Playing the Green Market

by Pameladevi Govinda   photographed by Kenneth Chen

2

Pop!
Goes the Artist

3

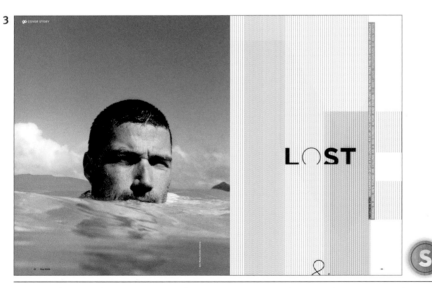

LOST

1 CREATIVE FIRM: **Morris Visitor Publications - New York, NY** CREATIVE TEAM: **Anna Ratman - Art Director; Joanna Foucheux - Designer; Jodie Love - Photo Editor** CLIENT: **IN New York** 2 CREATIVE FIRM: **Kosak Design - Pittsburgh, PA** CREATIVE TEAM: **Tom Kosak - Creative Director, Designer; Tom Altany - Photographer; Burton Morris - Illustrator; Robert Mendelson - Executive Editor** CLIENT: **Carnegie Mellon University** URL: **www.kosakdesign.com** 3 CREATIVE FIRM: **INK Publishing - New York, NY** CREATIVE TEAM: **Shane Luitjens - Art Director/Graphic Design; Bret Love - Writer** CLIENT: **Airtran Airways**

creativity 38 annual awards

1 CREATIVE FIRM: Sellier Design, Inc. - Marietta, GA CREATIVE TEAM: Carl Bradford - Creative Director; Julie Cofer - Senior Graphic Designer CLIENT: iMi Agency 2 CREATIVE FIRM: Morris Visitor Publications - New York, NY CREATIVE TEAM: Anna Ratman - Art Director; Joanna Foucheux - Designer; Jodie Love - Photo Editor CLIENT: IN New York 3 CREATIVE FIRM: Morris Visitor Publications - New York, NY CREATIVE TEAM: Anna Ratman - Art Director; Joanna Foucheux - Designer; Jodie Love - Photo Editor CLIENT: IN New York 4 CREATIVE FIRM: Direct Focus Marketing Communications Inc. - Winnipeg, MB, Canada CREATIVE TEAM: Direct Focus Marketing Communications Inc. CLIENT: Loewen 5 CREATIVE FIRM: HenryGill Advertising - Denver, CO CREATIVE TEAM: Mark Cohen - Creative Director; Lisa Rundall - Art Director CLIENT: Wild Blue Yonder Magazine 6 CREATIVE FIRM: Levine & Associates - Washington, D.C. CREATIVE TEAM: Scott Miller, Greg Sitzmann, Monica Snellings, Kerry McCutcheon CLIENT: AARP

236

PLATINUM P

CREATIVE FIRM: **Hafenbrack Marketing - Dayton, OH**

CREATIVE TEAM: **Jon Brooks - Creative Director; Cherissa Fenwick - Production; Melissa Wyatt, Casey Bowers - Copy**

CLIENT: **F&S Harley-Davidson**

One Sweet Ride

The assignment of reworking a brand doesn't always mean the rebranding agency gets carte blanche to do whatever they want. "Rebranding efforts can be real heartbreakers," says Dayton's Hafenbrack Marketing of the ongoing quest to match the firm's vision with the client's typically "paler and homogenized" preferences. Which is why Hafenbrack was thrilled to find a client as enthusiastic as they: In this case, F&S Harley-Davidson, Ohio's largest Harley-Davidson dealership. "It's equally a treat and a triumph to find a truly cool client willing to jump right in—or on, in this case—and take off down that road with you," the agency says.

Equipped with this enthusiasm, Hafenbrack helped make F&S the fastest-growing and most successful Harley dealer in the region by taking riders' pride and passion for the hometown shop, injecting equal parts Harley attitude and F&S family-friendliness—then tying everything to a tagline that says it all: "The Journey Starts Here."

Hafenbrack showed F&S how to lead the pack by furnishing a shiny new logo, an ambitious campaign and a full-on marketing push aimed toward today's rider, crowned with a quarterly newsletter especially for Hog enthusiasts: *The Ride.* "'The Journey' required a guidebook for its travelers and *The Ride* delivered," the agency says of the publication, which evokes an image as clean, sleek and high-end as its namesake bikes. "It utilizes high-resolution, close-up photography for the cover shot, placing the emphasis where it should be—on the bike," Hafenbrack says, adding that inside, the signature orange and black palette complements the very brand attitude Harley-Davidson enthusiasts have come to expect.

Riders may want to keep their eyes on the road, but the inaugural issue of *The Ride* proved to be its own kind of required reading, ahead of a map that freewheeling Harley lovers might care to leave behind. "Keeping riders, customers and casuals tuned in to everything F&S, the publication offers dealer and product information, promotions, coupons, an events schedule and even the occasional history lesson," Hafenbrack says. "It's one sweet *Ride*."

1

Using Your Prescription Drug Benefit

Medical and Prescription Drug Plans

2

A HISTORIC PROPERTY OF
FULLER E. CALLAWAY FOUNDATION

Hills & Dales
ESTATE

the
PORTICO
News from Hills & Dales Estate

ISSUE NO. 3 FALL 2007
www.hillsanddalesestate.org

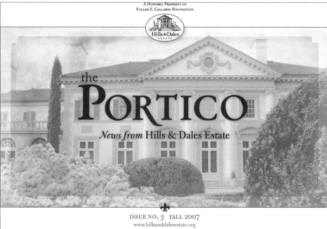

Guest Lecturer:
WILLIAM R. MITCHELL, JR.

1 CREATIVE FIRM: **Beth Singer Design** - Arlington, VA CREATIVE TEAM: **Beth Singer** - Principal; **Suheun Yu** - Graphic Designer; **Sucha Snidvongs** - Senior Graphic Designer CLIENT: **American Red Cross**

2 CREATIVE FIRM: **Kelsey Advertising & Design** - LaGrange, GA CREATIVE TEAM: **Brant Kelsey** - Creative Director; **Niki Studdard** - Designer CLIENT: **Hills & Dales Estate**

creativity 38 annual awards

1

G

2

3

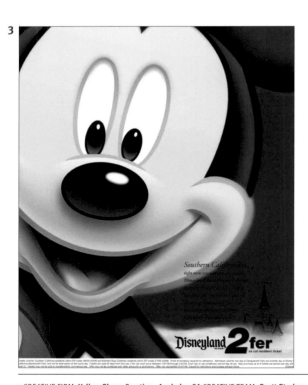

4

S

1 CREATIVE FIRM: **Yellow Shoes Creative - Anaheim, CA** CREATIVE TEAM: **Scott Starkey - Art Director; Wes Clark - Copywriter; Greg Trombo - Illustrator; Marty Muller - Sr. VP Global Creative, Walt Disney Parks & Resort; Joe Schneider - VP Global Creative; Jacquelyn L. Moe - Director of Creative** CLIENT: **Disneyland Resort** 2 CREATIVE FIRM: **MENDES PUBLICIDADE - Belém, Brazil** CREATIVE TEAM: **Oswaldo Mendes - Creative Director; Oswaldo Mendes - Copywriter; Marcel Chaves - Art Director** CLIENT: **Magazan.** 3 CREATIVE FIRM: **Yellow Shoes Creative - Anaheim, CA** CREATIVE TEAM: **Scott Starkey - Art Director; Wes Clark - Copywriter; Marty Muller - Sr. VP Global Creative, Walt Disney Parks & Resort; Joe Schneider - VP Global Creative; Jacquelyn L. Moe - Director of Creative** CLIENT: **Disneyland Resort** 4 CREATIVE FIRM: **360 Communications Limited - Hong Kong** CREATIVE TEAM: **David Chow - Executive Creative Director; Michael Hart - Creative Director; Caver Chu - Associate Creative Director; Teresa Zhang - Account Director; Jacqueline Chong - Senior Art Director; Nelson Cheung - Photographer** CLIENT: **Sincere Department Store**

With all of the other unsightly ads, we thought you could use a clean moment.

Download Coupons at WD40.com/CleanMoments

creativity 38 annual awards

PLATINUM P

Clean Moments

CREATIVE FIRM: **Alcone Marketing - Irvine, CA**

CREATIVE TEAM: **Luis Camano - SVP, Creative Director; Carlos Musquez - Creative Director; Justin Wright - Designer**

CLIENT: **WD-40**

Everyone knows WD-40 can keep your door hinges from squeaking, but the household chemical's maker makes more than just the lubricant in the blue and yellow can. "[We had to raise] awareness of these four really good WD-40 products that not many people knew about," says Alcone Marketing, "and convey the fact that all these products can measure up to the competition and outperform them."

The agency faced several challenges in breaking out of WD-40's single-brand image. "First, trying to find a single idea that would bring all four products together, and secondly, selling the notion of the absence of coupons in a medium that is all about coupons," they say of the campaign, dubbed "Clean Moments."

The theme of cleanliness extends to the ad's image itself—and beyond. "Overall, we [tried] to create the cleanest ad you will find in the Sunday newspaper inserts," Alcone says. "The reward to the consumer was a respite, almost a break, while going through a very busy land-scape. The hope was for the consumer to relate the cleanliness of the ad with the products themselves."

1

BOSS

Any job you want. Almost any. **JobsDB.com**
Interactive Recruitment Network

O mundo é uma eterna descoberta.

Um dia, o homem sonhou com terras distantes, atravessou mares e conquistou continentes.
Foi além: deu asas à imaginação e realizou o sonho de voar feito um passarinho.
Sonhou ainda mais alto e, com a cabeça na lua, não demorou para colocar, lá, também os pés.
Enquanto o homem não perder a capacidade de sonhar e mantiver desperta a sua vontade de sempre
aprender, o mundo será uma eterna descoberta.
Por tudo isso, homenageamos os homens e as mulheres que, tendo abraçado a missão de estimular a
descoberta de conhecimentos, são os primeiros a contribuir para que a vida de cada um de nós seja uma
sublime conquista de cada dia.
Aos mestres, o nosso agradecimento.

15 de outubro. Dia do Professor.

Unama
UNIVERSIDADE
DA AMAZÔNIA
Educação para o desenvolvimento da Amazônia
www.unama.br

One gram with weight

An unprecedented 300 billion won invested to make Korea a center of development excellence.
It's Pfizer's determination to help people live healthier and happier that carries the most weight of all.

Pfizer **Pfizer Korea**

1 CREATIVE FIRM: **Ad Planet Group - Singapore** CREATIVE TEAM: **Teck Chong Leo - Executive Creative Director; Alfred Teo - Associate Creative Director; Yi Long Chen - Art Director; Joy Lee - Senior Copywriter** CLIENT: **Jobs DB** 2 CREATIVE FIRM: **MENDES PUBLICIDADE - Belém, Brazil** CREATIVE TEAM: **Oswaldo Mendes - Creative Director; Dalmiro Freitas - Copywriter; Marcel Chaves - Art Director** CLIENT: **Unama - Universidade da Amazônia.** 3 CREATIVE FIRM: **Leo Burnett Korea - Seoul, South Korea** CREATIVE TEAM: **Jung-Tae Kim - Executive Creative Director; Soo-Hee Yang - Creative Director; Bong-Ho Jeon - Associate Creative Director; Yong-Jin Kim - Senior Art Director; Sun-Young Kim - Senior Copywriter; Suk-Joon Jang - Photographer** CLIENT: **Pfizer Korea**

S

1

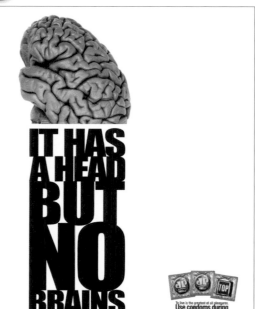

2

G

3

S

1 CREATIVE FIRM: DC3 Unicom - Belém, Brazil CREATIVE TEAM: Glauco Lima, Haroldo Valente - Creative Directors; Alexandre Helmut - Copywriter, Account Executive; Antônio Coelho - Art Director CLIENT: Jovern Pan 2 CREATIVE FIRM: L3 Advertising Inc. - New York, NY CREATIVE TEAM: Jo Chan - Creative Director, Art Director; Lawrence Lee - Copywriter; Seray Sun - Graphic Designer CLIENT: Harrah's Entertainment Inc. 3 CREATIVE FIRM: Yellow Shoes Creative - Anaheim, CA CREATIVE TEAM: Scott Starkey - Art Director; Wes Clark - Illustrator; Marty Muller - Sr. VP Global Creative, Walt Disney Parks & Resort; Joe Schneider - VP Global Creative; Jacquelyn L. Moe - Director of Creative CLIENT: Disneyland Resort

242

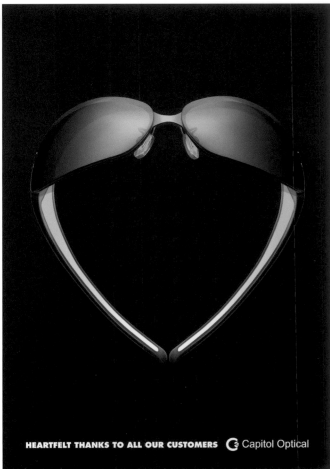

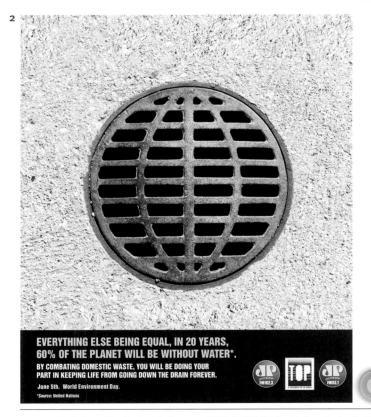

1 CREATIVE FIRM: **Planet Ads & Design P/L - Singapore** CREATIVE TEAM: **Hal Suzuki - Executive Creative Director; Eran Husni Amir Husni - Art Director; Rachel Lee - Senior Account Executive; Suzanne Lauridsen - Senior Copywriter; Takahiro Kiyota - Photographer; Jolene Goh - Retoucher** CLIENT: **Capitol Optical** 2 CREATIVE FIRM: **DC3 Unicom - Belém, Brazil** CREATIVE TEAM: **Glauco Lima, Haroldo Valente - Creative Directors; Alexandre Helmut - Copywriter, Account Executive; Glauco Lima - Copywriter; Paulo Sérgio - Art Director** CLIENT: **Jovem Pan**

Why not the world?

— Lea Salonga

Dare to ask.
Be an Inquirer.
PHILIPPINE DAILY
INQUIRER

creativity 38 annual awards

How hard can it be?
— Romi Garduce

Dare to ask.
Be an Inquirer.
INQUIRER

Why can't I come home?
— Ninoy Aquino

Dare to ask.
Be an Inquirer.
INQUIRER

PLATINUM P

PDI Dare to Ask Campaign

CREATIVE FIRM: **Philippine Daily Inquirer - Makati City, Philippines**
CREATIVE TEAM: **Philippine Daily Inquirer**
CLIENT: **Philippine Daily Inquirer**

A leading Philippines newspaper, facing a deteriorating reputation, asked itself some hard questions. "People were starting to see the *Philippine Daily Inquirer* as a newspaper that was antiestablishment and sensationalist," they say, "and we wanted to reverse that notion by [concentrating] on its strengths and putting forward its legacy of being a leader."

With the core creative idea and tagline, "Dare to ask. Be an *Inquirer*," the paper created a series of ads featuring iconic Filipinos making inquiries of their own. "How hard can it be?" says mountaineer Romi Garduce. Catholic leader Jaime Cardinal Sin poses, "How can we protect them?" And, perhaps most poignantly, the late politician Ninoy Aquino—who was assassinated upon his return from exile—asks, "Why can't I come home?"

"We featured Filipinos who dared to ask," the newspaper says. "They do not just conform to the norms of society, but have decided to push their limits further. And because of this attitude, they have

achieved so much in their lives. Their attitudes mirror the legacy of the *Philippine Daily Inquirer* as a newspaper that constantly provokes us to think and act, and not just be content on being bystanders in today's society."

The message, "Those who dare to ask can change their lives," drives home the newspaper's mission. "It provides news that matters to a nation who understands the issues and concerns of national consequences," they say. "It provides insights and thought-provoking articles that you need to know to help shape your opinion better."

PLATINUM P

CREATIVE FIRM: **Planet Ads & Design P/L - Singapore**

CREATIVE TEAM: **Hal Suzuki - Executive Creative Director; Hironori Kawaguchi - Art Director; Celine Tan - Account Manager; Suzanne Lauridsen - Senior Copywriter; Takahiro Kiyota - Photographer; Nelson Yu - Retoucher**

CLIENT: **Voi Jewellery Pte. Ltd.**

YOU. YOURSELF. YOURS.

Singapore-based agency Planet Ads & Design P/L was hired to raise awareness for a new brand of contemporary fine jewelry, Voi. "The client specifically wanted to convey the message that the brand was aimed at modern, confident women," they say. "As the brand name 'Voi' means 'you' in Italian, the tagline builds on the notion of self and self-indulgence - 'You. Yourself. Yours.' The inference is that when you find a piece of jewelry that you connect with, you literally find yourself in the piece."

Finding oneself in the jewelry itself is a recurring motif in the ads, which feature a close-up image of a woman wearing a piece of the jewelry, with that same woman in full interaction with the very piece. Says the agency: "The visual concept builds on this selfsame notion by depicting a beautiful and fashionable woman... sitting alongside a ring, swinging on an earring, and perched on a pendant."

While Planet found creating the juxta-position—combining separate images

of the model's face, the model's body and the jewelry in a seamless and aesthetically pleasing manner—challenging, the effect works by creating a mirror for the target market: "women who are accustomed to unapologetically indulging themselves and buying their own jewelry—rather than waiting for a man to buy it for them."

1

2

The newspaper that really absorbs you

3

Do you want to see more?
Pictures, videos, news and so much more-
The new address of our website services is **SK24.fi**.

SK24.fi

Do you want to see more?
Pictures, videos, news and so much more-
The new address of our website services is **SK24.fi**.

SK24.fi

SATAKUNNAN KANSA
giving you something new to talk about

SATAKUNNAN KANSA
giving you something new to talk about

1 CREATIVE FIRM: DC3 Unicom - Belém, Brazil CREATIVE TEAM: Glauco Lima, Haroldo Valente - Creative Directors; Alexandre Helmut, Glauco Lima - Copywriters; Paulo Sérgio - Art Director; Eduardo Ferreira - Account Executive CLIENT: ORM Cabo 2 CREATIVE FIRM: Zeeland Oy - Turku, Finland CREATIVE TEAM: Juuso Korpinen, Roy Gonzales - Art Director; Anna Korpi-Kyyny - Copywriter; Pia Gran - Planning Director CLIENT: Satakunnan Kansa 3 CREATIVE FIRM: Zeeland Oy - Turku, Finland CREATIVE TEAM: Juuso Korpinen - Art Director; Anna Korpi-Kyyny - Copywriter; Pia Gran - Planning Director CLIENT: Satakunnan Kansa

creativity 38 annual awards

1

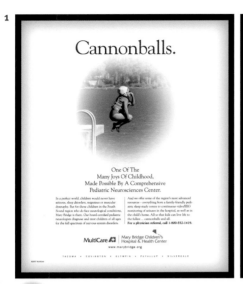

Cannonballs.

One Of The
Many Joys Of Childhood,
Made Possible By A Comprehensive
Pediatric Neurosciences Center.

Mud Pies.

One Of The
Many Joys Of Childhood,
Made Possible By
Exceptional Pediatric Heart Care.

Tadpoles.

One Of The
Many Joys Of Childhood,
Made Possible By A Comprehensive
Pediatric Cancer Program.

2

THEY UNDERSTOOD
I WAS SCARED DELIVERING
TRIPLETS
TEN WEEKS EARLY

THEY UNDERSTOOD
I DIDN'T WANT MY CAREER
TO SKIP
A BEAT

THEY UNDERSTOOD
I DIDN'T WANT LEUKEMIA
TO TAKE ME
OUT OF THE GAME

3

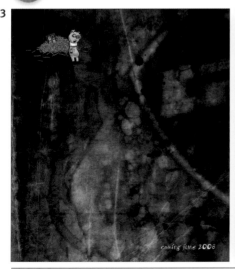

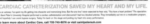

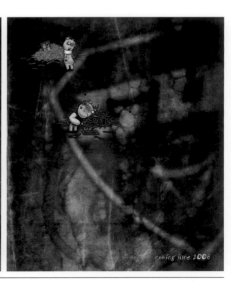

And the goalies lived
happily ever after

1

2

3

4

1 CREATIVE FIRM: **TIME - New York, NY** CREATIVE TEAM: **Ray Rualo - Art Director** CLIENT: **TIME** 2 CREATIVE FIRM: **Yellow Shoes Creative - Anaheim, CA** CREATIVE TEAM: **Scott Starkey - Art Director; Wes Clark - Copywriter; Marty Muller - Sr. VP Global Creative, Walt Disney Parks & Resort; Joe Schneider - VP Global Creative; Jacquelyn L. Moe - Director of Creative** CLIENT: **Disneyland Resort** 3 CREATIVE FIRM: **Fixgo Advertising (M) Sdn Bhd - Subang Jaya, Malaysia** CREATIVE TEAM: **Chua Cheng Kee - Creative Director; Elyse Liew - Copywriter; Aaron Liau - Art Director** CLIENT: **Melco Sales Malaysia Sdn Bhd** 4 CREATIVE FIRM: **Fixgo Advertising (M) Sdn Bhd - Subang Jaya, Malaysia** CREATIVE TEAM: **Chua Cheng Kee - Creative Director; Elyse Liew - Copywriter; Aaron Liau - Art Director** CLIENT: **Melco Sales Malaysia Sdn Bhd**

1

UM DIA PARA
SER RISCADO DO
CALENDÁRIO.

4 de julho é o Dia Mundial das Crianças
Vítimas de Agressão.
Um dia que nem deveria existir.
Porque cobre de vergonha a humanidade.
E que só depende de nossa vontade riscar
do calendário. Não aceitando de braços
cruzados a violência contra crianças.
Denunciando. Colaborando com gestos,
atitudes e palavras. Colaborando com as
autoridades.
Trabalhar duro para acabar com a violência
contra crianças é um dos nossos
compromissos de governo.
Um compromisso de um Pará de Direitos.
Hoje e em todos os dias do ano.

Pará
GOVERNO POPULAR

EM CASO DE DENÚNCIA,
LIGUE PARA (91) 4009-2734.

2

TH!NK

Opening presents under the tree
won't be the same if you're not there to see.

yuh think?

please drive responsibly

bp
Trinidad and Tobago

3

June 26
International Day
in Support of
Victims of Torture

Inca Tanvir Advertising

Issued in the public interest by Khaleej Times

1 CREATIVE FIRM: **MENDES PUBLICIDADE - Belém, Brazil** CREATIVE TEAM: **Oswaldo Mendes - Creative Director, Copywriter; Marcelo Amorim - Art Director** CLIENT: **Governo do Estado do Pará.**
2 CREATIVE FIRM: **All Media Projects Limited - Port of Spain, Trinidad & Tobago** CREATIVE TEAM: **Cathleen Jones - Creative Director/Art Director; Aisha Provoteaux - Graphic Artist/Copywriter;**
Josiane Khan - Senior Account Executive CLIENT: **BPTT** 3 CREATIVE FIRM: **Inca Tanvir Advertising Llc - Sharjah, UAE** CREATIVE TEAM: **Tanvir Kanji - Creative Director; Max D'Lima - Art Director; Sunil**
Anand, Ernest Desai, Rhea Dixit CLIENT: **Khaleej Times**

248

1

Sattu ihan kama-lasti ja mä itkin. Sitten Mikko laittoi kipsin ja kohta mä voin taas pelata!

Veera, koripalloilija

21 000 ammatti-laista tarkoittaa, että joka päivä joku jää äitiyslomalle, vuorotteluvapaalle tai eläkkeelle.

HUS
tarvitsee
uusia osaajia
jatkuvasti.

✖HUS

www.hus.fi

Loppujen lopuksi, elä-mässä on pahempia-kin asioita kuin rinta-syöpä. Tällä hetkellä voin erittäin hyvin.

Anja, kukkakauppias

21 000 ammatti-laista tarkoittaa, että joka päivä joku jää äitiyslomalle, vuorotteluvapaalle tai eläkkeelle.

HUS
tarvitsee
uusia osaajia
jatkuvasti.

✖HUS

www.hus.fi

Tiedän tekeväni tärkeää työtä.

Mikko, sairaanhoitaja

21 000 ammatti-laista tarkoittaa, että joka päivä joku jää äitiyslomalle, vuorotteluvapaalle tai eläkkeelle.

HUS
tarvitsee
uusia osaajia
jatkuvasti.

✖HUS

www.hus.fi

Minulle HUSlaisuus on parasta hoitoa potilaille.

Merja, sairaanhoitaja

21 000 ammatti-laista tarkoittaa, että joka päivä joku jää äitiyslomalle, vuorotteluvapaalle tai eläkkeelle.

HUS
tarvitsee
uusia osaajia
jatkuvasti.

✖HUS

www.hus.fi

1 CREATIVE FIRM: Zeeland Oy - Turku, Finland CREATIVE TEAM: Teija Himberg - Art Director; Piia Gran - Planning Director; Ulla Jämä - Account Planner CLIENT: HUS

1

1 CREATIVE FIRM: **All Media Projects Limited - Port of Spain, Trinidad & Tobago** CREATIVE TEAM: **Cathleen Jones - Creative Director/Art Director; Leon Murray - Senior Graphic Artist; Damon Leon - Copywriter; Adonna Da Costa-Headley - Senior Account Executive** CLIENT: **Government Information Service**

FILM & VIDEO

1

2

1 CREATIVE FIRM: Crabtree + Company - Falls Church, VA CREATIVE TEAM: Susan Angrisani - Creative Director; Lisa Suchy - Production Manager; Rodrigo Vera - Art Director; Billy Weinheimer - Production Artist CLIENT: NASA - National Aeronautics & Space Administration 2 CREATIVE FIRM: DoubleJay Creative - Knoxville, TN CREATIVE TEAM: Larsen Jay - Executive Producer; Brandon Ward - Producer; Dominic Moore - Creative Director; Brian Ford - Editor CLIENT: School of the Art Institute of Chicago

1

254

izzy is...people

...making a difference

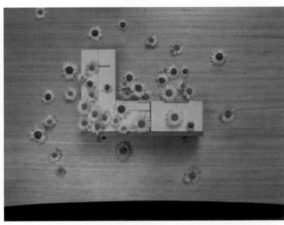

...making us better

izzydesign.com

1 CREATIVE FIRM: **People Design Inc - Grand Rapids, MI** CREATIVE TEAM: **Michele Brautnick - Design Director; Yang Kim - Creative Director; People Design - Photographer; Ryan Lee - Production; Kristin Tennant - Copywriting; Creo Productions - Sound** CLIENT: **izzydesign**

1

Francesca Onwitt

Online Account Funding

Identity to Account Match

10:01a

VAL

"Fraud Is Not Black And White"

2

1 CREATIVE FIRM: Doublelay Creative - Knoxville, TN CREATIVE TEAM: Larsen Jay - Executive Producer; Brandon Ward - Producer; Dominic Moore - Creative Director; Brian Ford - Editor CLIENT: Museum of Science & Industry 2 CREATIVE FIRM: Merestone - Scottsdale, AZ CREATIVE TEAM: Nancy Waller-Stults - Executive Producer; David DeRosier - Director of Creative Services CLIENT: Early Warning

1

256

2

1 CREATIVE FIRM: **Groovy Like a Movie - San Diego, CA** CREATIVE TEAM: **Greg Smith - Producer** CLIENT: **Digium** 2 CREATIVE FIRM: **NBC Universal Global Networks Italia - Rome, Italy** CREATIVE TEAM: **NBC Universal Global Networks Italia** CLIENT: **Steel**

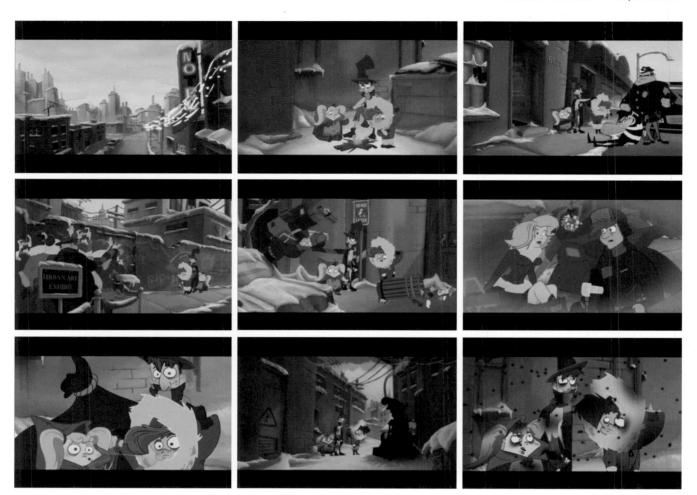

PLATINUM Ⓟ

CREATIVE FIRM: Animax Entertainment - Van Nuys, CA

CREATIVE TEAM: Al Rosson - Animation Director; Kat Kosmala - Lead Animator; Russell Jamison - Creator; Barry Kelly - Editor/Post Production; Adam Marin - Post Production

CLIENT: Animax Entertainment

The Orphan's Christmas Wish
A Coal-Black Comedy

A trio of vandals wreaks havoc one winter day—only to find their efforts not punished but rewarded. In the short film, "The Orphans' Christmas Wish," the Los Angeles animation studio Animax Entertainment imagined a darkly comic tale—a "coal-black comedy"—that harks back to holiday classics such as *A Christmas Carol* and *The Little Match Girl*, often with hilarious results steeped deeply in irony, as the urchins find their injurious efforts compounded with insult.

The result is offbeat—illustrated additionally by their staggered statures. "By giving them very different heights, we were always able to compose them as a triangle without worry of anyone's face being obscured," say the filmmakers. "By designing them as a set, we were also able to focus on giving each a very distinct silhouette shape."

Although the cycle of failed attempts at chaos shares a comically repetitive motif, it's never superfluous, and at a bit over two and a half minutes long—and with

very little dialogue—the tale transcends spoken language. "By keeping the orphans silent, the story remains simple and clear without being over-explained and the piece attains a more timeless quality," Animax explains, adding insight into the importance of a unifying musical score. "It's amazing the difference a few well-placed notes can make," they add. Lest there be any mistake, the film—which incorporates modern computer techniques while maintaining an old-school look—involves sight gags and comedy for all ages: "Suddenly the film's mood and timing came alive and the whole project began to feel like a real honest-to-goodness cartoon."

1

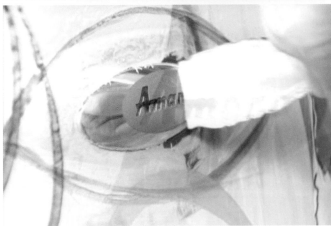

258

2

1 CREATIVE FIRM: **Creators Media Group - Pleasantville, NY** CREATIVE TEAM: **Anthony Trama - Director/Camera/Animator/Editor; Dana Barakat - Producer; Felipe Galindo** CLIENT: **Carmichael Lynch and Spong** 2 CREATIVE FIRM: **Clear Channel Creative Services Group - Atlanta, GA** CREATIVE TEAM: **Alphonso Dormun - Video Editor** CLIENT: **Clear Channel**

LIVE UP
LOVE. PROTECT. RESPECT.

www.iLIVEUP.com

PLATINUM P

CREATIVE FIRM: Inglefield, Ogilvy & Mather Caribbean Ltd. -
Port of Spain, Trinidad & Tobago

CREATIVE TEAM: David Gomez - Executive Creative Director; Paula
Obe - Senior Copywriter; Sara Camps - AV Production Manager;
Badger Smith - Director

CLIENT: Kaiser Foundation

Kaiser Family Foundation :
Live Up Questions And Answers

HIV/AIDS may be an open topic in the United States, but in the Caribbean, it's still a shameful secret. "For too long it has been swept under the carpet, and spoken off in hushed tones," reports Inglefield, Ogilvy & Mather Caribbean Ltd., which created the Kaiser Family Foundation's "Live Up" campaign for HIV/AIDS awareness in Trinidad and Tobago. "We wanted young people talking to their peers in a genre that will be appreciated—and paid attention to." The campaign also aimed to "encourage young people in the Caribbean to get informed about HIV/AIDS, to get tested, to respect those living with HIV/AIDS, and to be positive role models to their peers."

Ogilvy took care to present a realistic approach to HIV/AIDS prevention while not offending local mores. They tempered their biggest challenge, "to present a positive message without talking about abstinence, which has a religious connotation in the Caribbean," with universal messages about "'living up' in the face of HIV/AIDS... focusing on respect,

love, and protection." To this end, Ogilvy employed another universal medium: music. "Poetry and music were used, because of the growing poetry slams in the Caribbean. This is the reason real poets were used to give the message of being positive; of arming oneself with information on HIV and AIDS."

The power of music goes hand-in-hand with the power of knowledge. "We know that knowledge will help decrease the stigma about HIV and AIDS that currently exists," they say. "The ads were meant not only to encourage discussion on this topic, but also to encourage the viewer to get involved, to 'live up, love, protect, respect.'"

1

1 NBC Universal Global Networks Italia - Rome, Italy CREATIVE TEAM: NBC Universal Global Networks Italia CLIENT: Studio Universal

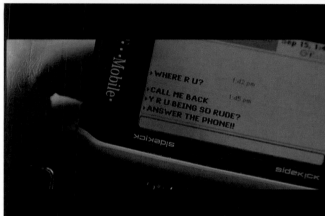

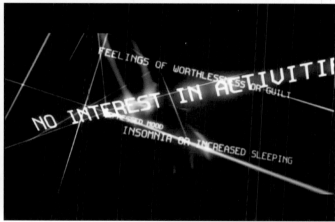

PLATINUM P

Half of Us: PSA's

CREATIVE FIRM: **MTV Networks - New York, NY**

CREATIVE TEAM: **Stephen Friedman - General Manager; Ross Martin - Head of Programming; Eric Conte - Executive Producer; Paul Ricci - Supervising Producer; Sophia Cranshaw - Vice-President, Director, On-Air Promotions; Gina Esposito - Director, Music & Talent; Gala Verdugo - Editor**

CLIENT: **JED Foundation**

It's no cliché that college is a time of great adjustments—and with these adjustments often come emotional problems. That is why mtvU, in conjunction with The JED Foundation, created a series of public service announcements to reach college students at risk for depression and other mental health-related afflictions. With the help of the Foundation's medical advisory board, mtvU carefully crafted the PSAs—depicting common scenarios of students struggling with mental health at college, and others highlighting emotional issues in the context of student activities such as music and sports—and directed students to the Half of Us Web site for more information and resources. ("Half of Us" refers to the number of college students affected by depression at some time.) "By abstractly showing a state of mind rather than a particular individual, these spots are meant to resonate with students of all backgrounds, encouraging them to seek help if they have ever felt the displayed emotions," says mtvU.

While depressed individuals may feel alone in their situation, mtvU wanted to make sure that they knew that their turmoil is by no means uncommon. "The challenges we faced in creating the PSAs included trying to depict scenarios that accurately reflect college life while still offering information about the symptoms of depression and making them appealing to college students," they report. "We created spots representing obvious signs of depression"— withdrawal from friends and family and feelings of anger and rage—"as well as more subtle signs"—disruptions of sleep, occasional excessive drinking and struggling to meet expectations—"to resonate with students from all different backgrounds." And while scaring off those who need help the most remained a major concern, it was crucial that the message got through to every person who heard it. "The words 'mental health' and 'depression' are scary words for anyone to hear," mtvU says. "A key challenge was ensuring these more subtle signs were distinguishable from the normal struggles many students face in their everyday lives. These PSAs encourage students to be attuned to warning signs in themselves and their friends, and empowers them to seek help."

public service film & video

1

---

sales film & video

G

2

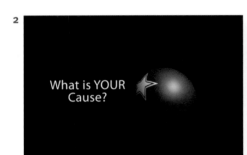

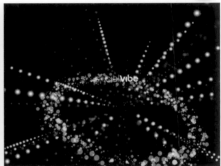

262

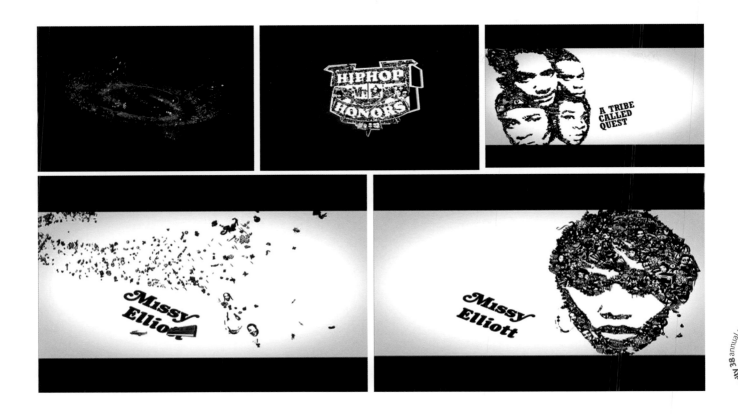

PLATINUM P

CREATIVE FIRM: MTV Networks - New York, NY

CREATIVE TEAM: Nigel Cox-Hagan - Creative Director: EVP Creative & Marketing, VH1; Phil Delbourgo - SVP Brand & Design, VH1; Nancy Mazzei, Amanda Havey - Art Directors; Wendell Wooten - VP Creative Production, VH1; Shannon Horan - Producer; Pascal Duval - Illustrator; EMBER - Design & Animation; Music by Antonio Gonzalez (the Score winner) and produced by Ahmir ?uestlove Thompson/Alex Moulton, Expansion Team

CLIENT: VH1

VH1- HHH Show Open

Hip hop took a mélange of influences to create an entirely new art form, and Dutch illustrator Pascal Duval similarly distilled a variety of components to create completely original portraits of some of hip hop's biggest stars. For VH1's signature Hip Hop Honors event, its parent company, MTV Networks, enlisted Duval to create illustrated portraits that would encapsulate each featured artist's history and significance. "The portraits are a composite of the ingredients of each of their lives and include a myriad of references related to the artist," MTV says, "and the portraits are also springboards to animation that reflect the dynamic and diverse range as well as the power of each of these artists." The campaign tagline, "Create. Innovate. Dominate." combined with Duval's signature style to make a recognizable and memorable campaign across a variety of media—television, billboards and print. As for the show itself, MTV says, "The main title used 3D animation to deconstruct each illustration into its ingredients and reform itself into the next one... The graphics act like a swarm of bees through animation in order to create a very fluid piece that reacts to the music."

1

2

3

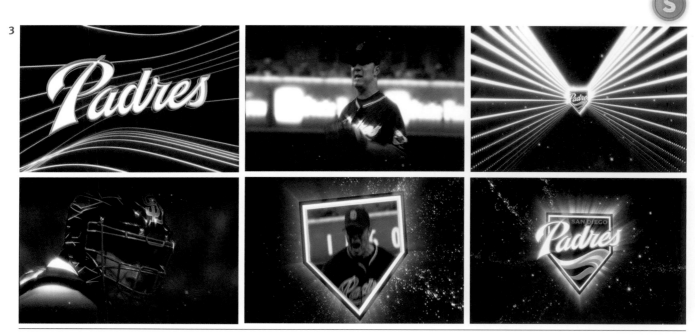

1 CREATIVE FIRM: **MTV Networks - New York, NY** CREATIVE TEAM: **David Bennett - Art Director; Michael Engleman - Creative Director; Emilie Schnick - Producer; Full Tank - Production Company/Design** CLIENT: **CMT 2** CREATIVE FIRM: **Cox Media/Channel 4 San Diego - San Diego, CA** CREATIVE TEAM: **Brian Jouan - Art Director/Animator/Editor; Brian Kim - Art Director/Animator; Tonya Alleyne, Tony Gross - Production Assistants; Jason Bott - Program Producer; Craig Nichols - Executive Producer** CLIENT: **Channel 4 San Diego 3** CREATIVE FIRM: **Cox Media/Channel 4 San Diego - San Diego, CA** CREATIVE TEAM: **Brian Jouan - Art Director/Animator; Mike Vaus - Music; Ed Barnes - Producer; Tom Ceterski - Program Director; Craig Nichols - Executive Producer** CLIENT: **Channel 4 San Diego** URL: www.youtube.com/watch?v=aVbUNe21pis

1

2

3

4

1 CREATIVE FIRM: Nickelodeon Preschool Brand Creative - New York, NY CREATIVE TEAM: Matthew Duntemann - VP - DESIGN: Nickelodeon Preschool Brand Creative; Melinda Beck - Designer/Illustrator; Kurt Hartman - Animator; Matthew Duntemann - Producer CLIENT: NOGGIN 2 CREATIVE FIRM: Nickelodeon Preschool Brand Creative - New York, NY CREATIVE TEAM: Matthew Duntemann - Art Director: Nickelodeon Preschool Brand Creative; Melinda Beck - Designer/Illustrator; Clark Stubbs - Writer: Nickelodeon Preschool Brand Creative; Mary Jacobson - Producer: Nickelodeon Preschool Brand Creative CLIENT: NOGGIN 3 CREATIVE FIRM: Nickelodeon Preschool Brand Creative - New York, NY CREATIVE TEAM: Jennifer Cast - Art Director: Nickelodeon Preschool Brand Creative; Matthew Duntemann - VP - DESIGN: Nickelodeon Preschool Brand Creative; Julia Rosner - Illustrator; Jenn Dewey - Producer: Nickelodeon Preschool Brand Creative CLIENT: Nick Jr. 4 CREATIVE FIRM: Cox Media, Channel 4 San Diego - San Diego, CA CREATIVE TEAM: Brian Kim - Art Director/Animator; Brian Jouan - Art Director; Craig Nichols - Executive Producer CLIENT: Channel 4 San Diego

1

2

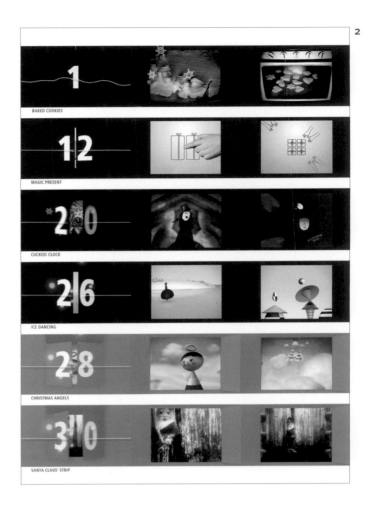

3

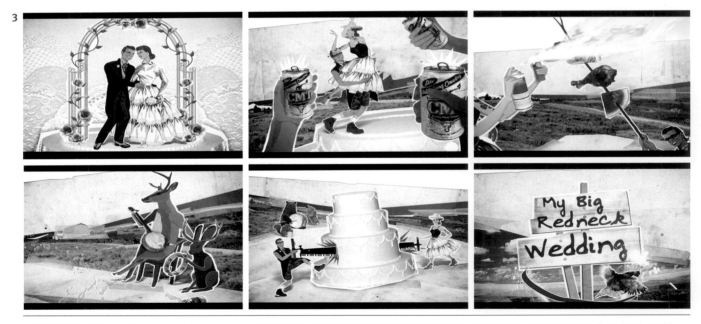

1 CREATIVE FIRM: **NBC Universal Global Networks Italia - Rome, Italy** CREATIVE TEAM: **NBC Universal Global Networks Italia** CLIENT: **Studio Universal** 2 CREATIVE FIRM: **Studio Nordwand - Munich, Germany** CREATIVE TEAM: **Klaus W Schuntermann - Creative Director On Air Design (MDR FERNSEHEN); Sandra Kather - Project Manager Design (MDR FERNSEHEN); Fabrice Gueneau - CEO/Global Creative Direction (Dream On); Peter Pedall - CEO/Global Creative Direction (Studio Nordwand)** CLIENT: **MDR FERNSEHEN (MDR tv), Leipzig/Germany** 3 CREATIVE FIRM: **MTV Networks - New York, NY** CREATIVE TEAM: **Jim Read - Art Director; Adam Gault, Carlo Vega - Designers; Michael Engleman, Jeff Nichols - Creative Directors** CLIENT: **CMT**

266

1

2

creativity 38 annual awards

1 CREATIVE FIRM: MTV Networks - New York, NY CREATIVE TEAM:Stephen Friedman - General Manager; Ross Martin - Head of Programming; Eric Conte - Executive Producer; Paul Ricci - Supervising Producer; James Cohan - Post Production Manager; Rodger Belknap - Sr. Director Design, MTV Off Air Creative CLIENT: mtvU 2 CREATIVE FIRM: MTV Networks - New York, NY CREATIVE TEAM: MTV Networks CLIENT: MTV2

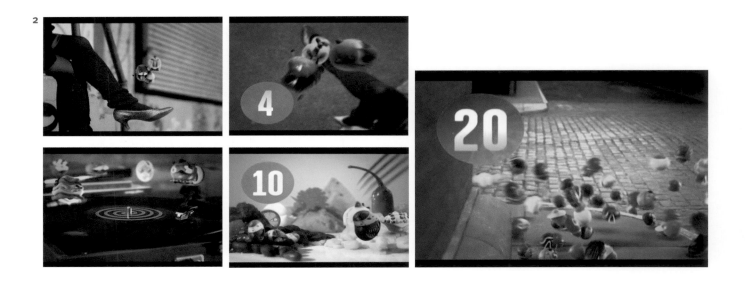

1 CREATIVE FIRM: **MTV Networks - New York, NY** CREATIVE TEAM: **MTV Networks** CLIENT: mtvU 2 CREATIVE FIRM: **MTV Networks - New York, NY** CREATIVE TEAM: **MTV Networks** CLIENT: Tr3s

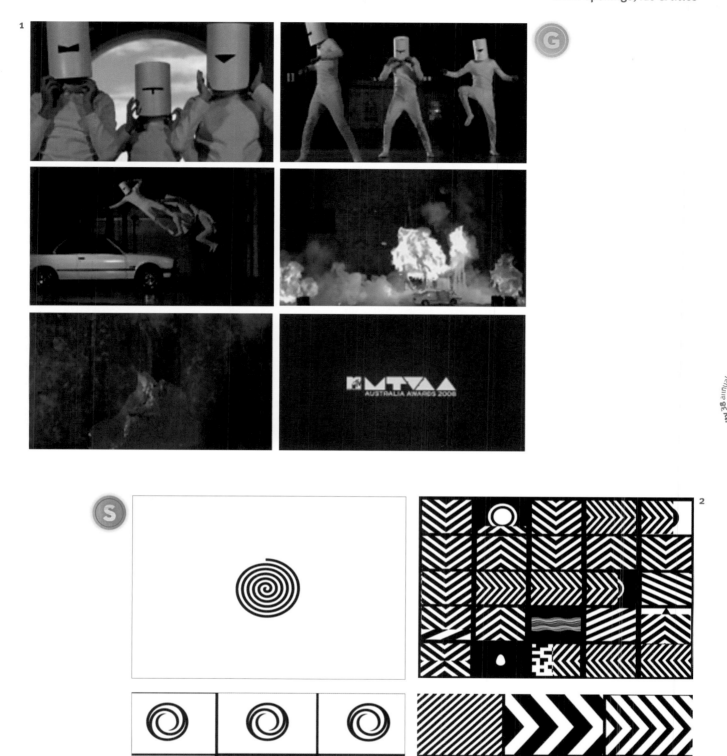

1 CREATIVE FIRM: **Collider - Sydney, Australia** CREATIVE TEAM: **Andrew van der Westhuyzen, Clemens Habicht - Directors; Tim Richardson - DOP** CLIENT: **MTV Australia** URL: **www.collider.com.au**
2 CREATIVE FIRM: **MTV Networks - New York, NY** CREATIVE TEAM: **MTV Networks** CLIENT: **MTV**

1

1 CREATIVE FIRM: **Sandia National Laboratories** - Albuquerque, NM CREATIVE TEAM: **Brent Peterson** - Director/Producer; **Mark Olona** - Sound/Light; **Chris Ranney, Alan Hudson** - Actors CLIENT: **Sandia National Laboratories**

POLITICAL

CREATIVITY **38** ANNUAL AWARDS

PLATINUM P

CREATIVE FIRM: **MTV Networks - New York, NY**

CREATIVE TEAM: **Stephen Friedman - General Manager; Ross Martin - Head of Programming; Eric Conte - Executive Producer; Brian DeCubellis - Supervising Producer; Joe Buoye - Director of Operations; Caroline Kim - Casting Coordinator**

CLIENT: **mtvU**

Editorial Boards: Bill Clinton

Bill Clinton was the first president elected by the so-called "MTV Generation" (remember "Boxers or briefs?"), so it's only fitting that when mtvU, MTV Networks' Peabody and Emmy Award-winning college network, launched a new programming series aimed at breaking down the walls between top student journalists and the influential national figures shaping the world, Clinton was the first participant in the network's Editorial Board series. Launched in March of 2008, the series, says mtvU, "built on the time-honored publishing tradition of the editorial board meeting, creating an unprecedented forum where top student journalists go well beyond canned answers and sound bites to the issues that greatly impact today's college students." These sessions gave selected writers and editors from mtvU's College Media Network—a collection of more than five hundred online college publications—unprecedented opportunity to press key national and global influencers on the issues that matter most to young adults.

The inaugural Editorial Board, featuring President Clinton, coincided with the inaugural meeting of CGI U, a new project from the Clinton Global Initiative (CGI). "These students, who were handpicked to participate in the series, have established themselves as among the smartest, most aggressive and enterprising student journalists in the country," says mtvU. *Politico* writer Mike Allen agrees, "The students were aggressive, and Clinton got a bit heated at a few points" when student reporters posited critical issues such as the current presidential campaign, gay marriage and the situation in Darfur.

CREATIVE FIRM: **Syrup - New York, NY**

CREATIVE TEAM: **Jakob Daschek - Creative Director; Robert Holzer - CEO; Jennifer Giroux - Account Director; Vineet Choudhary - CTO; Alex Lins - Design Director; Mike Manh - Lead Concept Programmer**

CLIENT: **cYclops form LLC**

1

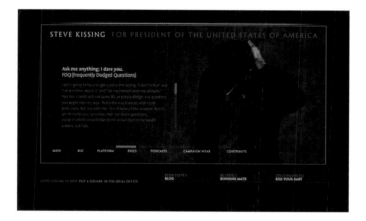

1 CREATIVE FIRM: **Barefoot - Cincinnati, OH** CREATIVE TEAM: **Steve Kissing - Creative Director, Copywriter; Adam George - Senior Designer; Bobby Uhlenbrock - Developer; Doug Worple - Executive Creative Director; TJ Vissing - Photographer, OMS Photography** CLIENT: **Steve Kissing**

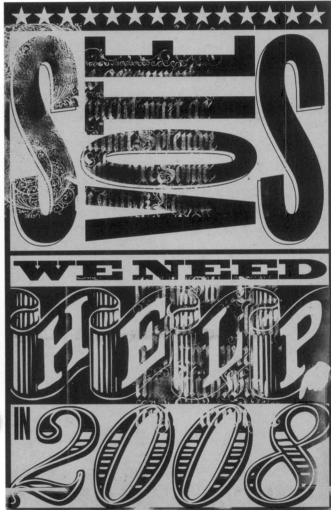

1 CREATIVE FIRM: **Nonperishable Design - Conshohocken, PA** CREATIVE TEAM: **Mitzie Testani - Designer** CLIENT: **AIGA**

ILLUSTRATION, PHOTOGRAPHY & TYPOGRAPHY

CREATIVITY 38 ANNUAL AWARDS

1

I was only fourteen when I first counted coup
by striking an enemy warrior's head
and earned my new name, "Sitting Bull."
It is a name of power and strength
that came to my father in a dream.
He gave me a shield painted with
sacred pictures to protect me.
I carried it always into battle.

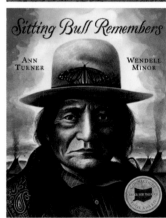

2

1 CREATIVE FIRM: Wendell Minor Design - Washington, CT CREATIVE TEAM: Wendell Minor - Illustrator; Matt Adamec - Designer; Martha Rago - Art Director CLIENT: HarperCollins URL: www.minorart.com 2 CREATIVE FIRM: Wendell Minor Design - Washington, CT CREATIVE TEAM: Wendell Minor - Illustrator; Sara Reynolds - Designer, Art Director CLIENT: Dutton URL: www.minorart.com

1

The buggy eased to a halt. Luke breathed a smell of metal mixed with the faint scent of lilacs. He climbed down and stood with his father close to the iron rails.

2

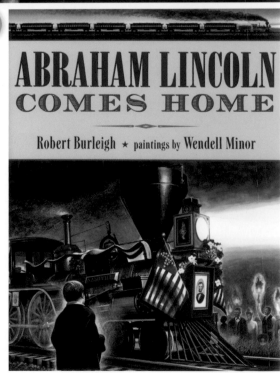

1 CREATIVE FIRM: **Wendell Minor Design - Washington, CT** CREATIVE TEAM: **Wendell Minor - Illustrator; Laurent Linn - Designer; Patrick Collins - Art Director** CLIENT: **Holt/Christy Ottaviano Books** URL: **www.minorart.com** 2 CREATIVE FIRM: **Purple Circle - Nottingham, UK** CREATIVE TEAM: **Simon Harrison - Creative Director; John Lyle - Director of Brands; Hannah Pearce - Project Manager; Steven Pearce - Illustrator** CLIENT: **BeWILDerwood**

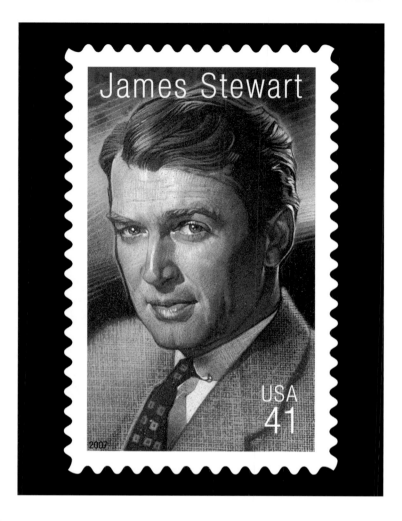

James Stewart Legends Of Hollywood Postage Stamp

CREATIVE FIRM: **United States Postal Service - Bethseda, MD**
CREATIVE TEAM: **Phil Jordan - Art Director; Drew Struzan - Artist**
CLIENT: **United States Postal Service**

It's a wonderful stamp—the thirteenth stamp in the United States Postal Service's Legend of Hollywood series, that is. The first-class label celebrates James Stewart, the film star whose lanky physique, drawling speech and naturalistic acting style made the characters he embodied American everymen. Basing the design on a portrait by Drew Struzan—who based his work on a publicity still for the 1949 baseball biopic *The Stratton Story*—art director Phil Jordan created an instantly identifiable image of the beloved actor. Additionally, the painting on the stamp's selvage, or background sheet, shows another Struzan-inspired image from *Mr. Smith Goes to Washington*, the 1939 film for which Stewart received the first of his five Academy Award nominations for Best Actor.

"The intent was to show Stewart in a way that would render him recognizable—at stamp size—to the greatest number of people," says Jordan. "The challenge, of course, is to create a good likeness. The art, though based on a publicity still, must function primarily as a portrait of Stewart himself, rather than recall his performance in any particular film."

1

2

4

3

1 CREATIVE FIRM: **United States Postal Service - Bethseda, MD** CREATIVE TEAM: **Carl Herrman, Michael Deas** CLIENT: **United States Postal Service** 2 CREATIVE FIRM: **Sabingrafik, Inc. - Carlsbad, CA** CREATIVE TEAM: **Tracy Sabin - Illustrator/Designer; Dave Henson - Art Director** CLIENT: **The Old Globe Theatre** 3 CREATIVE FIRM: **United States Postal Service - Bethseda, MD** CREATIVE TEAM: **Ethel Kessler - Art Director; Kam Mak - Artist** CLIENT: **United States Postal Service** 4 CREATIVE FIRM: **Dick Bobnick Illustration - Burnsville, MD** CREATIVE TEAM: **Dick Bobnick - Illustrator-Designer** CLIENT: **Self promotional** URL: **www.dickbobnick.com**

1

2

3

1 CREATIVE FIRM: Sue Todd Illustration - Toronto, ON, Canada CREATIVE TEAM: Sue Todd - Illustrator CLIENT: City of Waterloo 2 CREATIVE FIRM: United States Postal Service - Bethseda, MD CREATIVE TEAM: Richard Sheaff - Art Director CLIENT: United States Postal Service 3 CREATIVE FIRM: United States Postal Service - Bethseda, MD CREATIVE TEAM: Ethel Kessler - Art Director; Rafael Lopez - Artist CLIENT: United States Postal Service

Blue Light

CREATIVE FIRM: **Playboy Magazine - Chicago, IL**

CREATIVE TEAM: **Rob Wilson - Art Director; Gerard Dubois - Illustrator; John Updike - Writer**

CLIENT: **Playboy Magazine**

Illustrator Gérard DuBois had an opportunity to do a picture for Playboy, but it wasn't what you might think: He created an original design to accompany one of the, yes, articles—or, in this case, a short story. "The art director did not ask for anything specific, but [said] to enjoy myself," the Québécois artist said of his assignment for "Blue Light" (January 2008). "John Updike's short story was really subtle, the drama not overexposed, but still, you could feel this aging man's despair and loss," DuBois says of his inspiration for the portrait of a plump, past-his-prime man literally disintegrating before a mirror in a dusky blue room. "Starting from there, my intent was to depict his inner feelings, with an image as quiet as the text, lighted by a blue atmosphere, as a *clin d' œil* [wink] to the title."

1

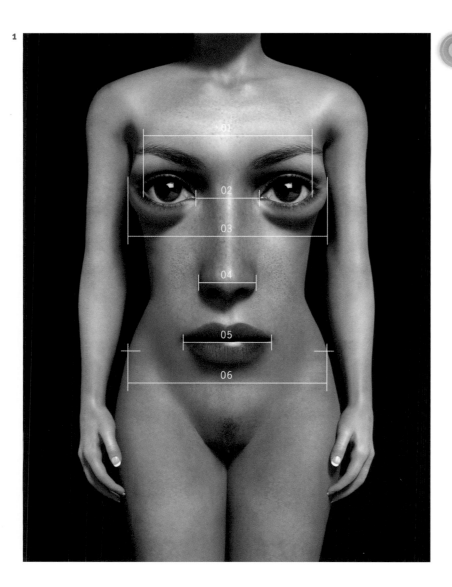

3

creativity 38 annual awards

1 CREATIVE FIRM: Playboy Magazine - Chicago, IL CREATIVE TEAM: Rob Wilson - Art Director; Mirko Ilic - Illustrator; Chip Rowe - Writer CLIENT: Playboy Magazine 2 CREATIVE FIRM: Playboy Magazine
- Chicago, IL CREATIVE TEAM: Rob Wilson - Art Director; Yuko Shimizu - Illustrator; Frank Owen - Writer CLIENT: Playboy Magazine 3 CREATIVE FIRM: Playboy Magazine - Chicago, IL CREATIVE TEAM:
Rob Wilson - Art Director; Jeffrey Smith - Illustrator; Robert Stone - Writer CLIENT: Playboy Magazine

1

2

3

1 CREATIVE FIRM: **Playboy Magazine - Chicago, IL** CREATIVE TEAM: **Rob Wilson - Art Director; Jason Holley - Illustrator; Jonathan Rendall - Writer** CLIENT: **Playboy Magazine** 2 CREATIVE FIRM: **Playboy Magazine - Chicago, IL** CREATIVE TEAM: **Rob Wilson - Art Director; Dave McKean - Illustrator; Kurt Vonnegut - Writer** CLIENT: **Playboy Magazine** 3 CREATIVE FIRM: **Playboy Magazine - Chicago, IL** CREATIVE TEAM: **Rob Wilson - Art Director; Phil Hale - Illustrator; Christian Parenti - Writer** CLIENT: **Playboy Magazine**

PLATINUM ⓟ

CREATIVE FIRM: Splash Productions Pte Ltd - Singapore

CREATIVE TEAM: Stanley Yap - Art Director, Photographer; Terry Lee, Evelyn Teng - Copywriters

CLIENT: Splash Productions Pte Ltd

Life's A Stage

Chinese street opera is a vanishing art—even in a country as populous as China, and it took a design team from a different nation to attempt to capture in book form what may be its last days. Singapore's Splash Productions Pte Ltd created a book, *Life's a Stage*, using seven nights of photographic documentation and three months of interviewing the craft's principals, then writing and laying it all out.

"The audience does not get any younger; the performing pool does not get any larger," the designers say. "Yet, there is eternity on stage; that is where the performers translate a lifelong passion into a language of grace and emotion. As designers, we relish in the opportunity to capture eternity in such a creative outlet."

The resulting book "approximates the stage and its icons as authentically as we ever wished," they report, "and we were drained from the exertion." After daring to take the first step of this huge under-taking, they had to "conquer our inertia, fear of rejection, self-doubt—all in one fell swoop. Once we got started, things fell into place relatively smoothly." Not only was it an emotional challenge, it was a financial one too: The team collaborated to create a beautiful volume—for not a lot of money. "We are glad we persisted with this book," they say. "It pays a psychic dividend that outweighs gold." Platinum, in fact.

1

2

"The real voyage of discovery consists not in seeking new landscapes, but in having new eyes."

Marcel Proust

arcus

2007 Annual Report

3

6

4

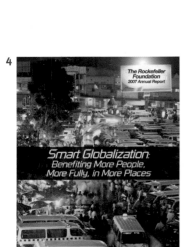

The Rockefeller Foundation 2007 Annual Report

Smart Globalization:
Benefiting More People,
More Fully, in More Places

5

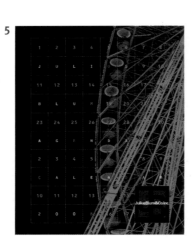

1 CREATIVE FIRM: QuadPhoto - New York, NY CREATIVE TEAM: Mark Van Amburgh - Photographer CLIENT: QuadPhoto 2 CREATIVE FIRM: Emerson Wajdowicz Studios Inc - New York, NY CREATIVE TEAM: Lisa LaRochelle - Art Director, Designer; Jurek Wajdowicz - Art Director, Designer, Photography; Manuel Mendez, Yoko Yoshida - Designer; Antonin Kratochvil - Photography CLIENT: Arcus Foundation 3 CREATIVE FIRM: Tcherevkoff Studio LTD. - New York, NY CREATIVE TEAM: Michel Tcherevkoff - Photographer CLIENT: self 4 CREATIVE FIRM: Emerson Wajdowicz Studios Inc - New York, NY CREATIVE TEAM: Lisa LaRochelle - Art Director, Designer; Jurek Wajdowicz - Art Director, Designer, Photography; Manuel Mendez, Yoko Yoshida - Designers; Jonas Bendiksen - Photography CLIENT: The Rockefeller Foundation 5 CREATIVE FIRM: Emerson Wajdowicz Studios Inc - New York, NY CREATIVE TEAM: Lisa LaRochelle, Jurek Wajdowicz - Art Director, Designers; Manuel Mendez, Yoko Yoshida - Designers CLIENT: Julius Blum & Co. Inc 6 CREATIVE FIRM: Tcherevkoff Studio LTD. - New York, NY CREATIVE TEAM: Michel Tcherevkoff - Photographer CLIENT: self

PLATINUM P

CREATIVE FIRM: **Mattel - El Segundo, CA**

CREATIVE TEAM: **Paul Jordan - Photographer; Mary Jordan - Stylist; Lars Auvinen - Set Design / Construction**

CLIENT: **Mattel**

Barbie Fashion Model Collection Je Ne Sais Quoi

Photographing an internationally known style icon for a fashion shoot may make some people nervous, but Mattel goes way back with their model. "Generally the biggest in hurdle in working with Barbie is scale," says Paul Jordan, who shot the doll photo for the Barbie Fashion Model Collection for advertising and catalog purposes. "My goal is always to make people believe that Barbie lives in the real world by choosing appropriate materials and colors to make the setting feel authentic," the El Segundo photographer explains. "This year, these dolls were French-themed, so naturally we chose to capture their beauty in a set resembling a city in France."

Despite the tiny size and un-diva-like attitude of the star, capturing the glamour girl's elegance was no game. Jordan thoroughly researched his setting, examining books and magazines such as vintage *VOGUE*, which, he says, "has always served as great inspiration for the collection." The images within helped create the color palate: rich, warm golden tones against a dark and dramatic background to suggest an evening out on the town. The combination proved to be the perfect complement to Barbie's stunning, detail-conscious couture. Says Jordan: "The collection is all about beauty, glamour and timelessness, so we created a setting that would elicit this type of imagery."

PLATINUM Ⓟ

CREATIVE FIRM: **Scanad - Odense C, Denmark**

CREATIVE TEAM: **Henry Rasmussen - Creative Director, Copywriter; Jan Maack - Art Director; Soren Hald - Photographer**

CLIENT: **Copenhagen Theatre Association**

Copenhagen Theatres campaign: Theatre is Now and Here

Drama doesn't have to be all seriousness—particularly when it comes to appealing to the masses, which would rather watch television than go to a play. In the land of Hamlet, Odense C design firm Scanad devised a campaign for the Copenhagen Theatres to bring them in.

The intent of the campaign, says Scanad, was to "'dramatize the drama' and convey that theatre is not 'museum art' but a contemporary art form, relevant in the lives of people today, and to show the main strength of theatre"—live action that happens in real time before your very eyes. Or, as the theme holds, "Theatre is Now and Here."

The whimsical photos capture the spirit of the playgoing experience without the boredom that so many would-be attendees fear. "The main challenge was to make photos real and believable, while at the same time being dramatic, absurd and funny, within the frames of everyday life," the agency says of tableaux that include everyday scenes twisted just

so. "It is a difficult photographic art to make slice-of-life seem realistic and not staged and lifeless."

The effect, whether depicting a pensive man in jeans with a sword protruding from his back or a hipster couple leaping in dance at a bus stop, is undeniably spontaneous. "We wanted to capture the life and the reality and achieved that by actually letting the models/actors/dancers go ahead and act out the scenes on real-life street locations, then catching the moment on camera with as little artificial lighting as possible," Scanad says.

1 CREATIVE FIRM: **Ron Berg Photography Inc - Kansas City, MO** CREATIVE TEAM: **Ron Berg - Photographer; Ky Miller, Claire Cunningham - Creative** CLIENT: **Wink** 2 CREATIVE FIRM: **Planet Ads & Design P/L - Singapore** CREATIVE TEAM: **Hal Suzuki - Executive Creative Director; Hironori Kawaguchi - Art Director; Celine Tan - Account Manager; Suzanne Lauridsen - Senior Copywriter; Shunsuke Mizoe - Photographer** CLIENT: **C.B. Fleet Co., Inc.** 3 CREATIVE FIRM: **DeMuth Design - Cazenovia, NY** CREATIVE TEAM: **Roger De Muth** CLIENT: **Syracuse International Film Festival**

1

2

1 CREATIVE FIRM: **Mattel - El Segundo, CA** CREATIVE TEAM: **Paul Jordan - Photography; Mary Jordan - Stylist; Lars Auvinen - Set Design / Construction** CLIENT: **Mattel** 2 CREATIVE FIRM: **MTV Networks - New York, NY** CREATIVE TEAM: **Matt Lehman - Designer; Lyndon Wade - Director/Photographer; Marge Casey - Production Company; James Hitchcock, Michael Engleman - Creative Director; Jason Skinner - Creative Director/Art Director** CLIENT: **CMT** 3 CREATIVE FIRM: **Scanad - Odense C, Denmark** CREATIVE TEAM: **Henry Rasmussen - Creative Director, Copywriter; Jan Maack - Art Director; Jakob Mark - Photographer** CLIENT: **Aalborg Energy Supply** 4 CREATIVE FIRM: **Morningstar Design, Inc. - Frederick, MD** CREATIVE TEAM: **Misti Morningstar - Photographer** CLIENT: **Maryland Ensemble Theatre**

PHOTO FEATURE

Q. How is kite photography different from other aerial photography?

I've shot thousands of pictures above India. More than any country in the world. From above, it's a completely new vision, new perspectives, new ways to understand the landscape, even though nature intended it to be seen at ground level. Some patterns, designs, unexpected aspects would show up in the results. Kites have the ability to carry my camera very close to roofs, clock towers, domes, minarets, any elevated building, and show a very close view of details. It is able to capture human profiles, fauna and flora so unobtrusively that it does not disturb the subject. I always use wide angle lenses, so the pictures are very exclusive, very challenging, and show our Earth from a very unusual angle.

I've flown these kites thousands of times. I build my own kites after the famous Japanese kite 'Rokkaku'. It has the largest span reaching 12 square metres (about 40 square feet). They are made out of siliconised nylon and carbon or fibre-glass sticks. I have adapted the traditional pattern of these kites to suit my own needs, but their proportions and designs vary, depending on weather conditions.

Students practising the ancient martial art form of Kalaripayattu at a beach in Kozhikode. "I love this picture for its shadow effect and graphic impact."
Next page: A unique shot of the dome of the Taj Mahal. "Only a kite can get so close to the dome. No man, chopper, crane could do it. It is a protected area."

CREATIVE FIRM: Mediascope Publicitas (I) Pvt Ltd - Mumbai, India

CREATIVE TEAM: Peter Morgan - COO -Content; Jit Ray - Creative Art Director; Lakshmi Narayan - Asst Art Director; Nicolas Chorier - Photographer

CLIENT: The Oberoi magazine Spring 2008

PHOTO FEATURE

Q. How do you put this programme into operation?

Frankly it's worked like a dream. The photographic equipment is mounted on a multicradle hanging on the line under the kite. The camera can be lifted up to a thousand feet, even though low altitudes are often more interesting. This whole rig weighs about two kilos, depending on the lens I mount, or on some extra battery. I use a Canon 5D, with mostly a 24 mm lens. This cradle with the camera is operated by remote control and can achieve a full 360-degree rotation and 90-degree tilt. An air-to-ground, video-link sends a signal which provides real-time monitoring on a portable TV screen for accurate framing. I set up my kite and fly it up to about 30 metres (100 feet).

Once I feel my kite flying nice and smooth, I rig up my camera on the line, about 100 feet below the kite. The whole apparatus can then be flown up to the required height. I hold the kite string under my arm. I carry my remote control on one shoulder and a video monitor around my neck. I can now shoot - the whole set-up being very flexible.

Previous page: Elephants enjoying a bath at Kodanad, an elephant training centre near Ernakulam, Kerala. "I see flying my kite roaring in realtime...but the junbos don't seem to care."
Left: Mehrangarh Fort, Jodhpur. "Hove this picture for the dynamics it affords. I know every single part of its rooftop terrace."

PLATINUM P

CREATIVE FIRM: **McGarry Bowen - New York, NY**

CREATIVE TEAM: **Annie Leibovitz - Photographer; Jeremy Lamin - Art Director; Jason Hunter - Copywriter; Gordon Bowen - Executive Creative Director; Marty Muller - Sr. VP Global Creative, Walt Disney Parks & Resort**

CLIENT: **Walt Disney Parks & Resorts**

A MAN, a boat, A LIFE

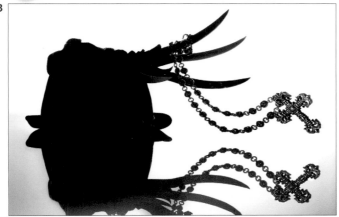

1 CREATIVE FIRM: **Mel Lindstrom Photography - San Francisco, CA** CREATIVE TEAM: **Mel Lindstrom - Photographer; Mary Sullivan - Art Director; Paulette Hurdlik - Creative Director** CLIENT: **Zehno Cross Media** 2 CREATIVE FIRM: **Mediascope Publicitas (I) Pvt Ltd - Mumbai, India** CREATIVE TEAM: **Peter Morgan - COO -Content; Jit Ray - Creative Art Director; Lakshmi Narayan - Asst Art Director; Sebastian Cortes - Photographer** CLIENT: **The Oberoi magazine Spring 2008** 3 CREATIVE FIRM: **Massimo Gammacurta Photographer - South Orange, NJ** CREATIVE TEAM: **Massimo Gammacurta - Photographer+Concept; Cat Baker - Styling; Charlie Matz - Prop Styling; Andi Kuonath - Retouching** CLIENT: **Surface Magazine Avant Guardian Winners Issue** URL: **www.gammacurta.com**

1

G

296

2

S

3

1 CREATIVE FIRM: **sophie pangrazzi photography - Seattle, WA** CREATIVE TEAM: **Sophie Pangrazzi - Seattle Metropolitan mag_Top Doctor** CLIENT: **Seattle Metropolitan mag** 2 CREATIVE FIRM: **The Standerd - Orlando, FL** CREATIVE TEAM: **James Krawczyk - Editor/Art Direction; Joey Meddock, Josh Letchworth - Editor/Senior Photographers** CLIENT: **The Standerd** 3 CREATIVE FIRM: **The Standerd - Orlando, FL** CREATIVE TEAM: **James Krawczyk - Editor/Art Direction; Joey Meddock, Josh Letchworth - Editor/Senior Photographers** CLIENT: **The Standerd**

1

IMPRESSIONS FROM CHINA

PHOTOGRAPHS BY JAMES WHITLOW DELANO

2

3

peripheral vision

---

1 CREATIVE FIRM: **Mediascope Publicitas (I) Pvt Ltd - Mumbai, India** CREATIVE TEAM: **James Whitlow Delano - Photography; Peter Morgan - Editor & COO, Content; Jit Ray - Art Director** CLIENT: **The Oberoi magazine Winter 2007-2008 2** CREATIVE FIRM: **Jeff Harris Photography - New York, NY** CREATIVE TEAM: **Jeff Harris Photography** CLIENT: **Spread Magazine 3** CREATIVE FIRM: **The Standerd - Orlando, FL** CREATIVE TEAM: **James Krawczyk - Editor/Art Direction; Joey Meddock, Josh Letchworth - Editor/Senior Photographers** CLIENT: **The Standerd**

1

PORTFOLIO   PORTFOLIO

58

2

3

1 CREATIVE FIRM: **Mediascope Publicitas (I) Pvt Ltd - Mumbai, India** CREATIVE TEAM: **Monica Denevan - Photography; Lakshmi Narayan - Art Director; Peter Morgan - Editor** CLIENT: **The Oberoi magazine Winter 2007-2008 2** CREATIVE FIRM: **Massimo Gammacurta Photographer - South Orange, NJ** CREATIVE TEAM: **Massimo Gammacurta - Photographer+Concept; Kali Abdullah - Styling; Andi Kuonath - Retouching** CLIENT: **Style Montecarlo Magazine** URL: **www.gammacurta.com 3** CREATIVE FIRM: **Jeff Harris Photography - New York, NY** CREATIVE TEAM: **Jeff Harris Photography** CLIENT: **Slam Magazine**

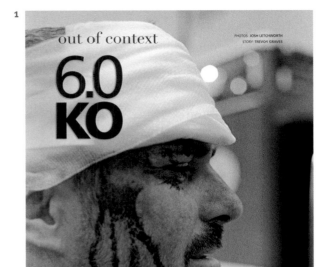

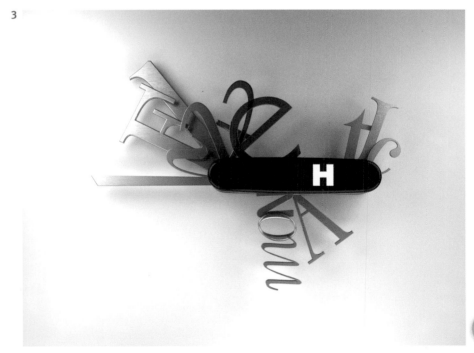

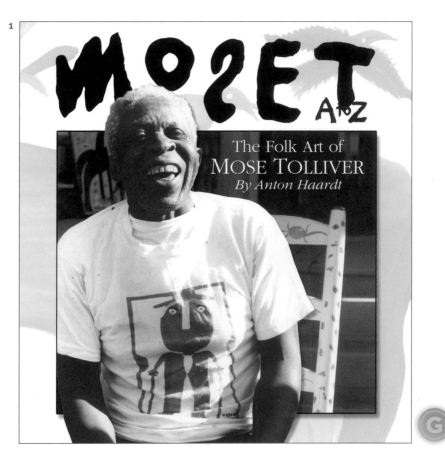

1 CREATIVE FIRM: **Saturno Press - Montgomery, AL** CREATIVE TEAM: **Anton Haardt - Author; Saturno Press - Publisher** CLIENT: **Anton Haardt** **2** CREATIVE FIRM: **Emphasis Media Limited - North Point, Hong Kong** CREATIVE TEAM: **Percy Chung - Associate Creative Director; Teresita Khaw - Art Director; Davis Kwok - Senior Designer; Eva Chan - Photo Editor** CLIENT: **SilkAir**

NEW MEDIA &
WEB DESIGN

CREATIVITY 38 ANNUAL AWARDS

For the Love of Food - Seduction Meals

CREATIVE FIRM: **Tara del Mar Productions Inc. - New York, NY**

CREATIVE TEAM: **Terry Dagrosa - Founder/Publisher; Brad Carter, Brian Hayes - Designers**

CLIENT: **Seduction Meals**

"If music be the food of love," wrote Shakespeare, "play on, play on!" A modern-day Bill may find inspiration with Seduction Meals, a Web site "about food and romance and the excitement and passion behind creating a special culinary rendezvous for two," says New York's Tara del Mar Productions. "It's a lifestyle brand that is inspirational, fun and accessible, with a variety of content targeting home cooks, romantics and food enthusiasts."

The site is sensuality defined, featuring exquisite photographs of food that beg to be enjoyed, slowly, in an intimate setting. But mention "food porn" and the designers might take raise an objection. "The main goal of the design was to create a look and feel that would quickly capture the essence of that experience in an elegant, modern and somewhat flirtatious manner," they say. "At the same time, we wanted the design to entice users to explore the various content of the site — all of which is part of orchestrating a special moment." Logistical tools include

a database of recipes, tips on cooking with spices, must-have books and cookbooks and a playlist of sexy, cool tunes to set the mood.

Seduction Meals may look rich, but it's not — and it's not cheap, either. The designers' biggest challenges were "working with a very limited budget, and finding a CMS solution that was scalable and easy to work with. We used a combination of Moveable Type and Typepad." Tara del Mar carefully chose the color palette to evoke certain emotions and best showcase the luscious images. "Red was used in the main header as a color suggestive of seduction and love," they report, "and we leveraged a white background in order for the [pictures] and ads to pop. The preferred photographic style is close-up imagery to show the texture, color and composition of the food so you really got a sense of the meal you might want to cook."

1

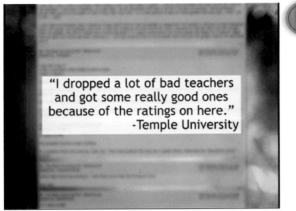

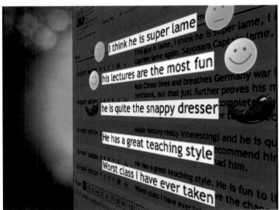

RECENT POSTS:

"NOT A HAPPY LEARNING EXPERIENCE"

RATE MY PROFESSORS

RATE MY PROFESSORS

PROFESSOR HAINES

WILLIAM PATERSON UNIVERSITY

Rate this professor

2

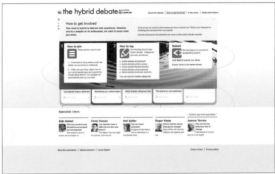

1 CREATIVE FIRM: MTV Networks - New York, NY CREATIVE TEAM: Stephen Friedman - General Manager; Ross Martin - Head of Programming; Eric Conte - Executive Producer; Brian DeCubellis - Supervising Producer; Sophia Cranshaw - Vice-President, Director, On-Air Promotions; Peter Nilsson - VP Technology & Ops; Paul DeGeorges - Online Producer CLIENT: mtvU 2 CREATIVE FIRM: Lateral - London, England CREATIVE TEAM: Owen Priestly - Head of Design; Simon Crabtree - Creative Director CLIENT: Lexus URL: ads.lateral.net

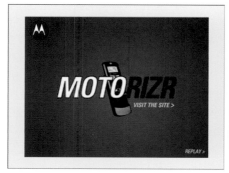

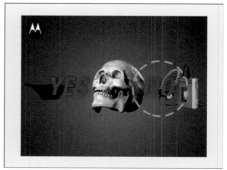

PLATINUM P

CREATIVE FIRM: **Draftfcb - New York, NY**

CREATIVE TEAM: **David Bryant - Executive Creative Director; Luke Bailey - Group Creative Director; Jason Koxvold, Nick Goodey - Associate Creative Directors; Bruce Doscher - Senior Art Director; Tina Whelski - Copywriter**

CLIENT: **Motorola**

Motorola "Hipster Tips"

Draftfcb may be an agency with a long pedigree—in previous incarnations, it was Foote, Cone & Belding and Draft— but that doesn't mean it's stuck in the past. For Motorola, it produced a Web show called "The Burg," parodying the hipsters of Williamsburg, Brooklyn. "We developed a unique set of ads to run during nine episodes," they explain. Draftcfb created the recurring theme of "Hipster Tips" as a wink to viewers, testing how hip they *really* are. Rather than traditionally interrupting content, the ad runs in a ticker crawl at the bottom of the screen asking a true or false question related to a moment in the script. "The answers?" Draftcfb asks. "Sheep in trucker caps. Marching kidneys. All brought to you by MOTORIZR—very hip."

1 CREATIVE FIRM: AKQA - London, England CREATIVE TEAM: Daniel Bonner - Co-Chief Creative Office; Duan Evans - Creative Director; Nick Bailey - Associate Creative Director; Daniel Whitehead - Designer; Emile Swain - Creative Developer CLIENT: Nike 2 CREATIVE FIRM: AKQA - London, England CREATIVE TEAM: James Capp, Colin Byrne - Creative Director; Jamen Percy - Senior Designer; Belinda Nichols - Project Manager; Tom Kordys, Dennis Ippel - Creative Developers CLIENT: Yell Group URL: www.akqa.com 3 CREATIVE FIRM: Lateral - London, England CREATIVE TEAM: Owen Priestley - Head of Design; Simon Crabtree - Creative Director; Geoff Donegan - Designer CLIENT: Which? URL: ads.lateral.net/ 4 CREATIVE FIRM: AKQA - London, England CREATIVE TEAM: Daniel Bonner - Co-Chief Creative Officer; Duan Evans - Associate Creative Director; Jamie Thompson - Designer; Rick Williams - Associate Creative Development Director; James Hay - Creative Developer CLIENT: Nike 5 CREATIVE FIRM: Unicast - New York, NY CREATIVE TEAM: Unicast CLIENT: Unicast URL: www.unicast.com

1

2

3

1 CREATIVE FIRM: AKQA - London, England CREATIVE TEAM: James Capp, Colin Byrne - Creative Directors; Shahpour Abbasvand - Art Director; Claire Langler - Project Manager; Abraham Azam - Creative Developer CLIENT: Yell Group 2 CREATIVE FIRM: Hitchcock Fleming & Associates Inc. - Akron, OH CREATIVE TEAM: Rene McCann - Sr. Art Director/Interactive; Eric Hartline - Web Developer; Amy Weegar - Account Manager; Nick Betro - Executive Creative Director; Larry Yoder - Manager/Interactive Production CLIENT: Goodyear Tire & Rubber Co. 3 CREATIVE FIRM: Hitchcock Fleming & Associates Inc. - Akron, OH CREATIVE TEAM: Rene McCann - Art Director; Nick Betro - Executive Creative Director; Cheryl Boehm - Writer; Kathy Szczesny - Web Developer; Shelly Morton - Account Manager; Larry Yoder - Manager/Interactive Production CLIENT: Goodyear Tire & Rubber Co.

banner advertising

1

2

---

1 CREATIVE FIRM: **Draftfcb - New York, NY** CREATIVE TEAM: **Christoph Becker - Chief Creative Officer; Luke Bailey - Group Creative Director; Bruce Doscher - Senior Art Director; Nick Goodey - Associate Creative Director; Sam Barr - Project Manager** CLIENT: **Citizens Crime Commission of New York City** 2 CREATIVE FIRM: **Groove11 - San Rafael, CA** CREATIVE TEAM: **Tito Chazo - Lead Designer; Joel Berghoff - Lead Programmer; Freda Byrne - Account Executive; Mike McGinty - Creative Lead** CLIENT: **Citrix** URL: **home.groove11.com**

1

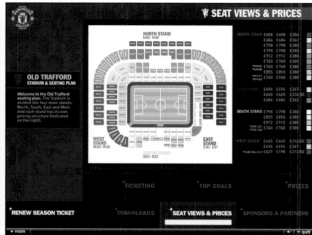

2

3

4

1 CREATIVE FIRM: **Serious - New York, NY** CREATIVE TEAM: **Vince Allen - Creative Director; Laura Smith - Art Director; Nelson Almanzar, Greg Flores - Designers; Ed Mundy - Animator; Marcus Milius - Music and Sound Design** CLIENT: **Manchester United** 2 CREATIVE FIRM: **American Specialty Health - San Diego, CA** CREATIVE TEAM: **Dawn Ta - Senior Manager; Rey Santiago - Flash Designer; Ernesto Sillas - Associate Flash Designer; Donny Carpio - Senior Flash Designer** CLIENT: **members** 3 CREATIVE FIRM: **Serious - New York, NY** CREATIVE TEAM: **Vince Allen - Creative Director; Laura Smith - Art Director; Bryan Green - Illustrator; Ed Mundy - Animator; Marcus Milius - Music and Sound; Byron Karlevics - Video Editor** CLIENT: **DKNY** 4 CREATIVE FIRM: **Kutoka Interactive - Montreal, QC, Canada** CREATIVE TEAM: **Kutoka Interactive** CLIENT: **Kutoka Interactive**

1

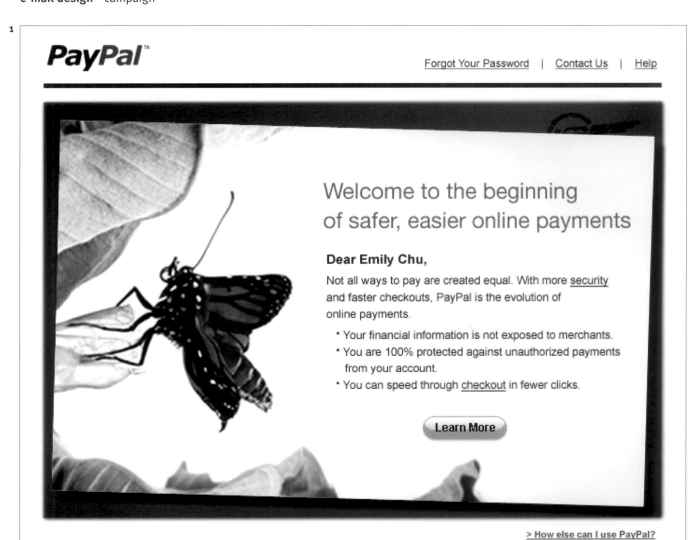

PayPal™

<u>Forgot Your Password</u> | <u>Contact Us</u> | <u>Help</u>

Welcome to the beginning of safer, easier online payments

Dear Emily Chu,

Not all ways to pay are created equal. With more <u>security</u> and faster checkouts, PayPal is the evolution of online payments.

* Your financial information is not exposed to merchants.
* You are 100% protected against unauthorized payments from your account.
* You can speed through <u>checkout</u> in fewer clicks.

Learn More

> How else can I use PayPal?

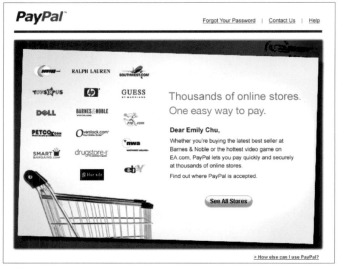

PayPal™

<u>Forgot Your Password</u> | <u>Contact Us</u> | <u>Help</u>

Thousands of online stores. One easy way to pay.

Dear Emily Chu,

Whether you're buying the latest best seller at Barnes & Noble or the hottest video game on EA.com, PayPal lets you pay quickly and securely at thousands of online stores.

Find out where PayPal is accepted.

See All Stores

> How else can I use PayPal?

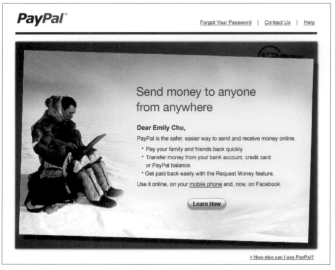

PayPal™

<u>Forgot Your Password</u> | <u>Contact Us</u> | <u>Help</u>

Send money to anyone from anywhere

Dear Emily Chu,

PayPal is the safer, easier way to send and receive money online.

* Pay your family and friends back quickly.
* Transfer money from your bank account, credit card or PayPal balance.
* Get paid back easily with the Request Money feature.

Use it online, on your <u>mobile phone</u> and, now, on Facebook.

Learn How

> How else can I use PayPal?

G

1 CREATIVE FIRM: **Red Bricks Media - San Francisco, CA** CREATIVE TEAM: **Theresa Lee - Creative Director; BorFang Su - Designer; Peter Vaughan - Copywriter; Ben Kou - Account Manager** CLIENT: **PayPal**

310

Keeping the world's largest running club up to speed

CREATIVE FIRM: **AKQA - London, England**

CREATIVE TEAM: **Daniel Bonner - Co-Chief Creative Officer; Nick Bailey - Associate Creative Director; Paul Anglin - Copywriter; Ignacio Gonzalez - Designer**

CLIENT: **Nike**

A lone runner doesn't have to be lonely—which is the overall theme of Nike+, an online community for novice and experienced running enthusiasts. London agency AKQA developed the Web site at Nikeplus. com and its attendant newsletter to provide "a window into their world... A way of showing each member the breadth and depth of their running community and providing quick links into it," the firm says.

"Runners are always looking for tips to help improve their performance," AKQA says, "so the newsletter uses editorial, promotional and product content to link to sections on Nikeplus.com, giving first-time runners and seasoned veterans practical tips and deepening their engagement with the Nike+ community." In addition to this support, Nike+ gives runners fresh from a run instant performance feedback on their time, distance, pace and calories burned.

Nike+, billed as "the world's largest running club," allows members to swap performance tips in the forums, run against one another in challenges and train in virtual teams. "Through the Nike+ newsletter, we help motivate runners to stay on track, introduce them to new Nike+ features and the latest content, show members how to make the most of the service and update them on the latest Nike events," AKQA reports. And, while runners may have time to themselves to think while out on the track or trail, they may not always have a lot of leisure to browse the site. "Our audience is information-hungry but time-poor," the agency says, "so we developed the newsletter to be clean and easy to scan."

A straightforward navigational tab at the top of the newsletter gives readers easy access to all main areas of Nikeplus.com; its look and feel make the newsletter a seamless extension of that world. "The clear, simple magazine format starts with one recognizable lead story, followed by a number of easily digestible content modules," AKQA explains, adding that the ease of use and targeted content is also a runaway success in results: "The Nike+ newsletter leads the field, with above industry average open rates of up to thirty-five percent and click-through rates as high as fifteen percent."

1

3

4

1 CREATIVE FIRM: **SKAGGS Design - New York, NY** CREATIVE TEAM: **Bradley Skaggs, Jonina Skaggs - Creative Directors; Samantha Edwards - Senior Designer; Elspeth Maxwell, Joseph Guzman - Designers** CLIENT: **SKAGGS Design** URL: **www.skaggsdesign.com** 2 CREATIVE FIRM: **Tara del Mar Productions Inc. - New York, NY** CREATIVE TEAM: **Terry Dagrosa - Founder/Publisher** CLIENT: **Seduction Meals** 3 CREATIVE FIRM: **Dustin W Design - Los Angeles, CA** CREATIVE TEAM: **Dustin Woehrmann - Creative Director, Designer; Leslie Pollock - Editor, Copywriter** CLIENT: **Dustin W Design** 4 CREATIVE FIRM: **Merestone - Scottsdale, AZ** CREATIVE TEAM: **Camille Hill - President; Ian Jones - Animator/Graphic Artist; David DeRosier - Director of Creative Services** CLIENT: **Merestone**

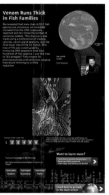

PLATINUM P

DNA Discovery Center Kiosk

CREATIVE FIRM: 15 letters inc. - Chicago, IL

CREATIVE TEAM: 15 letters inc.

CLIENT: the Field Museum

URL: www.15letters.com

In May of 2008, Chicago's Field Museum of Natural History opened a new permanent exhibit designed to put DNA—DNA research, at least—into visitors' hands. Local creative agency 15 letters brought the idea to life by creating a touch-screen kiosk programmed with ever-changing content—a dynamic interactive exhibit that museum employees could continually update as the museum's scientists and researchers advance their work on DNA research.

"We developed a robust environment that allows employees to log in remotely to a content management system as either an editor or publisher to add, remove or edit the content for the kiosk," 15 letters says. "Ensuring that this system was intuitive and flexible enough to allow the kiosk to be successfully updated and managed into the future was the biggest hurdle we overcame in the development process."

On the front end—which is obviously the most visible—15 letters designed an interface for visitors of all ages to explore a wide range of research projects in several interesting, near-tangible ways. "They can choose to touch and spin a large 3D globe covered with research site locations or rotate through iconic images of organisms, and then select featured projects from a status menu on the main page of the kiosk," the agency explains. Once visitors choose a project, they can learn more by drilling down to reveal a synopsis, a headshot and brief bio of the scientist and the project's site on a digital globe—but that's only the surface: "Each project page also features a large media gallery to spotlight relevant images, videos and audio clips from the field, plus an interactive quiz and the ability to link to another related project," 15 letters says. "It conveys the breadth of active DNA research projects taking place around the globe by the museum's many scientists and researchers today and for years to come."

1

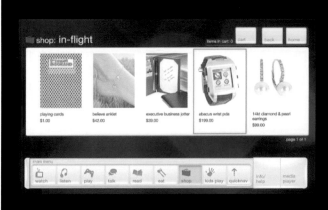

1 CREATIVE FIRM: Wunderman, Irvine - Irvine, CA CREATIVE TEAM: Anthony DiBiase - Executive Creative Director; Susie Lim - Creative Director; Candy Ho - Associate Creative Director; Angela Tu - Senior Art Director; Brian Song - Multimedia Designer; Vincent Hudson - Information Architect; Ben Peters - Copywriter CLIENT: Virgin America

PLATINUM ℗

Slip

CREATIVE FIRM: **AKQA** - London, England

CREATIVE TEAM: **James Hilton** - Co-Chief Creative Officer; **Kevin Russell** - Associate Creative Director; **Barney Howells** - Director, Partizan Films; **Miles Wilkes** - Producer; **Golden Square Post Production** - Post Production; **Adelphoi** - Music Production

CLIENT: **Xbox**

A daring acrobat runs up walls and somersaults over reflecting pools. He performs hair-raising stunts on the streets of London while passersby go about their business, oblivious to his peril—and to his confidence. AKQA created this short film to coincide with the launch of three new Japanese games for the Xbox 360: Project Sylpheed, Vampire Rain and Tenchu Z. The agency used the theme, "Master Your Environment," as the linchpin and launching pad to depict the young man's actions "beyond the bounds of the traditionally possible, and [the video] highlights what you can achieve when you break free of mental and physical obstacles and truly master your environment."

Filmed with four HD cameras and capturing 1,000 frames per second, AKQA says that the "Slip" clip is "the first time that cameras have been attached to a freerunner in motion, giving a real sense of being at one with the film's protagonist, Chase Armitage." The agency then seeded the film through the Xbox community and

popular video Web sites such as YouTube as key campaign drivers in generating buzz around the new games. "The success of these games can be attributed to the power of 'Slip' and the overwhelming impact of the 'Master Your Environment' campaign," AKQA says.

creativity 38 annual awards

1

YOUR MEAT ISN'T GOING
TO GRILL ITSELF

2

For when it's over

1 CREATIVE FIRM: **Y&R Advertising, Irvine - Irvine, CA** CREATIVE TEAM: **Anthony DiBiase - Executive Creative Director; Miles Turpin - Creative Director; Jeff Heath - Associate Creative Director, Copywriter; Brian Morgan - ACD, Art Director; Christopher Coleman - Executive Producer; David Jellison - Director** CLIENT: **BBQ Galore** 2 CREATIVE FIRM: **Zero Gravity Design Group - Smithtown, NY** CREATIVE TEAM: **Jennifer Mariotti, Chuck Killorin - Partners** CLIENT: **myDivorceCertificate.com**

1

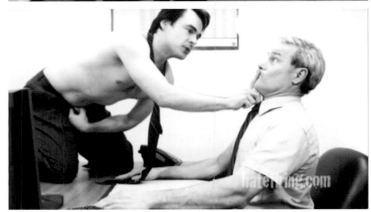

2

1 CREATIVE FIRM: **Supercool Creative + SpotZero - Los Angeles, CA** CREATIVE TEAM: **David Murdico - Creative Director/Director/Writer; Vince Murdico - Producer; Timothy Brennen - Writer** CLIENT: **Hatefiring.com** 2 CREATIVE FIRM: **Choice Hotels International- Cambria Suites - Silver Spring, MD** CREATIVE TEAM: **Cathy Poinsett - Senior Director, Brand Management; Amanda Morgan - Director, Brand Management; Kourtnie Perry - Project Manager, Brand Management** CLIENT: **Cambria Suites**

1

Rap isn't just a boy's
game anymore.

2

1 CREATIVE FIRM: **MTV Networks - New York, NY** CREATIVE TEAM: **Nigel Cox-Hagan - Creative Director: EVP Creative & Marketing, VH1; Wendy Weatherford-Marks - VP Consumer Marketing, VH1; Tony Maxwell - VP On-Air Promos; Wendell Wooten - VP Creative Production, VH1; Sean Salo - Senior Director Consumer Marketing; Jessica Rademaker - Manager Consumer Marketing; Doreen Rokhsar - Coordinator Consumer Marketing; BAM (Bradley and Montgomery) - Agency; Melissa Bolton-Klinger - Director Multi-Platform Promotion** CLIENT: **VH1** 2 CREATIVE FIRM: **MTV Networks - New York, NY** CREATIVE TEAM: **Nigel Cox-Hagan - Creative Director: EVP Creative & Marketing, VH1; Amanda Havey, Jimmy Fingers - Art Directors; Wendell Wooten - VP Creative Production, VH1; Julie Ruiz - Designer; Dan Tucker - Writer; Gary Encarnacion, Jon Wallach - Producers; Jonathan Cooper - Animator; Orba Squara - Audio/Composer** CLIENT: **VH1**

1

2

1 CREATIVE FIRM: **AKQA - London, England** CREATIVE TEAM: **James Hilton - Co-Chief Creative Officer; Colin Byrne - Creative Director; Emily Bull - Head of Production; Rowena Minhas - Account Director** CLIENT: **Unilever** 2 CREATIVE FIRM: **Fitting Group - Pittsburgh, PA** CREATIVE TEAM: **Travis Norris - Creative Director; Andrew Ellis - Designer** CLIENT: **Fitting Group** URL: fittingroup.com

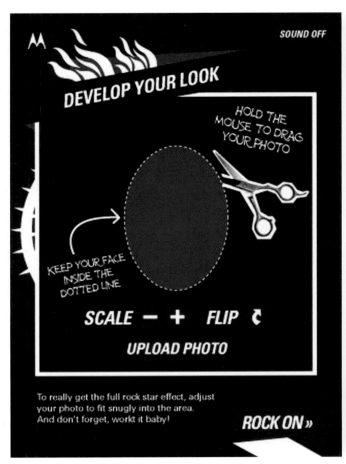

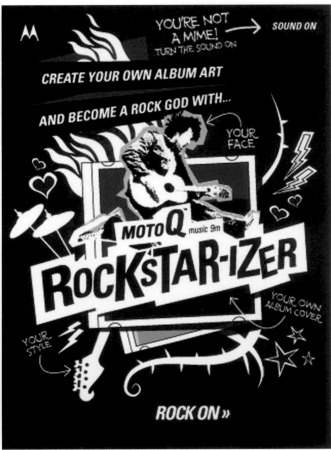

PLATINUM P

CREATIVE FIRM: **Draftfcb - New York, NY**

CREATIVE TEAM: **Christoph Becker - Chief Creative Officer; David Bryant - Executive Creative Director; Luke Bailey - Group Creative Director; Dexter Cruz - Associate Creative Director; Bruce Doscher, Mira Alibek - Senior Art Directors**

CLIENT: **Motorola**

Motorola "Rockstar-izer"

As any Facebook user knows, there seems to be an infinite number of applications to try and groups to join, so any developer wanting a following has to make his or her one especially memorable. For Motorola, the mission—creating a "sponsored group" to recruit young professionals to join their MOTO-sponsored group—fell to New York's Draftfcb to execute.

The agency took a basic idea and turned it up to eleven. "To unleash those young professionals' inner rock stars, we developed the Rockstar-izer, a digital campaign that allows users to create and distribute their own album art." To assist users in experiencing the MOTO Q "smartphone" differentiators, including its vast array of music capabilities, the Rockstar-izer lets would-be Facebook rock gods and armchair Guitar Heroes warm up for the big time. "[They can] upload their photos, customize their album covers and send their new art to friends, post it to their Facebook profiles or create desktop wallpaper," Draftfcb says.

1

WHO IS BIANCA?

"Never judge a book by its cover." That's the best way to describe Bianca Turner.

At The House of Champagne couture fashion company, Bianca is the cool-headed, competent right-hand to temperamental head designer Franc.

Bianca grew up watching her mother, Coco, create high style on a low budget in her tiny neighborhood boutique. Playing 'dress up' was all fun and games, but it was here she learned how to succeed in the fashion business.

Mom's world of beauty and glamour was Bianca's refuge when she missed her father, James. He spent most of her childhood overseas dedicated to a demanding and clandestine job for the US Government. Brief times with Daddy meant more fun and games. Little did she know that he, too, was teaching her the tools of his secretive trade.

Now Bianca will need every skill she's ever learned to unravel the mystery that has suddenly become her life. And a little help from her friends.

THIS WEEKS EPISODE
THE SELL OUT

Just when she thinks the story is over, Bianca's life takes a twist that no one saw coming. The person she thought had her back has plotted against her the whole time. Will karma kick in just in time to put her back on top? She'll need your help to set her world right side up.

PLAY NOW ▶

2

3

4

1 CREATIVE FIRM: Burrell - Chicago, IL CREATIVE TEAM: Munier Sharrieff - Creative Director; Mike Willis - Art Director; Debbie Amsden - Producer; Lewis Williams - Chief Creative Officer CLIENT: Toyota
2 CREATIVE FIRM: GA Creative, Inc. - Bellevue, WA CREATIVE TEAM: Wally Lloyd - Principal; Jeff Welsh - Creative Director; Rebecca Laughlin - Account Manager, Writer; Jeremy Parton - Designer; Mosaic Company - Producer CLIENT: Microsoft URL: design.gacreative.com 3 CREATIVE FIRM: Clear Channel Creative Services Group - Atlanta, GA CREATIVE TEAM: Liz Smith - Creative Director; Terry Yormark, Geoff Kirsch - Copywriters; Mike O'Connor - Copywriter & Producer; Rich Moyer, Richard Florence - Art Design & Animation CLIENT: Lauren Diamonds Ltd. Jewelers 4 CREATIVE FIRM: MTV Networks - New York, NY CREATIVE TEAM: Stephen Friedman - General Manager; Ross Martin - Head of Programming; Eric Conte - Executive Producer; Noopur Agarwal - Manager Public Affairs, mtvU Marketing; Claudia Bojorquez - Coordinator Pro Social, mtvU Marketing; Sophia Cranshaw - Vice-President, Director, On-Air Promotions; Peter Nilsson - VP Technology & Ops; Chris McCarthy - VP mtvU Marketing and Strategic Development CLIENT: mtvU

1 CREATIVE FIRM: **SightWorks, Inc. - Portland, OR** CREATIVE TEAM: **Eric Dayton - Creative Director** CLIENT: **Hungry Man Entertainment** 2 CREATIVE FIRM: **Arkadium - New York, NY** CREATIVE TEAM: **Jeremy Mayes - Director of Game Production** CLIENT: **National Geographic Channel** 3 CREATIVE FIRM: **Very Memorable Design - New York, NY** CREATIVE TEAM: **Gwenevere Singley - Illustration, Character Animation & Game Design; Michael Pinto - Creative Director; Roger Widicus - Producer** CLIENT: **PBS Kids & Scholastic Media** 4 CREATIVE FIRM: **15 letters inc. - Chicago, IL** CREATIVE TEAM: **15 letters inc.** CLIENT: **Orbitz Worldwide** URL: www.15letters.com 5 CREATIVE FIRM: **Animax Entertainment - Van Nuys, CA** CREATIVE TEAM: **David Wilson - Producer; Alex Gonzalez - Graphic Designer; Craig Pierson - Programmer; Paul Manchester - Art Director** CLIENT: **Ad Council** 6 CREATIVE FIRM: **MTV Networks - New York, NY** CREATIVE TEAM: **Seth Madej - Senior Producer/Writer, The N Digital; Eric Leuschner - Producer, Smashing Ideas; Chad Otis - Creative Director/Designer, Smashing Ideas; Craig Downey - Designer, Smashing Ideas; Scott Porterfield - Animator, Smashing Ideas; Rob Chapple - QA Coordinator, Smashing Ideas** CLIENT: **The-N.com** 7 CREATIVE FIRM: **Big Spaceship - Brooklyn, NY** CREATIVE TEAM: **Big Spaceship - Crew; Cramer-Krasselt/Chicago** CLIENT: **A&E**

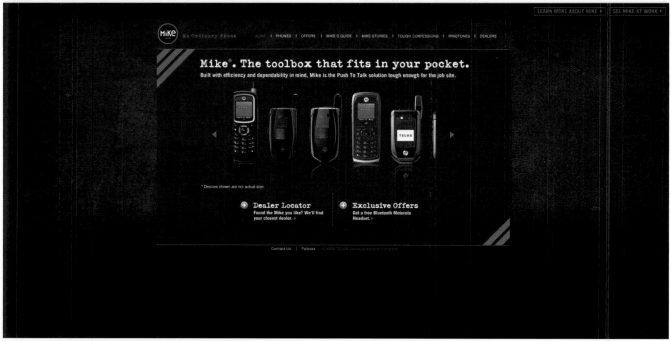

PLATINUM Ⓟ

CREATIVE FIRM: **Tribal DDB - Vancouver, BC, Canada**

CREATIVE TEAM: **Cosmo Campbell - Creative Director; Kelly Hale - Art Director; Tony Nichols - Writer; Jonathan Coe - Programmer; Ryan McCormick - Producer; Marty Yaskowich - Account Director**

CLIENT: **Telus Business Solutions**

Are you man enough for MiKE?

Are you man enough to own a Mike phone? Vancouver's Tribal DDB Canada was charged to revitalize TELUS' existing Mike brand—while at the same time dispelling rumors of its demise. Says Tribal: "We needed to dial up the Mike brand personality even further. The customers are... tough guys who can spot B.S. from a mile away. We needed to be authentic and speak to a truth they could relate to."

To cut through the aforementioned B.S., Tribal set out to differentiate this particular line from the rest of the pack. The push-to-talk handsets "require a different brand identity in order to really connect with the blue- and gray-collar workers that the handsets are intended for," the agency says. "The Mike brand speaks with a tough-guy attitude... Its rugged, stand-up-to-anything handsets and super-productive push-to-talk technology [are] its main benefits."

Tribal developed NoOrdinaryPhone.com like an online magazine Web site, "similar to *Maxim* or *FHM*—something that our target audience would be familiar with." After visitors answered a suitably "manly" question (about tools, poker, cars, etc.), they would gain admission to the site. "Depending on their answer, they were directed to a 'fake' site and given the chance to try again—or, if they got the answer right, into the Mike site." Once inside, visitors could explore an illustrated "Mike's Guide" showing the reader how Mike would handle tough situations—along with "tough" ringtones (chainsaw, anyone?) and other goodies designed to appeal to the Steve McQueen in all of us—and, of course, take a look at the handset lineup and promotional offers.

"These 'guy's guys' understand and respect what it means to earn your way in life," Tribal says. "We wanted these guys to feel that a Mike handset was desirable enough that you should have to work a little to earn it."

1

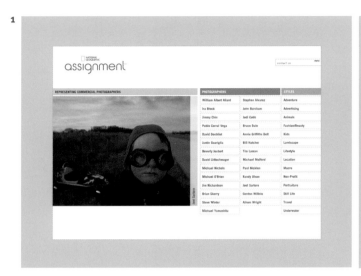

2

3

1 CREATIVE FIRM: **Lost Luggage/Brand Envy - Seattle, WA** CREATIVE TEAM: **Nadine Stellavato - Designer; Laurie Becharas - Production** CLIENT: **National Geographic Assignment 2** CREATIVE FIRM: **brandUNITY Inc - Rollingbay, WA** CREATIVE TEAM: **Ann J Warman - Creative Director; Harumi Nishiyama - Designer; atelier-r-hata - Photographer** CLIENT: **Lost Arts LLC 3** CREATIVE FIRM: **Davis Design Partners - Holland, OH** CREATIVE TEAM: **Matt Davis, Karen Davis - Designers; Patrick Poer - Senior Developer; Nick Wilcox - Developer** CLIENT: **Associated General Contractors of California**

1

2

3

4

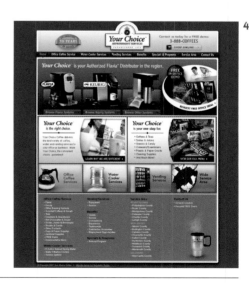

creativity 38 annual awards

---

1 CREATIVE FIRM: **Fitting Group - Pittsburgh, PA** CREATIVE TEAM: **Travis Norris - Creative Director; Jeff Fitting - Technical Projects Director; Tim Emanuel - Programmer** CLIENT: **Rolf Glass** 2 CREATIVE FIRM: **Bayshore Solutions - Tampa, FL** CREATIVE TEAM: **Bayshore Solutions** CLIENT: **Kforce Professional Staffing** 3 CREATIVE FIRM: **Singularity Design - Philadelphia, PA** CREATIVE TEAM: **Jeff Greenhouse - President; Owen Linton - Sr. Designer** CLIENT: **Service By Air** 4 CREATIVE FIRM: **Singularity Design - Philadelphia, PA** CREATIVE TEAM: **Jeff Greenhouse - President; Owen Linton - Sr. Designer** CLIENT: **Your Choice Coffee**

1

2

3

4

1 CREATIVE FIRM: **Wirestone San Diego Office - San Diego, CA** CREATIVE TEAM: **Molly O'Shea - Creative Services Manager; Lee Scott - Designer; Alex Oyler - Video Design & Execution; Jason Haberman - Lead Programmer; Joel Clausen - Lead Flash Developer** CLIENT: **Limelight Networks** 2 CREATIVE FIRM: **Q - Wiesbaden, Germany** CREATIVE TEAM: **Marcel Kummerer, Thilo von Debschitz** CLIENT: **Passione Bici** 3 CREATIVE FIRM: **Silver Communications Inc - New York, NY** CREATIVE TEAM: **Christina Weissman - Creative Director; Nelia Vishnevsky - Senior Designer; Gregg Sibert - President** CLIENT: **Clearbrook Financial** 4 CREATIVE FIRM: **Boston Interactive - Boston, MA** CREATIVE TEAM: **Boston Interactive** CLIENT: **ConforMIS**

1

2

3

1 CREATIVE FIRM: **The UXB - Beverly Hills, CA** CREATIVE TEAM: **NJ Goldston - CEO and Founder** CLIENT: **Lumeta** 2 CREATIVE FIRM: **GEM Group - New York, NY** CREATIVE TEAM: **George Bradshaw - VP, Creative Director; Steve Garvey - Creative Director** CLIENT: **NBC Universal** 3 CREATIVE FIRM: **Cahan & Associates - San Francisco, CA** CREATIVE TEAM: **Bill Cahan - Creative Director, Art Director; Erik Adams, Sean McGuire - Designers; Christopher Wahl - Photographer; Paul Jaffe - Illustrator; Liisa Turan - Production Artist** CLIENT: **Gibson Dunn & Crutcher LLP**

1

2

S

S

S

3
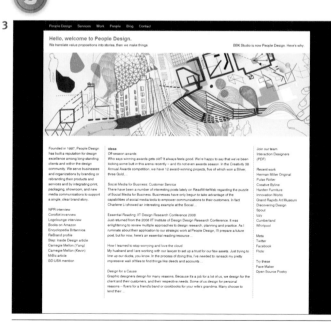

1 CREATIVE FIRM: **Zero Gravity Design Group - Smithtown, NY** CREATIVE TEAM: **Chuck Killorin, Jennifer Mariotti - Partners** CLIENT: **TechValidate** 2 CREATIVE FIRM: **Greenfield/Belser Ltd. - Washington, D.C.** CREATIVE TEAM: **Burkey Belser - Creative Director; Erika Ritzer - Account Manager; Aaron Thornburgh - Designer; Steve Gallagher - Web Manager; Paul Chang - Web/Interactive Project Manager** CLIENT: **Choate Hall & Stewart** 3 CREATIVE FIRM: **People Design Inc - Grand Rapids, MI** CREATIVE TEAM: **Kevin Budelmann, Yang Kim - Creative Directors; Victor Sirotek, Maire-Claire Camp - Interaction Designers; Scott Krieger - Lead Developer; Andy Weber - Developer** CLIENT: **People Design Inc**

1

2

3

1 CREATIVE FIRM: **People Design Inc - Grand Rapids, MI** CREATIVE TEAM: **Brian Hauch - Senior Designer; Ryan Lee - Interaction Designer/Flash Developer; Victor Sirotek - Interaction Designer; John Winkelman - Senior Developer; Kevin Budelman - Design Director** CLIENT: **Whirlpool** URL: **www.peopledesign.com** 2 CREATIVE FIRM: **Singularity Design - Philadelphia, PA** CREATIVE TEAM: **Jeff Greenhouse - President; Owen Linton - Sr. Designer** CLIENT: **Turnasure** 3 CREATIVE FIRM: **The UXB - Beverly Hills, CA** CREATIVE TEAM: **NJ Goldston - CEO and Founder** CLIENT: **Website**

Patio Gallery Website

CREATIVE FIRM: **Develisys - Hummelstown, PA**
CREATIVE TEAM: **Ian Schaefer - Creative Director; Nathan Baker - Web Designer; Matt Wilson - Web Developer; Aaron Sherrick - President**
CLIENT: **Patio Gallery**

Patio furniture has come a long way from molded plastic chairs that crack in the cold; today, the patio furniture *lifestyle* has become an object of desire in itself. "Patio Gallery is a new retail venture from one of our existing clients, Modern Bathroom, who sought to extend their reach in the luxury furnishings market," says Develisys, a design firm located in Hummelstown, Pennsylvania. In working with the Southern California-based showroom's extension to an e-commerce store, they sought to capture a sense of laid-back West Coast luxury online. The color palette—dubbed "Desert Oasis"—suggests warmer climes, with its sandy shades and bright blues evoking a sense of breezy poolside relaxation. The palette also provides a neutral background for large, richly detailed product photos. "Creating an immersive, effortless and satisfying shopping experience demands attention to the finest, often-overlooked details, architecture designed for the products at hand and consistent execution throughout," they say.

But making the merchandise seem tactile on a Web site, even with all-new photog-raphy, became a challenge—along with the question of how to best represent such a large selection. "Our client felt strongly that their customers should be able browse products through a variety of means without being forced to follow a one-size-fits-all taxonomy," Develisys says. "Although winnowing-style navigation may have worked in this situation, budget constraints and the initially small number of items in the catalog made this impractical. Our solution emphasizes the merchandising of complete sets of patio furniture and allows a customer to browse by color, style or material. Individual product pages are designed to make it easy to locate similar sets or browse individual pieces from those sets." Develisys addressed this by creating a product page that encourages continued exploration of related items and, by removing the left-hand category navigation, freeing up considerable screen real estate "for the things that matter most in a customer's purchase decision: large product images, concise specifications and measurements and engaging product descriptions."

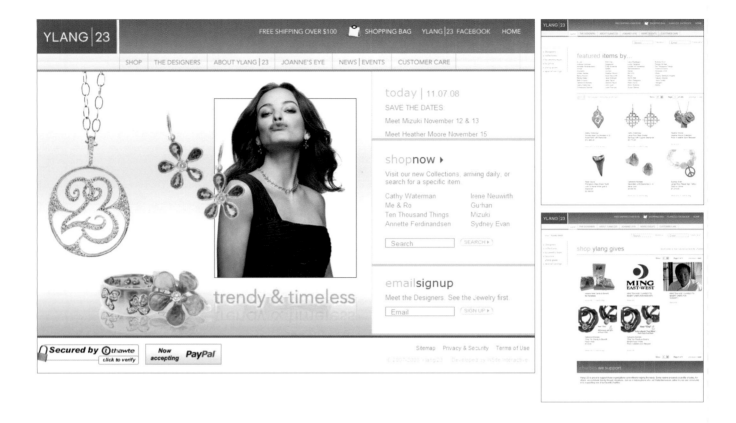

 PLATINUM P

Ylang | 23 Website re-design

CREATIVE FIRM: **InSite Interactive - Dallas, TX**
CREATIVE TEAM: **InSite Interactive**
CLIENT: **Ylang | 23**

Ylang | 23, a specialty jewelry store in Dallas' upscale Galleria Mall, attracts customers who appreciate its high-end, original designer jewelry and dedication to customer service. To sustain this gold standard of product and service, the store's owners enlisted local design firm InSite Interactive to create their e-commerce Web site. The main objectives, says InSite, were to "create a unique and high-profile online presence to compete with majors in the market, showcase the uniqueness of the designers' brands and creativity of their one-of-a-kind pieces, provide an online shopping experience that is both upscale and exciting and build management tools that allow the store's staff to add, change and remove pieces in real time."

Ylang | 23 charged InSite with creating a clean, elegant and modern site that uses both design and animation to reflect Ylang | 23's image. Beyond the cosmetic upgrades, however, InSite updated the look of the site while upgrading internal functionality—including

remote administration of a section featuring the store's jewelry designers, the addition of an administrator to a News & Events section, an improved Scene@23 section (with photos from special events, such as the store's twenty-third anniversary celebration)—and external, including an "E-mail a Friend" feature and an option for users to relate products to one another in order to create their own collections.

"One of the biggest challenges of this project was to implement feature updates and upgrades with a completely new look and feel while leaving a huge amount of the infrastructure intact, building on the old foundation," says InSite. "The site also needed to reinforce the store's dedication to high levels of customer service. Easy access to Ylang | 23's expertise and customer-centric team is the focus of the site."

creativity 38 annual awards

1

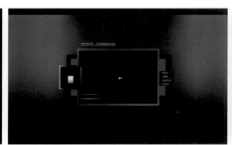

2

3

4

5

---

1 CREATIVE FIRM: **Dolce&Gabbana srl - Milan, Italy** CREATIVE TEAM: **Dennis Valle - VP of Group Digital Mktg & Comm. at Dolce&Gabbana** CLIENT: **Dolce&Gabbana srl** URL: **eng.dolcegabbana.it/2009/dolcegabbana/eng/index.html** 2 CREATIVE FIRM: **POP - Seattle, WA** CREATIVE TEAM: **POP** CLIENT: **Raleigh Bikes** 3 CREATIVE FIRM: **POP - Seattle, WA** CREATIVE TEAM: **POP** CLIENT: **Nintendo** 4 CREATIVE FIRM: **POP - Seattle, WA** CREATIVE TEAM: **POP** CLIENT: **EA** 5 CREATIVE FIRM: **POP - Seattle, WA** CREATIVE TEAM: **POP** CLIENT: **Ubisoft**

1

the film   video   images   adventure   live wild blog   experience

Inspired by a true story

Emile Hirsch
Marcia Gay Harden
William Hurt
Jena Malone
Catherine Keener
Brian Dierker
Vince Vaughn
Zach Galifianakis
Kristen Stewart
and Hal Holbrook

in theaters September 21

INTO THE WILD

screenplay and directed by Sean Penn

142

FAIRBANKS CITY TRANSIT SYSTEM

2

3

4

5

6

creativity 38 annual awards

1 CREATIVE FIRM: **Dustin W Design - Los Angeles, CA** CREATIVE TEAM: **Dustin Woehrmann - Creative Director; Leslie Pollock - Web Content Producer; Joshua Sassoon, Amanda Kaay - Flash Programmers; Brian Sugden - Design and Programming; River* - Design** CLIENT: **Paramount Vantage 2** CREATIVE FIRM: **Develisys - Hummelstown , PA** CREATIVE TEAM: **Ian Schaefer - Creative Director; Nathan Baker - Web Developer; Aaron Sherrick - President** CLIENT: **Adventure Sports in Hershey 3** CREATIVE FIRM: **B3 Interactive - Cleveland, OH** CREATIVE TEAM: **Brad Fagan - President & Creative Director; Shelley Barney - Director of Accounts & Strategy; Nicholas Latkovic - Interactive Designer; Lisa Ambrose - Account Coordinator; Joel Burke, Amar Vankireddy - Developers** CLIENT: **Stouffer's 4** CREATIVE FIRM: **1919 Creative Studio - New York, NY** CREATIVE TEAM: **Peter Klueger - Creative Direction, Graphic Designer,Photographer; Nick Wollner - Copywriter; Alex Motzenbacher - Flash Design** CLIENT: **Ritz- Carlton 5** CREATIVE FIRM: **CDKWeb, Inc. - St. Charles, MO** CREATIVE TEAM: **Nicholas Sneed - Senior Web Designer** CLIENT: **Roemer Originals 6** CREATIVE FIRM: **CDKWeb, Inc. - St. Charles, MO** CREATIVE TEAM: **Nicholas Sneed - Senior Web Designer** CLIENT: **Beans for Hope**

1

Click to view episode

EPISODE
06 Meet Vasava and Creative Suite 4
with "Melted Thoughts: An Allegory"

2

3

4

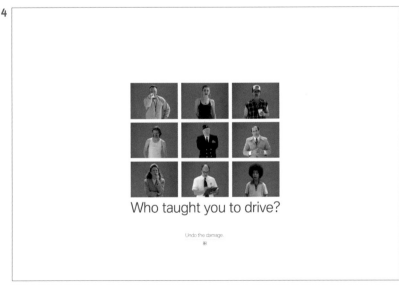

Who taught you to drive?

Undo the damage.

5

---

1 CREATIVE FIRM: Juxt Interactive - Newport Beach, CA CREATIVE TEAM: Todd Purgason - Creative Director; Alex Mustacich - Art Director; Ann-Marie Harbour - Project Manager; Gary Stasiuk - Flash Development; Karen LeFever - Executive Producer; Marcelo Baldin - Sound Designer CLIENT: Adobe URL: review.juxtinteractive.com 2 CREATIVE FIRM: 19Blossom - Singapore CREATIVE TEAM: Rina Lim - Art Director CLIENT: Sky Tower Pte Ltd 3 CREATIVE FIRM: AKQA - London, England CREATIVE TEAM: Daniel Bonner - Co-Chief Creative Officer; Andrew Tuffs - Associate Creative Director; Paul Anglin - Copywriter; James Hay - Creative Developer CLIENT: Nike 4 CREATIVE FIRM: Juxt Interactive - Newport Beach, CA CREATIVE TEAM: Mark Ray - Group Creative Director; Chad Laughlin - Art Director; Scott Staab - Interactive Art Director; Ryan Martindale - Copywriter; Lani DeGuire - Creative Project Manager; Aaron Kovan - Broadcast Producer CLIENT: BMW 5 CREATIVE FIRM: Fitting Group - Pittsburgh, PA CREATIVE TEAM: Travis Norris - Creative Director; Andrew Ellis - Designer CLIENT: Red Hot & Blue

1

G

S

2

3

S

4

S

creativity 38 annual awards

1 CREATIVE FIRM: Juxt Interactive - Newport Beach, CA CREATIVE TEAM: Emily Spangler - Account Director; Kim Phillips - Project Manager; Todd Purgason - Creative Director; Victor Allen - Flash Development; Jorge Fino - Art Direction; Edward Herda - Copywriter CLIENT: Coca-Cola URL: review.juxtinteractive.com 2 CREATIVE FIRM: ZAAZ - Seattle, WA CREATIVE TEAM: Jim Chesnutt - Account Director; Kent Pearson - Program Manager; Jud Holliday - Developer; David Buckley - Art Director; Justin Marshall - User Experience Specialist; David Koppy - Senior Web Analyst CLIENT: Helio 3 CREATIVE FIRM: ZAAZ - Seattle, WA CREATIVE TEAM: Rob Mapes - Program Manager; Karrie Gaylord - Project Manager; Ryan Turner - User Experience Architect; Graeme Asher, Roger McGary - Flash Developers; David Buckley - Art Director CLIENT: Microsoft 4 CREATIVE FIRM: Push Button Productions - Gainesville, FL CREATIVE TEAM: Push Button Productions - Creative Team; Dicks, Nanton & Glass - Strategic Partner; Next Level Media - Creator; River City Consulting - Graphic Design; Studio AKT - Logo Design CLIENT: Push Button Productions URL: www.pushbuttonproductions.com

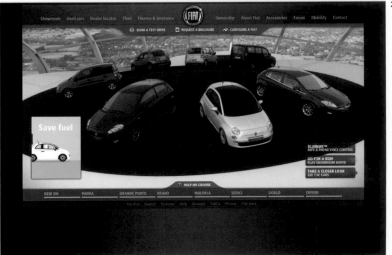

1 CREATIVE FIRM: **Y&R Advertising, Irvine - Irvine, CA** CREATIVE TEAM: **Anthony DiBiase - Executive Creative Director; Susie Lim, Craig Evans - Creative Directors; Josh Lieber - Associate Creative Director; Pieck Panikabutr - Art Director; Ryan Lindsey - Flash Designer; Ronnie Lee, Brian Marabello - Copywriters; Kristen Myers - Executive Producer; Sam Ayres - Producer; Albert Woo, Eric Lim - Developers; Aron North - Account** CLIENT: **Toshiba** URL: **www.explore.toshiba.com/fusionfinish** 2 CREATIVE FIRM: **AKQA - London, England** CREATIVE TEAM: **Nick Turner - Creative Director; Kerry Robinson - Copy Lead; William Lidstone - Group Account Director; Robert Marshall - Project Director; Greg Sharp - Technical Director; Ella Norton - Head of UE** CLIENT: **Fiat** 3 CREATIVE FIRM: **AKQA - London, England** CREATIVE TEAM: **James Hilton - Co-Chief Creative Officer; Miles Unwin - Associate Creative Director; Suzanne Mucci - Copywriter; Rodrigo Sobral - Art Director; Emily Bull - Head of Production; Abraham Azam - Creative Developer** CLIENT: **Fiat** 4 CREATIVE FIRM: **JPL Productions - Harrisburg, PA** CREATIVE TEAM: **Jessica Scarlato - Art Director; Melissa Wimbish - Designer; Mike Wilt - Project Manager** CLIENT: **The Hershey Company** 5 CREATIVE FIRM: **JPL Productions - Harrisburg, PA** CREATIVE TEAM: **Chelsie Markel - Art Director; Katy Jacobs - Lead Designer; Ryan Pudloski - Flash Developer; Jamy Kunjappu - Web Developer; Krysti Blessing, Mike Wilt - Project Managers** CLIENT: **The Hershey Company** 6 CREATIVE FIRM: **IDENTITY AFRICA Advertising Agency - Kigali, Rwanda** CREATIVE TEAM: **Marija Kovacevic - Co-Owner, Creative Director, Designer; Dan Barlow - Co-Owner, Managing Director, Photographer; Anna Behm Masozera - Copywriter; Meddy Saleh Hemed - Cinematographer** CLIENT: **SPREAD Project/USAID**

1

2

3

4

5

6

1

2

3

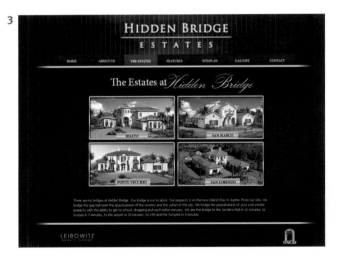

4

1 CREATIVE FIRM: **AKQA - London, England** CREATIVE TEAM: **Daniel Bonner - Co-Chief Creative Officer; Colin Byrne - Creative Director; Matt Longstaff, Per Nielsen - Copywriters; Rowena Minhas - Account Director; Joel Godfrey - Project Manager** CLIENT: **Cadbury Trebor Bassett/Trident 2** CREATIVE FIRM: **Syrup - New York, NY** CREATIVE TEAM: **Jakob Daschek - Creative Director; Robert Holzer - CEO; Kansas Waugh - Account Director; Vineet Choudhary - CTO; Amy Martino - Lead Designer; Mike Manh - Lead Mapping/Core Programmer** CLIENT: **Mammoth Toys, a Division of NSI International 3** CREATIVE FIRM: **SethJoseph & Co., LLC - West Palm Beach, FL** CREATIVE TEAM: **Seth J. Katzen - CEO - Chief Evolution Officer; Kevin Blandon - Web Designer/Developer** CLIENT: **Hidden Bridge Estates 4** CREATIVE FIRM: **MTV Networks - New York, NY** CREATIVE TEAM: **Martin Clayton - VP/GM CMT Digital; Donna Priesmeyer - Executive Producer, CMT.com; Laurens Glass - Producer, CMT.com; Marshall Woksa, Brandy Byrd - Sr. Web Designers, CMT.com; Jason Hill - Sr. Director of Product Development and Strategy** CLIENT: **CMT/CMT.com**

1

2

3

4

1 CREATIVE FIRM: **Hornall Anderson Design Works - Seattle, WA** CREATIVE TEAM: **Jamie Monberg - Creative Director; Nate Young, Joseph King - Designers; Gordon Meuller, Matt Frickelton - Programmers; Erica Goldsmith - Senior Producer** CLIENT: **Tommy Bahama** 2 CREATIVE FIRM: **Octavo Designs - Frederick, MD** CREATIVE TEAM: **Sue Hough - Art Director; Mark Burrier - Designer, HTML** CLIENT: **The Cinefamily** 3 CREATIVE FIRM: **MTV Networks - New York, NY** CREATIVE TEAM: **Robin Richardson - Sr. Producer, CMT.com; Brandy Byrd, Marshall Woksa - Sr. Web Designers, CMT.com; Tyson Tune, Ryan Kaldari, Rick Kelchner - Web Developers, CMT.com** CLIENT: **CMT/CMT.com** 4 CREATIVE FIRM: **MTV Networks - New York, NY** CREATIVE TEAM: **Robin Richardson - Sr. Producer, CMT.com; Brandy Byrd, Marshall Woksa - Sr. Web Designers, CMT.com; Ryan Kaldari, Tyson Tune, Rick Kelchner - Web Developers** CLIENT: **CMT/CMT.com**

1

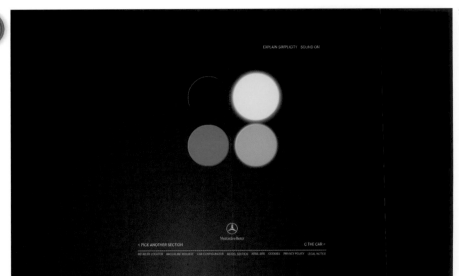

2

340

4

3

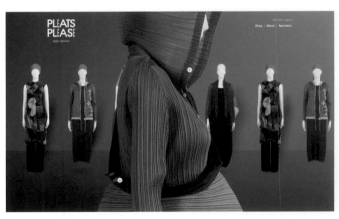

1 CREATIVE FIRM: **Agency Republic - London, England** CREATIVE TEAM: **Gavin Gordon-Rogers - Creative Director; Alistair Campbell - Copywriter; Richard Hale - Art Director; Robin Wong - Technical Developer; Jay Gelardi - Sound** CLIENT: **Mercedes Benz** URL: **agencyrepublic.net** 2 CREATIVE FIRM: **Stone Interactive Group - Ann Arbor, MI** CREATIVE TEAM: **Joel Beals - Creative Director; Jennifer Belaire - Project Manager; Jamie Larsen, Harry Pannu - Programmers** CLIENT: **Hiller's** 3 CREATIVE FIRM: **Syrup - New York, NY** CREATIVE TEAM: **Jakob Daschek - Creative Director; Robert Holzer - CEO; Elin Svegsjö - Account Manager; Clayton Crocker - Art Director; Iling Chen - Lead Developer; Oskar Tilly - Back End Developer** CLIENT: **Issey Miyake** 4 CREATIVE FIRM: **Groove11 - San Rafael, CA** CREATIVE TEAM: **Rainey Straus - Design Director; Todd Hedgpeth - Lead Designer; Mike McGinty - Creative Director; Kristin Nielsen - Producer; Sean Dunn - Account Executive** CLIENT: **Copia**

1

2

3

4

5

creativity 38 annual awards

1 CREATIVE FIRM: **Singularity Design - Philadelphia, PA** CREATIVE TEAM: **Jeff Greenhouse - President; Owen Linton - Sr. Designer** CLIENT: **Kensington** 2 CREATIVE FIRM: **FindLaw - Eagan, MN** CREATIVE TEAM: **Greg Jorgenson - Web Designer; Karl Ness - Web Developer** CLIENT: **Brian D. Primes** 3 CREATIVE FIRM: **Leibowitz Communications - New York, NY** CREATIVE TEAM: **Rick Bargmann - Creative Director/Designer; Brian Eliseo - Art Director/Web Developer** CLIENT: **The Royce Funds** 4 CREATIVE FIRM: **Zero Gravity Design Group - Smithtown, NY** CREATIVE TEAM: **Chuck Killorin, Jennifer Mariotti - Partners** CLIENT: **myPhotopipe** 5 CREATIVE FIRM: **Zero Gravity Design Group - Smithtown, NY** CREATIVE TEAM: **Jennifer Mariotti, Chuck Killorin - Partners; Matt Hogeboom - Designer** CLIENT: **myDivorceCertificate.com**

1

2

3

342

4

5

1 CREATIVE FIRM: **Singularity Design - Philadelphia, PA** CREATIVE TEAM: **Sean Trapani - Creative Director/ Art Director/Designer; Owen Linton - Sr. Designer; Jeff Mills - Interactive Developer** CLIENT: **Carlisle Wide Plank Floors** 2 CREATIVE FIRM: **Singularity Design - Philadelphia, PA** CREATIVE TEAM: **Sean Trapani - Creative Director/Art Director; Alex Hohlov - Sr. Designer; Laura Haldis - Interactive Developer** CLIENT: **Healthy Directions** 3 CREATIVE FIRM: **Code and Theory - New York, NY** CREATIVE TEAM: **Brandon Ralph - Executive Creative Director; Pablo Caro - Senior Designer; Graham Milton - Interaction Designer; Vincent Tuscano - Associate Technical Director** CLIENT: **Starwood Preferred Guest** 4 CREATIVE FIRM: **Code and Theory - New York, NY** CREATIVE TEAM: **Brandon Ralph - Executive Creative Director; Jeremy Davis - Art Director; Roberto Gonzalez-Rey - Senior Designer; Chenta Yu - Designer; Jon Harris - Engineer; Graham Milton - Interaction Designer** CLIENT: **Dr Pepper Snapple Group** 5 CREATIVE FIRM: **People Design Inc - Grand Rapids, MI** CREATIVE TEAM: **Geoffrey Mark - Design Director; Victor Sirotek - Lead Interaction Designer; Ryan Lee - Interaction Designer/Flash Developer; Andy Weber - Lead Developer; Aaron Vanderzwan - Developer; John Winkelman - Senior Developer** CLIENT: **Grand Rapids Art Museum**

1

2

3

4

1 CREATIVE FIRM: Phinney Bischoff Design House - Seattle, WA CREATIVE TEAM: Geoffrey Smith - Interactive Designer; Dean Hart - Creative Director; Ryan Scherler - Interactive Developer CLIENT: Queen Mary Tea 2 CREATIVE FIRM: People Design Inc - Grand Rapids, MI CREATIVE TEAM: Geoffrey Mark - Information Architect, Design Director; Marie-Claire Camp - Lead Interaction Designer; Ryan Lee - Interaction Designer/Flash Developer; Aaron Vanderzwan, Andy Weber - Developers; John Winkelman - Senior Developer CLIENT: Creative Byline 3 CREATIVE FIRM: Phinney Bischoff Design House - Seattle, WA CREATIVE TEAM: Cody Rasmussen - Senior Designer; Geoffrey Smith - Interactive Designer; Leslie Phinney - Creative Director; Devin Liddell - Copywriter; Ryan Scherler - Interactive Developer; Mark Burgess - Information Architecture CLIENT: Phinney Bischoff Design House 4 CREATIVE FIRM: Draftfcb - New York, NY CREATIVE TEAM: Luke Bailey - Group Creative Director; Jason Koxvold - Creative Director; Dexter Cruz - Associate Creative Director; William Tran, Billy Custer - Copywriters; Ashley Steen - Designer CLIENT: Motorola

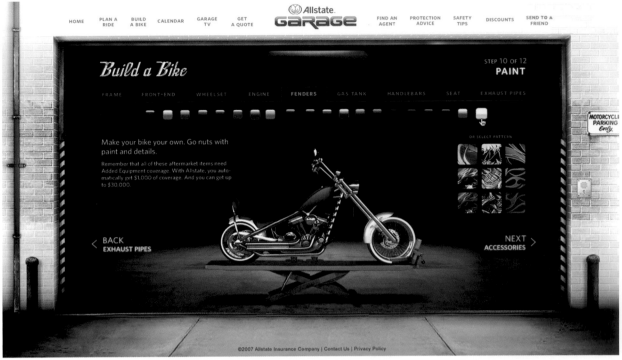

Build a Bike

STEP 10 OF 12

PAINT

FRAME · FRONT-END · WHEELSET · ENGINE · **FENDERS** · GAS TANK · HANDLEBARS · SEAT · EXHAUST PIPES

Make your bike your own. Go nuts with paint and details.

Remember that all of these aftermarket items need Added Equipment coverage. With Allstate, you automatically get $1,000 of coverage. And you can get up to $30,000.

OR SELECT PATTERN

‹ BACK
EXHAUST PIPES

NEXT ›
ACCESSORIES

©2007 Allstate Insurance Company | Contact Us | Privacy Policy

1 CREATIVE FIRM: **Domani Studios - Brooklyn, NY** CREATIVE TEAM: **Domani Studios** CLIENT: **Allstate (Agency: Leo Burnett)** 2 CREATIVE FIRM: **People Design Inc - Grand Rapids, MI** CREATIVE TEAM: **Marie-Claire Camp - Lead Interaction Designer; Ryan Lee - Interaction Designer; Victor Sirotek - Interaction Designer; Aaron Vanderzwan - Lead Developer; John Winkelman - Senior Developer; Geoffrey Mark - Design Director** CLIENT: **Harden Furniture** 3 CREATIVE FIRM: **Code and Theory - New York, NY** CREATIVE TEAM: **Brandon Ralph - Executive Creative Director; Jeremy Davis - Art Director; Vincent Tuscano - Associate Technical Director; Ed Burnett - Engineer; Chenta Yu - Designer** CLIENT: **Lenny Kravitz** 4 CREATIVE FIRM: **15 letters inc. - Chicago, IL** CREATIVE TEAM: **15 letters inc.** CLIENT: **Orbitz Worldwide**

1

CAMPAIGNS   DRINKS   ABOUT ABSOLUT   PRESS

IN AN ABSOLUT WORLD

ABSOLUT LOVES VISIONS. WE LOVE THEM SO MUCH THAT WE TURN VISIONS INTO REALITIES. CHECK OUT THE REALIZED VISIONS BELOW.
THEN SUBMIT A VISION OF YOUR OWN AND STAY TUNED FOR MORE REALIZED VISIONS. MAYBE YOURS IS NEXT?

CHOOSE VIEW:

REALIZED
VISIONS

TERMS & CONDITIONS   PRIVACY POLICY   REALIZED VISIONS   **SUBMITTED VISIONS**   SUBMIT YOUR VISION   THE BLOG   FULL SCREEN   VOLUME

2

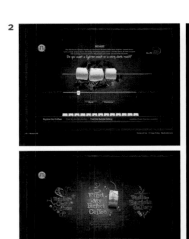

Caffè Verona®

Combine the juicy flavor of Latin
American beans with the earthy
aroma of Asia/Pacific coffee; then a
bit of Italian Roast, for added depth,
and you get the toasty sweet taste of
this popular multi-region blend.
Bellissimo.

GROWING REGION: Multi-Region Blend
KEY TERM: Complex
CLASSIFICATION: Bold
AVAILABLE IN: Ground & Decaffeinated
Ground, Whole Bean &
Decaffeinated Whole Bean

DID YOU KNOW...

Explore Our Coffees   **Find My Perfect Coffee**   Visit the Barista Gallery   Available Where You Buy Groceries

Sound Off   Terms of Use   Privacy Policy   Starbucks.com

creativity 38 annual awards

1 CREATIVE FIRM: **Great Works Stockholm - Stockholm, Sweden** CREATIVE TEAM: **Magnus Wålsten - Global Account Director; Jenna Moran - Account Director; Ted Persson - Global Creative Director; Fredrik Carlström - Creative Director; Charlotta Rydholm, Kaj Bouic - Account Managers; Eva Nilsson - Account Producer; Jacob Åström, Jakob Nielsen - Art Director/Designers; Ola Persson - 3D Design; Jocke Wissing - Technical Production Manager; Mikael Zetterberg, Saher Sidholm - Planners; Ernie Klein - Production Supervisor/Visionary; Carlos Ulloa - Papervision/Flash; Jonas Quant - Music; Deborah Moss - Copywriter; MYP - Motion; Stickybeat & AlbertKen - Miscellaneous** CLIENT: **V&S ABSOLUT SPIRITS** URL: projects.greatworks.se 2 CREATIVE FIRM: **Draftfcb - New York, NY** CREATIVE TEAM: **Christoph Becker - Chief Creative Officer; David Bryant - Executive Creative Director; Dexter Cruz, Nick Goodey - Associate Creative Directors; Luke Meseke - Senior Art Director; Tina Whelski - Copywriter** CLIENT: **Kraft Foods Inc.**

1

2
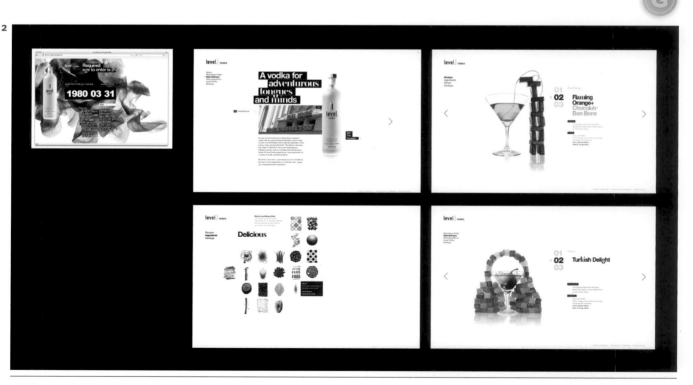

1 CREATIVE FIRM: **Barefoot - Cincinnati, OH** CREATIVE TEAM: **Steve Kissing - Creative Director, Copywriter; Jodi Greene - Creative Director; Rob Sloan - Associate Creative Director, Designer, Developer; Sarah Knott - Copywriter; Michael Krisher - Developer** CLIENT: **Miller Brewing Company** 2 CREATIVE FIRM: **Great Works - New York, NY** CREATIVE TEAM: **Fredrik Carlstrom - Concept & Creative Direction, Producer; Mathias Krigh, Brad Dixon - Art Directors; Patrik Persson, Jenna Moran - Account Directors; Ernie Klein, Lotta Linde - Account Managers; Mitchell Feinberg - Photography; Sonia dos Santos - Photo Assistant; Victoria Granof, Sara Crawford, Elizabeth Buckley, Charlotte Puckette - Food Stylists; LaRetoucherie - Retouching; Frederic Puigvert-Fabren - Director; Jill-Morgan Aubert - Editor; Natur'Dom - Music; Jens Karlsson (Your Majesty) - Creative Director; Kalle Thyselius (Your Majesty) - Flash Developer; Jessica Siegel (Your Majesty) - Producer** CLIENT: **Level Vodka**

1

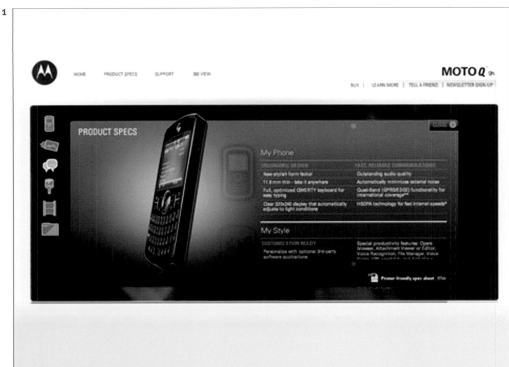

2

3

4

1 CREATIVE FIRM: Draftfcb - New York, NY CREATIVE TEAM: David Bryant - Executive Creative Director; Tim Doherty - Creative Director; Nick Goodey, Matt Zavala - Associate Creative Directors; Pitchaya Sudbanthand - Copywriter; Mira Alibek - Senior Art Director CLIENT: Motorola 2 CREATIVE FIRM: Wunderman - Team Detroit (Primary)/Oddcast (Secondary) - New York, NY CREATIVE TEAM: Stuart O'Neil - Group Creative Director (Wunderman); Sue Driscoll - Creative Director/Writer (Wunderman); Doug Kohnen (Wunderman), James Salanitri (Oddcast) - Art Directors; Tony Lamberty - Animator (Oddcast) CLIENT: Ford 3 CREATIVE FIRM: Object 9 - Baton Rouge, LA CREATIVE TEAM: Object 9 CLIENT: Fire & Flavor Grilling Company 4 CREATIVE FIRM: Think Studio - New York, NY CREATIVE TEAM: Herb Thornby - Creative Director/Designer/Programmer; John Clifford - Creative Director/Designer CLIENT: Rothschild Safaris

creativity 38 annual awards

1

2

3

5

4

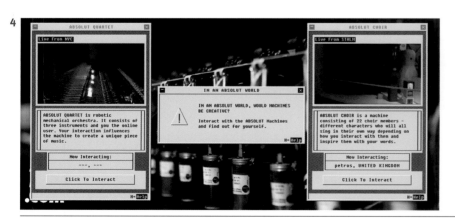

1 CREATIVE FIRM: **15 letters inc. - Chicago, IL** CREATIVE TEAM: **15 letters inc.** CLIENT: **Orbitz Worldwide** 2 CREATIVE FIRM: **Coastlines Creative Group Inc. - Vancouver, BC, Canada** CREATIVE TEAM: **Byron Dowler - Creative Director; Scott Morgan - Photographer; Graham Winterbottom - Assistant; Jeremy Thorp - Programmer; Chris Freeman - Designer; Vanessa Caruso - Talent** CLIENT: **Trafalgar Trading Co.** 3 CREATIVE FIRM: **TM&N Design and Brand Consultants Ltd. - Hong Kong** CREATIVE TEAM: **Leila Nachtigall - Managing Director/Brand Consultant; Jillian Lee - Creative Director/Brand Consultant; Samson Sung - Design Manager** CLIENT: **Mission Hills Spa** 4 CREATIVE FIRM: **Great Works Stockholm - Stockholm, Sweden** CREATIVE TEAM: **Magnus Wålsten - Global Account Director; Charlotta Rydholm, Kaj Bouic, Christelle Delarue (TBWA Paris), Cilla Winbladh (Frankenstein) - Project Management; Saher Sidholm, Mikael Zetterberg, Joe Konietzko (TBWA New York) - Planners; Linn Tornérhielm, Jocke Wissing - Production Management; Ted Persson, Pontus Frankenstein (Frankenstein), Sebastien Vacherot (TBWA Paris) - Creative Directors; Mathias Päres - Art Director; Fredrik Karlsson - Designer; Micke Emtinger - Technical Director; Erik Hagman, Sesse Lind - Photography; Fredrik Karlsson, Ola Löfgren, David Anderson (Katamari) - Production; Dan Paluska, Jeff Liebermann (Plebian Design), Jesper Kouthoofd, David Erikkson, Björn Sjölén, Jens Rudberg (Teenage Engineering) - Machine Creation; Jung & Noise Marketing - PR; Knock - Event Team** CLIENT: **V&S ABSOLUT SPIRITS** 5 CREATIVE FIRM: **Ferroconcrete - Los Angeles, CA** CREATIVE TEAM: **Yolanda Santosa - Designer/Creative Director; Sunjoo Park, Wendy Thai - Designers; Christina Peters - Photographer; Luellen Renn - Copywriter; Ronny Widjaja - Programmer** CLIENT: **Pinkberry, Inc.**

1

2

3

4

1 CREATIVE FIRM: **Plumbline Studios, Inc - Napa, CA** CREATIVE TEAM: **Dom Moreci - Creative Director; Robert Burns - Design Director; Tim Brocato - Designer/Producer; Peter Nochisaki - Production Director; Melinda Swenson - Flash Developer; Dom Moreci - Photographer** CLIENT: **Empire Communities** 2 CREATIVE FIRM: **Plumbline Studios, Inc - Napa, CA** CREATIVE TEAM: **Dom Moreci - Creative Director; Robert Burns - Design Director; Tim Brocato - Designer/Producer; Peter Nochisaki - Production Director; Melinda Swenson - Flash Developer** CLIENT: **Empire Co./Prestige Homes** 3 CREATIVE FIRM: **Plumbline Studios, Inc - Napa, CA** CREATIVE TEAM: **Dom Moreci - Creative Director; Robert Burns - Design Director; Tim Brocato - Designer/Producer; Dom Moreci - Photographer** CLIENT: **Empire Communities** 4 CREATIVE FIRM: **Great Works Stockholm - Stockholm, Sweden** CREATIVE TEAM: **Jesper Versfeld - Art Director; Kristoffer Triumf, David Sundin - Creative; Anna Ottosson - Production Manager; Mikael Zetterberg - Planner; Björn Wissing, Erik Nygren - Designers; Sebastian Bäckström, Martin Landquist - Music; Illianced - Flash** CLIENT: **H&M** URL: **projects.greatworks.se**

PLATINUM P

CREATIVE FIRM: **Draftfcb - New York, NY**

CREATIVE TEAM: **Timothy Bruns - Executive Creative Director; Luke Bailey - Group Creative Director; Johanna Thompson-Cook - Creative Director; Bruce Doscher, Nathaniel Jones - Senior Art Directors; Jodie Leopold - Senior Copywriter**

CLIENT: **National Youth Anti-Drug Media Campaign**

NYADMC "SketchPad"

A significant number of marketing ideas start out as a doodle on a notepad, but in the case of the National Youth Anti-Drug Media Campaign, the final product looked pretty much the same as the original pen-on-paper concept. "[The late Madison Avenue legend] Mach Arom challenged us to come up with an original idea that would engage teens to prevent and reduce drug and marijuana use," says Draftfcb, the agency charged with developing the message. "Teens watch videos, play games and download everything, and the sketchpad tapped into this."

This "experiential interactive experience," as Draftfcb calls it, faced one major hurdle: teen skepticism. "The biggest hurdle we faced was getting by teenagers bullshit radar," the agency says. "Teenagers especially these days are resistant to anything that [says,] 'This is bad for you, you shouldn't do it.' It's the natural need to rebel against 'tell me what to do' advertising." The sketchpad concept, they say, puts the control in the hands of the teens themselves, al-lowing them to explore, learn and—most importantly—think for themselves.

The sketchpad is replete with hidden and double meanings that even a sober teen—the intended audience, indeed—can find amusing. "One of my favorites is the Singing Blobs," Draftfcb says of the "under the influence" musical quartet whose playlist and amorphous shape are constant reminders to teens to stand up for themselves. Says the agency: "With songs such as 'Denial,' 'My Spine' and 'Identity Crisis,' teens are able to witness the downside of falling under the influence."

The Sketchpad concept, then, isn't just a flimsy sheet with no substance. Instead, Draftfcb says, "It allows us to deliver our brand message in an 'edu-taining' way, reinforcing the brand philosophy of 'Anything that makes me less than me is not for me.'"

creativity 38 annual awards

1

2

3

4

1 CREATIVE FIRM: **Square360 - New York, NY** CREATIVE TEAM: **Brian Milea, Nancy Smullen - Creative Directors; Rainne Wu, Sharon Nao - Interactive Designers; Sean Apparicio - Video Director** CLIENT: **New Jersey Department of Health and Senior Services** 2 CREATIVE FIRM: **JPL Productions - Harrisburg, PA** CREATIVE TEAM: **Chelsie Markel - Art Director; Melissa Wimbish - Lead Designer; Chris Buchholz - Illustrator; Ryan Pudloski - Flash Developer; Alison Fetterman - Project Manager; Kim Quigley - Web Developer** CLIENT: **Susan P. Byrnes Health Education Centers** 3 CREATIVE FIRM: **Ripe Media - Beverly Hills, CA** CREATIVE TEAM: **Heather Richman - Creative Director; Chris Simental - Director of Technology** CLIENT: **The Wildwoods Foundation** 4 CREATIVE FIRM: **CDKWeb, Inc. - St. Charles, MO** CREATIVE TEAM: **Nicholas Sneed - Senior Web Designer** CLIENT: **Connections to Success**

1

2

3

4

5

1 CREATIVE FIRM: **Agency Republic - London, England** CREATIVE TEAM: **Tim Gardiner - Producer/Director; Phil Wilce - Copywriter; Gavin Gordon-Rogers - Creative Director; Jay Gelardi - Art Director; Bertrand Carrara - Designer; George Penney - Flash Developer** CLIENT: **BBC Radio 1** 2 CREATIVE FIRM: **Zero Gravity Design Group - Smithstown, NY** CREATIVE TEAM: **Chuck Killorin, Jennifer Mariotti - Partners** CLIENT: **CTREE** 3 CREATIVE FIRM: **WhittmanHart Interactive - Los Angeles, CA** CREATIVE TEAM: **WhittmanHart Interactive** CLIENT: **Entertainment Industry Foundation** 4 CREATIVE FIRM: **Kelsey Advertising & Design - LaGrange, GA** CREATIVE TEAM: **Brant Kelsey - Creative Director; Brian Handley - Illustrator/Programmer** CLIENT: **Rape Response** 5 CREATIVE FIRM: **CivicPlus - Manhattan, KS** CREATIVE TEAM: **CivicPlus** CLIENT: **Hutto, TX**

1

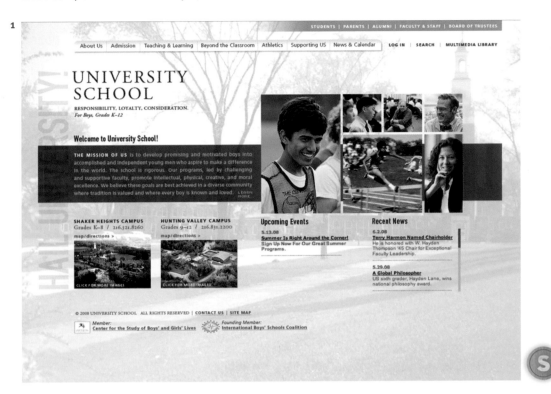

354

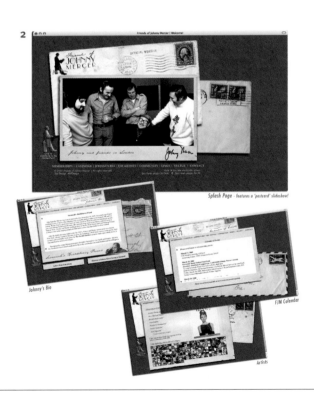

3

1

2

3

4

1 CREATIVE FIRM: **Syrup - New York, NY** CREATIVE TEAM: **Jakob Daschek - Creative Director; Robert Holzer - CEO; Jennifer Giroux - Account Director; Vineet Choudhary - CTO; Alex Lins - Design Director; Mike Manh - Lead Concept Programmer** CLIENT: **cYclops form LLC** 2 CREATIVE FIRM: **Magnani Caruso Dutton - New York, NY** CREATIVE TEAM: **John Caruso - Creative Director; John Dutton - Design Director; Chris Valley - Project Manager; Daniel Kolchinsky - Art Director; Ami Moore - Voice Over; Tim Carrier - Illustrator/Designer** CLIENT: **Partnership for a Drug Free America** 3 CREATIVE FIRM: **The UXB - Beverly Hills, CA** CREATIVE TEAM: **NJ Goldston - CEO and Founder** CLIENT: **Munchkin** 4 CREATIVE FIRM: **Singularity Design - Philadelphia, PA** CREATIVE TEAM: **Jeff Greenhouse - President; Owen Linton - Sr. Designer** CLIENT: **American Red Cross**

website • public service • **non-profit**

1

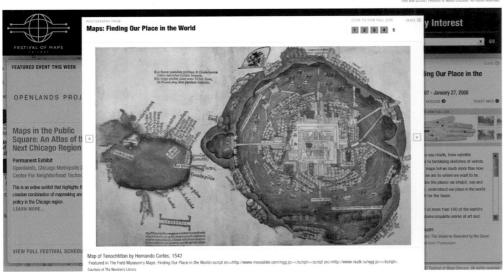

2

3

356

1 CREATIVE FIRM: **15 letters inc. - Chicago, IL** CREATIVE TEAM: **15 letters inc.** CLIENT: **Energy BBDO** 2 CREATIVE FIRM: **40olb.communications - Pittsburgh, PA** CREATIVE TEAM: **Nathan Kress - Creative Director; Clinton Godlesky - Lead Developer; Caulen Kress - Programmer; Rebecca Michalik - Designer** CLIENT: **StartingGate** 3 CREATIVE FIRM: **Greenfield/Belser Ltd. - Washington, D.C.** CREATIVE TEAM: **Burkey Belser - Creative Director; Liz Sullivan - Account Manager; Tae Jeong - Designer; Steve Gallagher - Web Manager; Paul Chang - Web/Interactive Project Manager** CLIENT: **DC Environmental Film Festival**

1

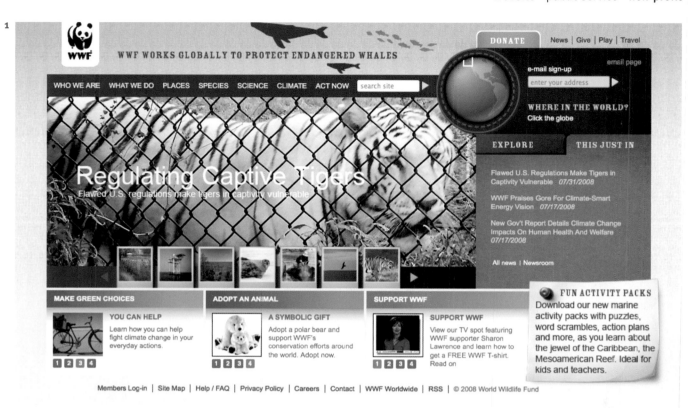

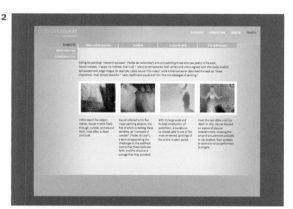

2

G

3

S

S

creativity 38 annual awards

1 CREATIVE FIRM: Greenfield/Belser Ltd. - Washington, D.C. CREATIVE TEAM: Burkey Belser - Creative Director; Shaun Quigley - Account Manager; Tae Jeong - Designer; Steve Gallagher - Web Manager; Paul Chang - Web/Interactive Project Manager CLIENT: World Wildlife Fund 2 CREATIVE FIRM: Behavior Design - New York, NY CREATIVE TEAM: Ralph Lucci - Project Lead; Chris Harrington - Information Architect; Daniel Hovey - Tech Lead; Anthony Armendariz - Visual Design Lead; Nick Keppol - Visual Designer; Al Johnson - Project Manager CLIENT: MoMA 3 CREATIVE FIRM: Taylor Design - Collingwood, Australia CREATIVE TEAM: Steve Habersang, Erin Cummings, Steve Dildarian, Cliff Huzienga CLIENT: Keep America Beautiful

website • self-promotion

PLATINUM P

358

CREATIVE FIRM: **Hornall Anderson - Seattle, WA**

CREATIVE TEAM: **Jamie Monberg - Art Director; Dana Kruse - Producer; Nathan Young - Designer; Chris Freed, Rachel Blakely - Production Designers; Adrien Lo - Lead Developer**

CLIENT: **Hornall Anderson**

Hornall Anderson Web Site

Hornall Anderson has its building in Seattle—and its Web site everywhere there's an available Internet connection. In order to keep visitors engaged and coming back to their virtual home, designers and developers spent hundreds of hours and plenty of thought to create a site that gets back to doing what any good interactive experience should. "It makes its point in the moment, it lets you drive and it shows you—not tells you," they say. "It conveys a message of authenticity and transparency, focusing on usability and ease of navigation."

New developments include the use of the keyboard's arrow keys to navigate, the ability to start typing anywhere as an intuitive search application, the application of tags to move laterally through the work and the overarching theme of transparency throughout the site, including a truly democratic blog platform. "The blog makes this site a more accurate representation of who Hornall Anderson is as a firm," the agency says. "It can be added to by anyone in the firm and cover any

topic—from a haiku to honor a seagull who hangs out on the ledge outside the kitchen to coverage of the firm's social events or photo essays about sneaker styles around the office." Bird poetry aside, the company states unequivocally that the goal was "to create a site whose very fiber—its design, content, and navigation—shows what Hornall Anderson stands for and what it can do."

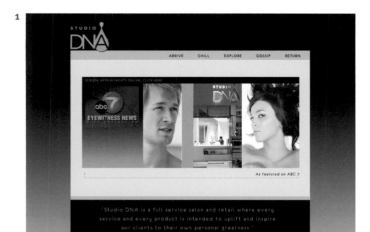

1 CREATIVE FIRM: Executionists, Inc. - Marina del Rey, CA CREATIVE TEAM: Richard Parr - Creative Director; Erin Tozour - Senior Designer; Julie Dwyer - Project Manager; Manuel Cabacungan - Web Developer CLIENT: Danny Leclair & Aubrey Loots 2 CREATIVE FIRM: MTV Networks Creative Services - New York, NY CREATIVE TEAM: Leslie Leventman - EVP/Creative Director; David Felton - SVP, Creative Consultant; Scott Wadler - SVP, Design; Cheryl Family - SVP, Editorial Director; Nick Gamma - Design Director; Houman Pourmand, Casey Stock - Designers; Matt Herron - Executive Producer/Director of Video; Elizabeth Boscoe, Tom Arnold - Producers of Video; Jon Zelenak - Editor of Video; Amanda Pecharsky, Hector Cardenas - Motion Graphics; Mark Malabrigo, Alan Perler - Technical Directors; Adam Wilson, Justin Cobb - Senior Developers; Ken Saji - Senior Copy Director; Patrick O'Sullivan - Copy Director; Tori Turner - Copywriter; Laura Calamari - Administrative Director CLIENT: MTV Networks 3 CREATIVE FIRM: Executionists, Inc. - Marina del Rey, CA CREATIVE TEAM: Richard Parr - Creative Director; Kaoru Wood - Designer; Temy Gu - Project Manager; Conrad Julian - Web Developer CLIENT: Christopher Laue 4 CREATIVE FIRM: Kelsey Advertising & Design - LaGrange, GA CREATIVE TEAM: Brant Kelsey - Creative Director/Programmer; Niki Studdard - Designer; Brian Handley - Programmer CLIENT: Kelsey Advertising & Design URL: www.kelseyads.com 5 CREATIVE FIRM: KNOCK inc. - Minneapolis, MN CREATIVE TEAM: Todd Paulson - Creative Director; Josh Clancy - Designer; Josh Clancy, Will Ecke - Illustrators; Josh Clancy - Flash Designer/Web Designer; Jill Palmquist - Copywriter CLIENT: TREAT and COMPANY 6 CREATIVE FIRM: The UXB - Beverly Hills, CA CREATIVE TEAM: NJ Goldston - CEO and Founder CLIENT: The UXB URL: www.theuxb.com

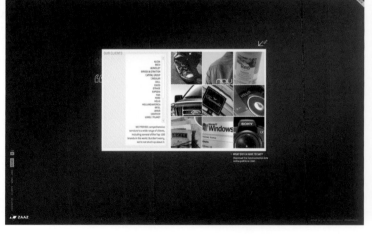

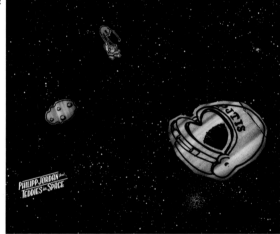

1 CREATIVE FIRM: **ZAAZ - Seattle, WA** CREATIVE TEAM: **Jon McVey, Tim Klauda - Creative Directors; Sarah Asher - Project Manager; Graeme Asher - Lead Interactive Developer** CLIENT: **ZAAZ** URL: **www. zaaz.com** 2 CREATIVE FIRM: **247 media studios - Cismar, Germany** CREATIVE TEAM: **Ingo Ramin - CEO/Creative Director** CLIENT: **Philipp Jordan**

1

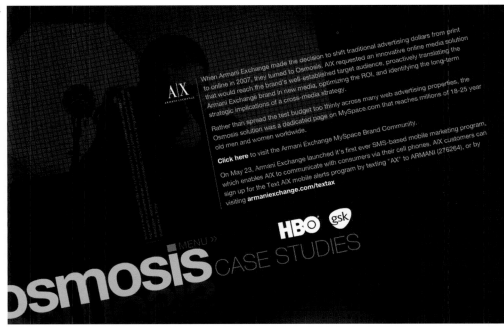

When Armani Exchange made the decision to shift traditional advertising dollars from print to online in 2007, they turned to Osmosis. AIX requested an innovative online media solution that would reach the brand's well-established target audience, proactively translating the Armani Exchange brand in new media, optimizing the ROI, and identifying the long-term strategic implications of a cross-media strategy.

Rather than spread the test budget too thinly across many web advertising properties, the Osmosis solution was a dedicated page on MySpace.com that reaches millions of 18-25 year old men and women worldwide.

Click here to visit the Armani Exchange MySpace Brand Community.

On May 23, Armani Exchange launched it's first ever SMS-based mobile marketing program, which enables AIX to communicate with consumers via their cell phones. AIX customers can sign up for the Text AIX mobile alerts program by texting "AX" to ARMANI (276264), or by visiting armaniexchange.com/textax

2

3

4

5

1 CREATIVE FIRM: Osmosis - New York, NY CREATIVE TEAM: Shawn Thomson - Executive Producer; Simone Davidson - Creative Director; Scott Kawczynski - Designer/Programmer CLIENT: osmosis URL: www.osmosis.net 2 CREATIVE FIRM: Fitting Group - Pittsburgh, PA CREATIVE TEAM: Travis Norris - Creative Director; Tim Emanuel - Programmer; Jeff Fitting - Technical Projects Director; Tony Jaffe - Copywriter; Andrew Ellis, Victoria Taylor - Designers CLIENT: Fitting Group URL: www.fittinggroup.com 3 CREATIVE FIRM: MTV Networks - New York, NY CREATIVE TEAM: Robin Richardson - Sr. Producer, CMT.com; Brandy Byrd, Marshall Woksa - Sr. Web Designers, CMT.com; Tyson Tune, Ryan Kaldari, Rick Kelchner - Web Developers, CMT.com CLIENT: CMT / CMT.com 4 CREATIVE FIRM: KAA Design Group, Inc. - Brand Experience Studio - Los Angeles, CA CREATIVE TEAM: Melanie Robinson - Creative Director; Annette Lee - Designer; Manolo Langis, Judith Kim - Illustrators; Anthony McLin, Fred J. Chasen - Web Developers CLIENT: HOM Escape in Style 5 CREATIVE FIRM: Zenith Design Group - Marietta, GA CREATIVE TEAM: Bonnie Buckner Reavis - Founder & CEO; Marc Parry - Interactive Developer CLIENT: Zenith Design Group URL: www.zenithdesigngroup.com

creativity 38 annual awards

1

2

3

4

5

6

1 CREATIVE FIRM: **MTV Networks - New York, NY** CREATIVE TEAM: **Kim Sorensen - Sr. Producer, CMT.com; Brandy Byrd, Marshall Woksa - Sr. Web Designers, CMT.com; Tyson Tune, Ryan Kaldari, Rick Kelchner - Web Developers, CMT.com** CLIENT: **CMT/CMT.com** 2 CREATIVE FIRM: **Taliana Design - Collingwood, Australia** CREATIVE TEAM: **Lisa Taliana, Andrea Maranzano - Graphic Designers** CLIENT: **Taliana Design** URL: **www.talianadesign.com.au** 3 CREATIVE FIRM: **Vilaitanarak & Knuesel - New York, NY** CREATIVE TEAM: **Orrawadee Vilaitanarak - Design/Interactions; Stephan Knuesel - Flash /Interactions** CLIENT: **Kevin Berrey, Filmmaker** 4 CREATIVE FIRM: **Vilaitanarak & Knuesel - New York, NY** CREATIVE TEAM: **Orrawadee Vilaitanarak - Design/Interactions; Stephan Knuesel - Flash/ Interactions** CLIENT: **G3 Architecture** 5 CREATIVE FIRM: **Kicksaints - Johannesburg, South Africa** CREATIVE TEAM: **Nick Bester, Brad Blundell - Creative Directors** CLIENT: **Sub urban** URL: **www.sub-urban.tv** 6 CREATIVE FIRM: **AKQA - London, England** CREATIVE TEAM: **Colin Byrne - Creative Director; Kevin Russell - Associate Creative Director; Colin Byrne - Writer; Joel Godfrey - Producer; David Wiltshire - Creative Developer; Groovy Gecko - Streaming** CLIENT: **AKQA**

1

2

3

4

5

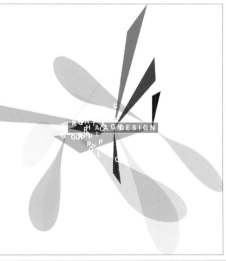

1 CREATIVE FIRM: **W. Lynn Garrett Art Direction + Design - Van Nuys, CA** CREATIVE TEAM: **Lynn Garrett - Client, Art Director, Designer, Copywriter, etc.** CLIENT: **W. Lynn Garrett Art Direction + Design** URL: **www.lynnster.com** 2 CREATIVE FIRM: **Vilaitanarak & Knuesel - New York, NY** CREATIVE TEAM: **Orrawadee Vilaitanarak - Design/Interactions; Stephan Knuesel - Flash/Interactions** CLIENT: **Uxor in Manu** 3 CREATIVE FIRM: **SKAGGS - New York, NY** CREATIVE TEAM: **Bradley Skaggs - Creative Director; Jonina Skaggs - Art Director; Joseph Guzman - Designer** CLIENT: **SKAGGS** URL: **www.skaggsdesign.com** 4 CREATIVE FIRM: **Singularity Design - Philadelphia, PA** CREATIVE TEAM: **Sean Trapani - Creative Director/Art Director; Owen Linton - Sr. Designer; Jeff Mills - Interactive Developer** CLIENT: **Singularity Design** URL: **www.singularitydesign.com** 5 CREATIVE FIRM: **Think Studio - New York, NY** CREATIVE TEAM: **Herb Thornby - Creative Director/Designer/Programmer; John Clifford - Creative Director/Designer** CLIENT: **Think Studio** URL: **www.thinkstudionyc.com**

1

2

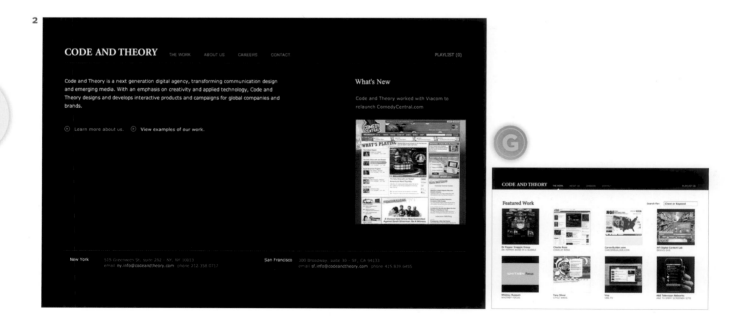

364

1 CREATIVE FIRM: **Valentine Group New York - New York, NY** CREATIVE TEAM: **Robert Valentine - Art Director & Designer** CLIENT: **Valentine Group New York** 2 CREATIVE FIRM: **Code and Theory - New York, NY** CREATIVE TEAM: **Brandon Ralph - Executive Creative Director; Jeremy Davis - Art Director; Vincent Tuscano - Associate Technical Director; Ed Burnett, Jon Harris - Engineers; Sapna Mia Gupta Ruiz-Escoto - Producer** CLIENT: **Code and Theory** URL: **codeandtheory.com**

COMMERCIALS,
TV & RADIO

CREATIVITY 38 ANNUAL AWARDS

PLATINUM (P)

CREATIVE FIRM: **Draftfcb - New York, NY**

CREATIVE TEAM: **Sandy Greenberg, Terri Meyer - Executive Creative Directors; Rob Rooney, Gerald Cuesta, Howie Ronay, Noah Davis - Creative Directors**

CLIENT: **Kraft Foods Inc.**

Planter's "Perfume"

A redheaded woman captivates every man whose path she crosses—on an elevator, at a coffee stand, on a bus (where male passengers crowd around her, leaving all the other seats empty) and on the street, to the peril of many. Her secret? It's not her Frida Kahlo-esque unibrow or flawless style, as anyone who catches her tugging on her pantyhose might attest: It's her scent that makes men go nuts for her. "She uses Planters Nuts as perfume," says New York agency Draftfcb, who produced the sixty-second spot that premiered during Super Bowl XLII. "For men, wanting Planters is more than desire. It's instinct."

creativity 38 annual awards

It doesn't matter how it happened,

... and that's how I got this stain, Mommy...

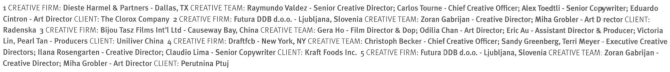

1 CREATIVE FIRM: **Dieste Harmel & Partners - Dallas, TX** CREATIVE TEAM: **Raymundo Valdez - Senior Creative Director; Carlos Tourne - Chief Creative Officer; Alex Toedtli - Senior Copywriter; Eduardo Cintron - Art Director** CLIENT: **The Clorox Company** 2 CREATIVE FIRM: **Futura DDB d.o.o. - Ljubljana, Slovenia** CREATIVE TEAM: **Zoran Gabrijan - Creative Director; Miha Grobler - Art D rector** CLIENT: **Radenska** 3 CREATIVE FIRM: **Bijou Tasz Films Int'l Ltd - Causeway Bay, China** CREATIVE TEAM: **Gera Ho - Film Director & Dop; Odilia Chan - Art Director; Eric Au - Assistant Director & Producer; Victoria Lin, Pearl Tan - Producers** CLIENT: **Uniliver China** 4 CREATIVE FIRM: **Draftfcb - New York, NY** CREATIVE TEAM: **Christoph Becker - Chief Creative Officer; Sandy Greenberg, Terri Meyer - Executive Creative Directors; Ilana Rosengarten - Creative Director; Claudio Lima - Senior Copywriter** CLIENT: **Kraft Foods Inc.** 5 CREATIVE FIRM: **Futura DDB d.o.o. - Ljubljana, Slovenia** CREATIVE TEAM: **Zoran Gabrijan - Creative Director; Miha Grobler - Art Director** CLIENT: **Perutnina Ptuj**

1

2

3

4

5

1 CREATIVE FIRM: **Dieste Harmel & Partners - Dallas, TX** CREATIVE TEAM: **Raymundo Valdez - Senior Creative Director; Carlos Tourne - Chief Creative Officer; Alex Toedtli - Senior Copywriter; Eduardo Cintron - Art Director** CLIENT: **The Clorox Company - Pine Sol** 2 CREATIVE FIRM: **GRAMM Werbeagentur GmbH - Düsseldorf, Germany** CREATIVE TEAM: **Uwe Köbbel - Chief Creative Officer; Norbert Streich - Executive Creative Director** CLIENT: **Volvo Car Germany GmbH** 3 CREATIVE FIRM: **MTV Networks - New York, NY** CREATIVE TEAM: **Lisa Bolton - Producer, Writer; Jim Read - Art Director; Michael Engleman, Jeff Nichols - Creative Directors** CLIENT: **CMT** 4 CREATIVE FIRM: **Burrell - Chicago, IL** CREATIVE TEAM: **Brenda Blonski - Creative Director; Kevin Miles, Carl Koestner - Associate Creative Directors; John Seaton - Producer; Lewis Williams - Chief Creative Officer; Anthony Hoffman - Director** CLIENT: **McDonalds** 5 CREATIVE FIRM: **Campbell-Ewald - Warren, MI** CREATIVE TEAM: **Bill Ludwig - Vice Chairman, Chief Creative Officer; Michael Stelmaszak, Duffy Patten - Writers; Robin Todd, Bob Guisgand - Art Directors** CLIENT: **Chevrolet**

1

The moment that you've been dreaming about the whole day.

G

2

S

3

4

1 CREATIVE FIRM: **Futura DDB d.o.o. - Ljubljana, Slovenia** CREATIVE TEAM: **Zoran Gabrijan - Creative Director; Miha Grobler - Art Director** CLIENT: **Telekom Slovenije** 2 CREATIVE FIRM: **Collider - Sydney, Australia** CREATIVE TEAM: **Andrew van der Westhuyzen - Director; Jay Russell, Bill Marceau - (CD GSD&Ms Ideacity)** CLIENT: **BMW** URL: **www.collider.com.au** 3 CREATIVE FIRM: **Bijou Tasz Films Int'l Ltd - Causeway Bay, China** CREATIVE TEAM: **Gera Ho - Film Director & Dop; Eric Au - Assistant Director & Producer; Victoria Lin - Producer; Odilia Chan - Art Director; Glendy Chiang, Sherry Huang - Copywriters/Creative** CLIENT: **Standard Foods Corporation** 4 CREATIVE FIRM: **MTV Networks - New York, NY** CREATIVE TEAM: **Michael Engleman, Jeff Nichols - Creative Directors; Scott Gerlock - Producer/Copywriter; Justin McClure - Designer; David Bennett - Art Director; Porter Gale - Director** CLIENT: **CMT**

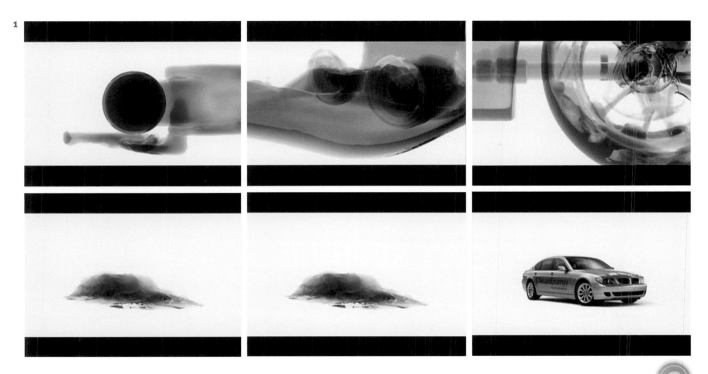

1 CREATIVE FIRM: Collider - Sydney, Australia CREATIVE TEAM: Andrew van der Westhuyzen - Director; Jay Russell, Bill Marceau - (CD GSD&Ms Ideacity) CLIENT: BMW URL: www.collider.com.au 2 CREATIVE FIRM: Y&R Advertising, Irvine - Irvine, CA CREATIVE TEAM: Anthony DiBiase - Executive Creative Director; Miles Turpin - Creative Director; Heather Stiteler - Creative Director, Copywriter; Theresa Menz - ACD, Art Director; Christopher Coleman - Executive Producer; David Jellison - Director CLIENT: BBQ Galore 3 CREATIVE FIRM: MTV Networks - New York, NY CREATIVE TEAM: Lisa Bolton - Director/Producer; R. Malcom Jones - Director; Michael Engleman, Jeff Nichols - Creative Directors; Dan Sutton - Editor CLIENT: CMT 4 CREATIVE FIRM: Bijou Tasz Films Int'l Ltd - Causeway Bay, China CREATIVE TEAM: Gera Ho - Film Director & Dop; Odilia Chan - Art Director; Victoria Lin - Producer; Eric Au - Assistant Director & Producer; Sunny Lee - Creative CLIENT: Jdb China

1

2

3

1 CREATIVE FIRM: **Campbell-Ewald - Warren, MI** CREATIVE TEAM: **Bill Ludwig - Vice Chairman, Chief Creative Officer; Debbie Karnowsky - Executive Creative Director; Mark Simon - Executive Creative Officer; Mike Conboy - Art Director; Neville Anderson - Writer; Jim Gilmore, John Haggerty - Executive Producers** CLIENT: **Kaiser Permanente** 2 CREATIVE FIRM: **Collider - Sydney, Australia** CREATIVE TEAM: **Joel Pront - Director; Peter Savieri - Production Designer** CLIENT: **Target** URL: **www.collider.com.au** 3 CREATIVE FIRM: **MTV On-Air Promos - New York, NY** CREATIVE TEAM: **Howard Grandison - Writer; Erin Hungerford, Seth Koen - Producers; Bryon Louie, Emmett Dzieza - Animators; Ian Stynes - Edit/Audio** CLIENT: **MTV**

1

2

3

4

1 CREATIVE FIRM: **Bijou Tasz Films Int'l Ltd - Causeway Bay, China** CREATIVE TEAM: **Gera Ho - Film Director & Dop; Eric Au - Assistant Director & Producer; Victoria Lin - Producer; Odilia Chan - Art Director; Dafung Li - Creative** CLIENT: **Jdb China** 2 CREATIVE FIRM: **Good Goliath, LLC - Round Rock, TX** CREATIVE TEAM: **Mat Harris - Chief Creative; Chris Wood - Art Director; Michael Hadwin - Production Director** CLIENT: **Christianson Enterprises** 3 CREATIVE FIRM: **Campbell-Ewald - Warren, MI** CREATIVE TEAM: **Bill Ludwig - Vice Chairman, Chief Creative Officer; Debbie Karnowsky - Executive Creative Director; Mark Simon - Executive Creative Director; Marie Abraham - Art Director; Chris Grenier - Writer; Jim Gilmore, John Haggerty - Executive Producers** CLIENT: **Kaiser Permanente** 4 CREATIVE FIRM: **G2 Media Group Inc. - Canton, OH** CREATIVE TEAM: **George Milnes II - Creative Director; Justin McCrea - Director of Photography; Brad Smitley - Art Director; Todd Archinal, Lucas Smithbauer - Grips** CLIENT: **Unilever Ice Cream**

1

2

3

1 CREATIVE FIRM: **Ardmore Advertising - Holywood, UK** CREATIVE TEAM: **Ashleigh Arthur - Art Director; Larry McGarry - Creative Director** CLIENT: **Translink** 2 CREATIVE FIRM: **GlobalWorks Group LLC - New York, NY** CREATIVE TEAM: **Caroline Fish - Creative Director; Nalini Alfonseca - Copywriter; Jorge Moret - Art Director; Israel Lugo, Gabriel Coss - Directors; Evelyn Badia - Agency Producer** CLIENT: **Cablevision Systems Corporation** 3 CREATIVE FIRM: **MTV Networks - New York, NY** CREATIVE TEAM: **Scott Gerlock - Producer/Director/Copywriter; Veva Burns, Warren Beck, Brian Abero - Designer/ Editors; Jim Parker - Sound Design; Jim Read - Art Director** CLIENT: **CMT**

1

2

3

Ryan McKee

Karen Eng

1 CREATIVE FIRM: Campbell-Ewald - Warren, MI CREATIVE TEAM: Bill Ludwig - Vice Chairman, Chief Creative Officer; Debbie Karnowsky - Executive Creative Director; Chip Kettering, Richard Bess - Art Director; John Dolab, Andy Stern - Writers; John Haggerty - Executive Producer CLIENT: Farmers Insurance 2 CREATIVE FIRM: Campbell-Ewald - Warren, MI CREATIVE TEAM: Bill Ludwig - Vice Chairman, Chief Creative Officer; Mark Simon - Executive Creative Director; Jim Millis - Creative Director; Jason Fetterman - Art Director; Mike O'Connell - Writer; John Burger, Heidi Verlinde - Producers CLIENT: Alltel 3 CREATIVE FIRM: Campbell-Ewald - Warren, MI CREATIVE TEAM: Bill Ludwig - Vice Chairman, Chief Creative Officer; Debbie Karnowsky - Executive Creative Director; Chip Kettering - Art Director; John Dolab - Writer; John Haggerty - Executive Producer CLIENT: Farmers Insurance 4 CREATIVE FIRM: Gotham Inc. - New York, NY CREATIVE TEAM: Gotham Inc. CLIENT: Yellowbook 5 CREATIVE FIRM: Gotham Inc. - New York, NY CREATIVE TEAM: Gotham Inc. CLIENT: Maybelline

1

2

3

4

5

1 CREATIVE FIRM: **Ardmore Advertising - Holywood, UK** CREATIVE TEAM: **Larry McGarry - Creative Director; Ashliegh Arthur - Art Director** CLIENT: **Belfast Visitor and Convention Bureau** 2 CREATIVE FIRM: **Gargoyle - Princeton, NJ** CREATIVE TEAM: **Dan Veltri - Creative Director and Director; Will Pang - Senior Art Director; Saul Katz - Copywriter; Scott Weitz, Sal Delgutis - Executive Producers** CLIENT: **Western Pest Services** 3 CREATIVE FIRM: **Quigley-Simpson - Los Angeles, CA** CREATIVE TEAM: **Gerald Bagg - Chief Executive Officer; Alissa Stakgold - Vice President; Desmond Burrows - Creative Director; Jeff Tinsley - President, reunion.com; Scott Moss, Bruce Somers - Producers** CLIENT: **reunion.com** 4 CREATIVE FIRM: **Quigley-Simpson - Los Angeles, CA** CREATIVE TEAM: **Gerald Bagg - Chief Executive Officer; Alissa Stakgold - Vice President; Desmond Burrows - Creative Director; Jeff Tinsley - President,reunion.com; Scott Moss, Bruce Somers - Producers** CLIENT: **reunion.com** 5 CREATIVE FIRM: **Quigley-Simpson - Los Angeles, CA** CREATIVE TEAM: **Gerald Bagg - Chief Executive Officer; Alissa Stakgold - Vice President; Desmond Burrows - Creative Director; Noah Michel - Copywriter; Sally Rosenberger-Wolfe - Director of North American Media & Marketing; Cindy Bashore - Producer - Upstream Media** CLIENT: **Walmart**

CREATIVE FIRM: **Animax Entertainment - Van Nuys, CA**

CREATIVE TEAM: **Dave Thomas - Creative Director;**
Al Rosson - Animation Director; Kat Kosmala - Lead Animator;
Barry Kelly - Editor/Post Production

CLIENT: **Animax Entertainment**

URL: **www.animaxinteractive.com**

Bob & Doug Trailer

Los Angeles may be a long way from the Great White North, but Canada's Global Television had no qualms about enlisting Animax Entertainment to redraw iconic characters Bob and Doug McKenzie as animated characters for a new television program. "Much care and consideration was given to how these characters would or would not behave in an animated world—and to what extent that might have an impact on their design," says Animax. The client wanted to "make sure that the main characters would retain the personalities and characteristics unique to each, and that the comic situations that they might find themselves in could be fully realized within the framework of an animated world."

Because the prototypes were actual people—and a thirty-year-old brand at that—creating two-dimensional McKenzies posed its own set of challenges. "The characters were live action comedians whose comedy was conveyed in subtle facial expressions and nuances, which were also difficult to transpose to animation," the studio explains. "Numerous photo references of

the live action characters were used to aid the animators in the creation of these facial expressions." Not only that, it was imperative that the overall effect be unmistakably McKenzie: "The designs had to capture the 'essence' of the comedy delivered by the live action characters and the 'acting' in the animation had to sell this comedy."

And, if viewers detect in-jokes reminiscent of other grown-up cartoons like "The Simpsons" or "Futurama," it's purely intentional. "Environment, the use of color and/or shapes will have a significant impact upon the mood of a setting or background and will largely determine its effectiveness," the animators explain. "Character, color, shapes and names all play a part in establishing a character's overall personality... A name might indicate a specific character trait, it might be a reference to an inside joke among artists and writers, or it may be selected simply because it sounds funny."

1

Studio Universal, we bring great cinema direct to your home, 24/7.

2

www.GroovyLikeaMovie.com

3

USE THEM OR LOSE THEM

Para Music Freaks.
mtvtr3s.com

PLATINUM (P)

CREATIVE FIRM: **MTV On-Air Promos - New York, NY**

CREATIVE TEAM: **Michel Rothschild - Writer/Director; David Grad - Producer; Alfonso Aguilar - Director of Photography; Brian Krupkin, Dan Sforza - Animators; Jose Maria Norton - Editor**

CLIENT: **MTV Tr3s**

Artist Speaking Tr3s - Julieta Venegas

The goal of MTV Tr3s' Artist Speaking Tr3s campaign is to create a series of promos positioning the Latin-themed Tr3s channel as a music authority with access to the biggest stars, resulting in unique content that can't be seen anywhere else. "The custom vignettes allow the artists to share different sides of themselves, such as where they find inspiration, their childhood heroes, social issues that matter to them and fun fantasies," says MTV of their on-air promos, which, in the case of Mexican songbird Julieta Venegas, posed a special kind of challenge. With Venegas' spot, they strove to create "fantastic and surreal worlds to express how she interacts with love—her muse—and at the same time create an engaging and fun connection with MTV Tr3s and its audience, all while working within a limited budget."

Besides creating engaging stories and worlds for the artist, MTV also developed a series of characters to brand the campaigns, featuring bright color palates, clean lines and carefully crafted art direc-

tion. "These creatures are conceptually made up of gadgets and instruments that represent the various ways in which our audience experience music," says MTV, "like headphones, boom boxes, speakers and MP3 players." MTV's designers then tailored the icons to fit certain categories, such as rock, hip hop and their Latin fusion, reggaetón. The team incorporated all the icons into the Venegas campaign, they say, "because we felt they were an imaginative way to show how the artist interacts with music as she works to make love a key element in the creation of her chosen art form."

1

2

3

1 CREATIVE FIRM: **MTV Networks - New York, NY** CREATIVE TEAM: **Terry McCorkmick - Creative Director; Laura Lundgren - Producer** CLIENT: **Nicktoons Network** 2 CREATIVE FIRM: **MTV On-Air Promos - New York, NY** CREATIVE TEAM: **Evan Silver - Writer/Director; Sheree Shu - Producer; Ericson Core - Director of Photography; Andre Sosnowski - Editor; Dave Huston - Audio; JP Riggle - Graphics** CLIENT: **MTV** 3 CREATIVE FIRM: **MTV On-Air Promos - New York, NY** CREATIVE TEAM: **Evan Silver - Writer/Director; Howard Grandison - Writer; Sheree Shu - Producer; Jerry Risius - Director of Photography; Carol Butrico - Editor; Dave Huston - Audio** CLIENT: **MTV**

1

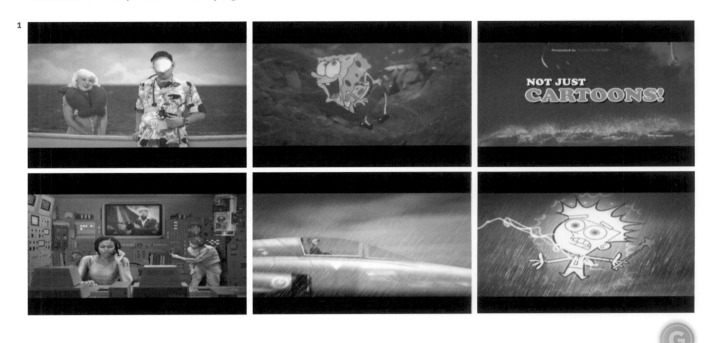

2

3

382

4

1 CREATIVE FIRM: **MTV Networks - New York, NY** CREATIVE TEAM: **Terry McCormick - Creative Director; Dave Berg - Producer/Director** CLIENT: **Nicktoons Network 2** CREATIVE FIRM: **MTV On-Air Promos - New York, NY** CREATIVE TEAM: **Dax Martinez-Vargas, Barry Flanagan - Writer/Directors; Jeff Woodton, Eve Frederick - Producers; Ben Williams - Editor/Graphics; Dave Huston - Audio** CLIENT: **mtvU 3** CREATIVE FIRM: **MTV Networks - New York, NY** CREATIVE TEAM: **Terry McCormick - Creative Director; Joseph Peptione - Producer; Michelle Kratchman - Art Director** CLIENT: **Nicktoons Network 4** CREATIVE FIRM: **MTV On-Air Promos - New York, NY** CREATIVE TEAM: **Joe Stevens, Rich Fulcher - Writers; Michael Bellino - Director; Adam Palmer - Producer; Peter Smokler - Director of Photography; Carol Butrico - Editor** CLIENT: **MTV**

1

2

corporate tv • single unit

3

4

---

1 CREATIVE FIRM: MTV Networks - New York, NY CREATIVE TEAM: Terry McCorkmick - Creative Director; Joseph Peptione - Producer; Michelle Kratchman - Art Director; Junichi Nakane, Milton Ladd - Designers CLIENT: Nicktoons Network 2 CREATIVE FIRM: MTV On-Air Promos - New York, NY CREATIVE TEAM: Evan Silver - Writer/Director; Howard Grandison - Writer; David Grad - Producer; Jerry Risius - Director of Photography; Michael Dart Wadsworth - Editor; Terressa Tate - Audio CLIENT: MTV Tr3s 3 CREATIVE FIRM: MENDES PUBLICIDADE - Belém, Brazil CREATIVE TEAM: Oswaldo Mendes - Creative Director, Copywriter; José Paulo Vieira - Director CLIENT: Governo do Estado do Pará. 4 CREATIVE FIRM: NBC Universal Global Networks Italia - Rome, Italy CREATIVE TEAM: NBC Universal Global Networks Italia CLIENT: Studio Universal URL: www.studiouniversal.it

BASIC HOUSE

www.re-creating.co.kr
Re-creating 'Emotions'

PLATINUM (P)

CREATIVE FIRM: **McCann Erickson Korea - Seoul, South Korea**

CREATIVE TEAM: **Jung hyun Shon - Senior Creative Director; Jung hyun Cho - Associate Creative Director; Won kuk Kim - Copywriter; Sang jin Kim - Art Director; Sang Youn Kim, Nam gil Kim - Agency Producers**

CLIENT: **The Basic House**

Re-Creating Spirit

South Korean clothing retailer Basic House plays upon its name by creating timeless, casual clothing with an eye for current fashion. McCann Erickson Korea's ad campaign took the natural next step in "re-creating spirit—bringing contemporary change and giving a twist to something basic, classic, traditional—which essentially captures the spirit and look" of their client. The Seoul-based agency explains: "We took dancing and music—which are easy and relevant for our audience—as creative subjects."

The resulting series of commercials effectively communicated Basic House's mission. "The client wanted to build strong brand equity with re-creating spirit; in addition, it wanted to have some image of globalism to be a potential global brand in the future," the agency says. "Therefore, we tried to feature various nationalities and cultures in each execution." Not only did McCann Erickson combine various human faces in the spots, but human *sounds* as well: Mozart is "played" with finger snaps and decid-

edly analog instruments, while a traditional Korean tune gets a new treatment from modern percussion devices such as plastic water bottles. And, in a startling twist, silent film icon Charlie Chaplin appears to dance alongside twenty-first century teens to a techno beat. "We were not allowed to make any changes in the original film," McCann Erickson says, "so we partially created the film, imitating the look and feel of the original."

1

2

3

1 CREATIVE FIRM: NBC Universal Global Networks Italia - Rome, Italy CREATIVE TEAM: NBC Universal Global Networks Italia CLIENT: Steel 2 CREATIVE FIRM: Cole & Weber United - Seattle, WA CREATIVE TEAM: Todd Grant - Creative Direction; Todd Derksen - Art Direction; Mike Tuton - Copywriting; Savant - Production Company; Jay Howard - Producer; Richard Carroll - Director CLIENT: Devon Energy 3 CREATIVE FIRM: MTV On-Air Promos - New York, NY CREATIVE TEAM: Alan Harris - Writer/Director; Matt Giulvezan - Producer; Joe Arcidiacono - Director of Photography; Tim Kafalas - Editor; Dave Huston - Audio; JP Riggle - Graphics CLIENT: MTV

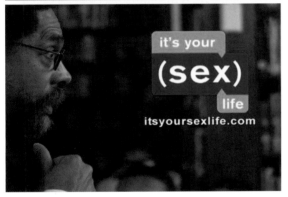

386

1 CREATIVE FIRM: **MTV On-Air Promos - New York, NY** CREATIVE TEAM: **Seyi Peter-Thomas, Kadine Anckle - Writer/Directors; Grayson Ross - Producer; Jerry Risius - Director of Photography; Andre Sosnowski, Kim O'Donnell - Editors** CLIENT: **MTV** 2 CREATIVE FIRM: **Vanguarda Propaganda - Belém, Brazil** CREATIVE TEAM: **Francisco Cavalcante - Creative Director; Phernando Silva - Art Director; Moana Luri - Copywriter** CLIENT: **Government of the State of Pará** 3 CREATIVE FIRM: **Dustin W Design - Los Angeles, CA** CREATIVE TEAM: **Raymond Rector - VP, Marketing and PR, Christopher Street West; Dustin Woehrmann - Creative, Copy, Animation, Designer; River* Bohanna, Gavin Sterley - Concept; Leslie Pollock - Copy; Abby Roccaforte - AfterEffects Production** CLIENT: **Christopher Street West** 4 CREATIVE FIRM: **Vanguarda Propaganda - Belém, Brazil** CREATIVE TEAM: **Francisco Cavalcante - Creative Director; Phernando Silva - Art Director** CLIENT: **Government of the State of Pará** 5 CREATIVE FIRM: **GIOVANNI+DRAFTFCB - São Paolo, Brazil** CREATIVE TEAM: **Adilson Xavier - President/Nacional Creative Director, Copywriter;L Cristina Amorim - Creative Director, Art Director** CLIENT: **MetaSocial**

PLATINUM P

CREATIVE FIRM: MTV Networks - New York, NY

CREATIVE TEAM: Stephen Friedman - General Manager; Ross Martin - Head of Programming; Eric Conte - Executive Producer; Paul Ricci - Supervising Producer; Sophia Cranshaw - Vice-President, Director, On-Air Promotions; Noopur Agarwal - Manager Public Affairs, mtvU Marketing; Chris McCarthy - VP mtvU Marketing and Strategic Development; Gina Esposito - Director, Music & Talent

CLIENT: JED Foundation

mtvU Half Of Us

Depression can be embarrassing—one study cites that seventy-five percent of sufferers hesitate to seek help because of feelings of awkwardness or anticipated humiliation. More critically, suicide is the second leading cause of death among college students—and suicide's primary cause is depression. To appeal to this demographic, mtvU teamed up with The JED Foundation in 2006 to create a multiplatform campaign called Half of Us. "The campaign represents the reality that nearly half of all college students have felt so depressed at one point they could not function," says mtvU. "Through on-air, online and on-campus initiatives, Half of Us raises awareness about the prevalence of mental health issues among college students, connects students to resources and assistance in their area and helps initiate a public dialogue to de-stigmatize mental health."

While leading people to a Web site is a big step, keeping them coming back is a larger endeavor. "[We had to] make it relevant over time so students would want to come back, even after receiving the help they needed, since emotional health—just like physical health—is something that must be maintained," the creators say. "Refreshing the site each semester with new student and celebrity stories to keep the site relevant was also challenging due to the stigma surrounding mental health issues and the reluctance of participants to share their personal stories publicly." Still, the collaboration continues to succeed as celebrities and students alike come forward to tell their stories. Such stories "serve as a reminder that mental health problems are not uncommon," says mtvU. "Ultimately, we hope the campaign will inspire others to share their own struggles."

1

2

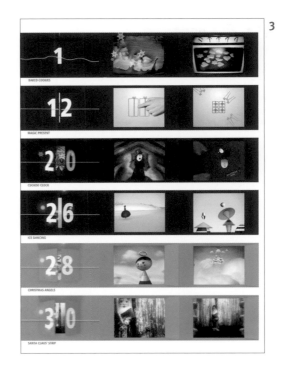

1 CREATIVE FIRM: **Draftfcb - New York, NY** CREATIVE TEAM: **Christoph Becker - Chief Creative Officer; Keith Ross, Rob Rooney - Creative Directors; Claudio Lima - Senior Copywriter; Daniel Prado - Art Director** CLIENT: **Office of National Drug Control Policy** 2 CREATIVE FIRM: **REVOLUCION - New York, NY** CREATIVE TEAM: **Alberto Rodriguez - Chief Creative Officer; Roberto Alcazar - Executive Creative Director; Mercedes Leonard - Producer** CLIENT: **Ad Council/Adopt-US-Kids** 3 CREATIVE FIRM: **Studio Nordwand - Munich, Germany** CREATIVE TEAM: **Klaus W Schuntermann - Creative Director On Air Design (MDR FERNSEHEN); Sandra Kather - Project Manager Design (MDR FERNSEHEN); Peter Pedall - CEO/Global Creative Direction (Studio Nordwand); Fabrice Gueneau - CEO/ Global Creative Direction (Dream On)** CLIENT: **MDR FERNSEHEN (MDR tv), Leipzig, Germany**

Planters Instincts

CREATIVE FIRM: **Draftfcb - New York, NY**

CREATIVE TEAM: **Christoph Becker - Chief Creative Officer; Sandy Greenberg, Terri Meyer - Executive Creative Directors; Rob Rooney - Creative Director; Matt Bottkol - Copywriter**

CLIENT: **Kraft Foods Inc.**

A male announcer is the first to admit it: "Men's instincts aren't always that good." For Planters Nuts, New York-based agency Draftfcb produced five thirty-second radio ads depicting common examples of misguided male instinct: ill-advised DIY automotive repair, inadvertently making their girlfriends jealous, attempting romance by getting their wives household appliances. "Men know what they want and follow their instincts. Due to this fact, they may get in trouble from time to time, but never when Planters is involved," the agency says. The tagline, heard in each radio spot, sums it up: "When it comes to nuts, men can always trust their instincts."

radio • campaign

Planters 'Kettle.' CREATIVE FIRM: **Draftfcb - New York, NY** CREATIVE TEAM: **Christoph Becker - Chief Creative Officer; Sandy Greenberg, Terri Meyer - Executive Creative Directors; Rob Rooney - Creative Director; Matt Bottkol - Copywriter** CLIENT: **Kraft Foods Inc.**

American Standard 'Extra Time.' CREATIVE FIRM: **Draftfcb - New York, NY** CREATIVE TEAM: **Christoph Becker - Chief Creative Officer; Rob Rooney - Creative Director; Matt Bottkol - Copywriter** CLIENT: **American Standard**

Wife/Rock Star Commercials. CREATIVE FIRM: **Choice Hotels International - Cambria Suites - Silver Spring, MD** CREATIVE TEAM: **Cathy Poinsett - Senior Director, Brand Management; Amanda Morgan - Director, Brand Management; Kourtnie Perry - Project Manager, Brand Management** CLIENT: **Cambria Suites**

American Standard 'You Need To Get Out.' CREATIVE FIRM: **Draftfcb - New York, NY** CREATIVE TEAM: **Christoph Becker - Chief Creative Officer; Rob Rooney - Creative Director; Matt Bottkol - Copywriter** CLIENT: **American Standard**

WESM Radio Network. CREATIVE FIRM: **HCP & Associates - Tampa, FL** CREATIVE TEAM: **Eric Polins - Creative Director; Nicklaus Fordham - Senior Account Manager** CLIENT: **DENTCO**

Mary Bridge Childrens Hospital. CREATIVE FIRM: **MultiCare Health Systems - Seattle, WA** CREATIVE TEAM: **Jenny Davidson - Project Manager; Julie Smith - Copywriter; Robin Pederson, Dean Driskell - Art Directors** CLIENT: **MultiCare Health Systems**

'Thanks Saint Peter's!' CREATIVE FIRM: **SGW Integrated Marketing Communications - Montville, NJ** CREATIVE TEAM: **Niles Wolfson - Chief Creative Officer; Chez Pari - Creative Director** CLIENT: **Saint Peter's University Hospital**

radio • single unit

'We Fixin' It' - Jingle. CREATIVE FIRM: **All Media Projects Limited - Port of Spain, Trinidad & Tobago** CREATIVE TEAM: **Anthony Moore - Creative Director/Copywriter; Sandra Rezende - Senior Account Executive; Richard Achong - Producer** CLIENT: **Water & Sewerage Authority**

Rough Rider Jingle. CREATIVE FIRM: **Inglefield, Ogilvy & Mather Caribbean Ltd. - Port of Spain, Trinidad & Tobago** CREATIVE TEAM: **David Gomez - Executive Creative Director; Paula Obe - Senior Copywriter; Sara Camps - AV Production Manager; Lorainne Orr - Senior Account Executive; Richard Achong - Producer** CLIENT: **Rough Rider**

Gig Harbor Medical Park Grand Opening. CREATIVE FIRM: **MultiCare Health Systems - Seattle, WA** CREATIVE TEAM: **Jenny Davidson - Project Manager; Julie Smith - Copywriter; Robin Pederson, Dean Driskell - Art Directors** CLIENT: **MultiCare Health Systems**

radio • self-promotion, campaign

Radio vs. Newspaper. CREATIVE FIRM: **Clear Channel Creative Services Group - Atlanta, GA** CREATIVE TEAM: **Liz Smith - Creative Director/Copywriter; Forrest Martin - Copywriter/ Producer** CLIENT: **Clear Channel**

GREEN
MARKETING

CREATIVITY **38** ANNUAL AWARDS

1

environmentally
responsible

Can a curtain wall be as environmentally responsible as a windmill?
If anyone will find out it will be Oldcastle Glass.' Why? Simple.
While many curtain wall manufacturers are jumping on the "green"
bandwagon—we are **the only curtain wall company that can also
custom manufacture glass.** So our perspective and opportunity are
unique. We call that opportunity Oldcastle Glass' Envelope.' It's a
commitment to forward-thinking technologies that lead
to **more responsible building envelope solutions.** We're
leaving our mark—just not on the environment. Call
us at **1-866-OLDCASTLE** (653-2278) or visit us online
at the new **www.oldcastleglass.com** to learn more.

111 South Wacker designed
by Goettsch Partners is
the first building to win
LEED-CS (Core and Shell)
Gold certification from the
U.S. Green Building Council.'
Curtain Wall custom-engi-
neered by Oldcastle Glass.'
*architecturalrecord.com

Our environmentally
friendly Curtain Walls
can incorporate our
exclusive SunGlass,'
which cuts energy
costs by reducing
the sun's heat gain.

Oldcastle Glass'   *Pushing the building envelope*'

G

creativity 38 annual awards

CREATIVE FIRM: **FORMO - Charleston, SC**

CREATIVE TEAM: **Caryn Baumgartner - Creative Director; Adam Boozer - Interactive Creative Director; Rich Wilson - Associate Creative Director, Copywriter; Joe Pohl, Elizabeth Hagin - Production Artists; Howard Bjornson - Photographer**

CLIENT: **The Greenbrier Sporting Club**

Green Homes Vision Brochure & Microsite

In the current economy, it's crucial that new housing developments, such as Green Homes at the Greenbrier, have an edge in attracting customers. That's where Charleston, South Carolina design firm FORMO came in. "The overall intent behind the design of the Green Homes brochure and microsite was to effectively design highly integrated components that would define 'green' in an authentic and believable manner," says FORMO of the West Virginia property, "as well as appropriately portray Green Homes at the Greenbrier to existing members and prospects."

Where "going green" is a popular buzz-word, FORMO made sure to walk the walk too. "The largest challenge came in communicating this initiative strongly and authentically so as to stand out in the midst of the gross overuse of people claiming to be 'green' through advertising hype only," FORMO says. "The client wanted us to effectively promote the legacy of [owners] DPS Sporting Club Development Company as a steward of the environment, and also convey that this 'green' initiative was a natural evolutionary step for their neighborhoods."

FORMO took the charge very seriously, creating a brochure that's green in both color and spirit. "There is a reason behind the selection of exclusively 'green' materials, just like there is a purpose behind building eco-friendly homes," the designers say. "We tell this story visually through beautiful detail portraits of botanical specimens, artfully crafted typography and design. Intellectually, we tell the story through the thoughtful consideration given to paper selection, printing and production." And as Web images go off into the ether, paper collateral for Green Homes at the Greenbrier also are designed to be enjoyed, then return to the earth. Says FORMO: "Like nature, this piece renews itself as an enduring work of art to be enjoyed for generations to come."

1

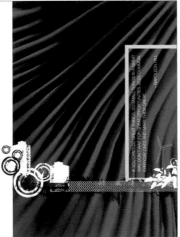

2

3

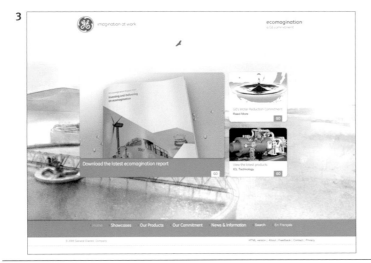

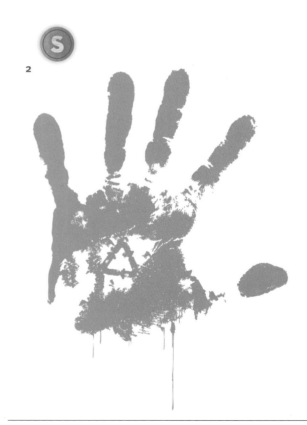

2

1 CREATIVE FIRM: **MJE Marketing Services Inc. - San Diego, CA** CREATIVE TEAM: **Marlee Ehrenfeld - Chief Creative Officer; Aaron Ishaeik - Art Director** CLIENT: **Port of San Diego** 2 CREATIVE FIRM: **Daniels College of Business, University of Denver - Denver, CO** CREATIVE TEAM: **Wendy Kent - Art Director; Jeff Doyle - Graphic Designer; Susan Passmore - Content Manager** CLIENT: **Daniels College of Business, University of Denver**

PLATINUM P

CREATIVE FIRM: **FORMO - Charleston, SC**

CREATIVE TEAM: **Caryn Baumgartner - Creative Director; Rich Wilson - Associate Creative Director, Copywriter; Joe Pohl, Elizabeth Hagin - Production Artists; Howard Bjornson - Photographer**

CLIENT: **The Greenbrier Sporting Club**

Green Homes Vision Brochure

In the current economy, it's crucial that new housing developments, such as Green Homes at the Greenbrier, have an edge in attracting customers. That's where Charleston, South Carolina design firm FORMO came in. "The overall intent behind the design of the Green Homes brochure and microsite was to effectively design highly integrated components that would define 'green' in an authentic and believable manner," says FORMO of the West Virginia property, "as well as appropriately portray Green Homes at the Greenbrier to existing members and prospects."

Where "going green" is a popular buzzword, FORMO made sure to walk the walk too. "The largest challenge came in communicating this initiative strongly and authentically so as to stand out in the midst of the gross overuse of people claiming to be 'green' through advertising hype only," FORMO says. "The client wanted us to effectively promote the legacy of [owners] DPS Sporting Club Development Company as a steward of the environment, and also convey that this 'green' initiative was a natural evolutionary step for their neighborhoods."

FORMO took the charge very seriously, creating a brochure that's green in both color and spirit. "There is a reason behind the selection of exclusively 'green' materials, just like there is a purpose behind building eco-friendly homes," the designers say. "We tell this story visually through beautiful detail portraits of botanical specimens, artfully crafted typography and design. Intellectually, we tell the story through the thoughtful consideration given to paper selection, printing and production." And as Web images go off into the ether, paper collateral for Green Homes at the Greenbrier also are designed to be enjoyed, then return to the earth. Says FORMO: "Like nature, this piece renews itself as an enduring work of art to be enjoyed for generations to come."

creativity 38 annual awards

1

2

3

1 CREATIVE FIRM: **Daniels College of Business, University of Denver - Denver, CO** CREATIVE TEAM: **R. Aaron Templer - Director of Marketing and Communications; Nicole Buettner - Art Director; Wendy Kent - Graphic Designer; Susan Passmore - Writer** CLIENT: **Daniels College of Business, University of Denver** 2 CREATIVE FIRM: **Greenfield/Belser Ltd. - Washington, D.C.** CREATIVE TEAM: **Burkey Belser - Creative Director; Erika Ritzer - Account Manager; Tae Jeong - Designer; George Kell - Copywriter; Gene Shaffer - Production Artist** CLIENT: **Nixon Peabody** 3 CREATIVE FIRM: **housemouse - Melbourne, Australia** CREATIVE TEAM: **Miguel Valenzuela - Creative Director; Andrea Taylor - Graphic Designer** CLIENT: **housemouse**

STUDENT

1

2

3

4

5

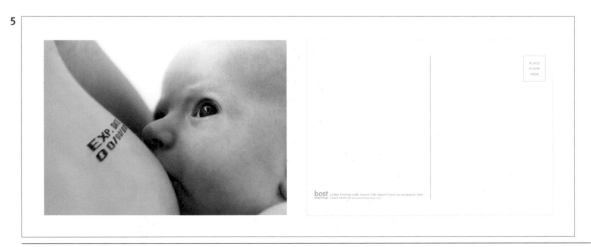

1 CATEGORY: **Ambient Media, Single Unit** CREATIVE FIRM: **Parsons The New School for Design - Jersey City, NJ** CREATIVE TEAM: **Ryan Wi - Art Director, Copywriter** CLIENT: **Johnson & Johnson Band-Aid** 2 CATEGORY: **Ambient Media, Single Unit** CREATIVE FIRM: **Parsons The New School for Design - Jersey City, NJ** CREATIVE TEAM: **Ryan Wi - Art Director, Copywriter** CLIENT: **Global Tree Campaign**
3 CATEGORY: **Ambient Media, Single Unit** CREATIVE FIRM: **Parsons The New School for Design - Jersey City, NJ** CREATIVE TEAM: **Ryan Wi - Art Director, Copywriter; Jiashan Wu, Yangjie Wee - Art Directors** CLIENT: **Grazia** 4 CATEGORY: **Guerilla Marketing, Single Unit** CREATIVE FIRM: **Parsons The New School for Design - Jersey City, NJ** CREATIVE TEAM: **Ryan Wi, Yangjie Wee, Jiashan Wu - Art Directors** CLIENT: **Grazia** 5 CATEGORY: **Ambient Media, Single Unit** CREATIVE FIRM: **School of Visual Arts - New York, NY** CLIENT: **Best Beginnings**

1

2

3

4

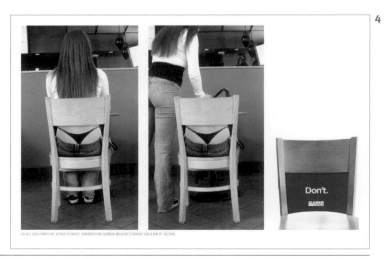

1 CATEGORY: **Guerilla Marketing, Single Unit** CREATIVE FIRM: **School of Visual Arts - New York, NY** CREATIVE TEAM: **School of Visual Arts** CLIENT: **Netflix** 2 CATEGORY: **Public Service Film/Video** CREATIVE FIRM: **Hawaii Student Television (HSTV) - Honolulu, HI** CREATIVE TEAM: **Hawaii Student Television (HSTV)** CLIENT: **Hawaii State Department of Health** URL: **www.HawaiiStudentTV.org** 3 CATEGORY: **Public Service Film/Video** CREATIVE FIRM: **Hawaii Student Television (HSTV) - Honolulu, HI** CREATIVE TEAM: **Hawaii Student Television (HSTV)** CLIENT: **Hawaii Youth Services Network** URL: **www.Hawaii-iStudentTV.org** 4 CATEGORY: **Guerilla Marketing, Single Unit** CREATIVE FIRM: **School of Visual Arts - New York, NY** CREATIVE TEAM: **Catherine Eccardt - Copywriter** CLIENT: **Glamour Magazine**

1 CATEGORY: **Repurposed Design** CREATIVE FIRM: **West Virginia University Senior Design Class - Morgantown, WV** CREATIVE TEAM: **Lauren Vause - Student** CLIENT: **WVU Division of Art and Design**
2 CATEGORY: **Illustration, Graphic Novel** CREATIVE FIRM: **Stephen F Austin State University - Nagodoches, TX** CREATIVE TEAM: **Yulia Kolonina** CLIENT: **SFA** 3 CATEGORY: **Photography, Book**
CREATIVE FIRM: **Modesto Junior College - Ceres, CA** CREATIVE TEAM: **Modesto Junior College** CLIENT: **Claudia** 4 CATEGORY: **Web Games & Entertainment** CREATIVE FIRM: **Drexel University Graphic**
Design Program, AWCoMAD - Philadelphia, PA CREATIVE TEAM: **Steve Nunes - Student Designer; Mark Willie - University Instructor** CLIENT: **Drexel University Graphic Design Program, AWCoMAD**
5 CATEGORY: **Illustration, Graphic Novel** CREATIVE FIRM: **Stephen F Austin State University - Nagodoches, TX** CREATIVE TEAM: **Yulia Kolonina** CLIENT: **SFA**

1 CATEGORY: **Website, Consumer** CREATIVE FIRM: **Berghs School Of Communication - Stockholm, Sweden** CREATIVE TEAM: **Tomas Jonsson - Art Director; Carl Fredrik Jannerfeldt - Copywriter** CLIENT: **Doritos**
2 CATEGORY: **Collateral Material, Single Unit** CREATIVE FIRM: **West Virginia University - Morgantown, WV** CREATIVE TEAM: **Brandy Gibson, Crystal Good, David Carenbauer - Students; Eve Faulkes - Professor**
CLIENT: **Fred Minnear, VP of WVU Health Sciences Program** 3 CATEGORY: **Collateral Material, Campaign** CREATIVE FIRM: **Academy of Art University - San Francisco, CA** CREATIVE TEAM: **Jang Soon Hwang - Art Director; Sung Jun Kim - Account Planner; Seong Bin Song - Photographer; Gabriel Johnson - Copywriter** CLIENT: **Bose (Quiet Comfort 2)** 4 CATEGORY: **Website, Consumer** CREATIVE FIRM: **Berghs School Of Communication - Stockholm, Sweden** CREATIVE TEAM: **Tomas Jonsson - Art Director; Carl Fredrik Jannerfeldt - Copywriter** CLIENT: **Maglite** 5 CATEGORY: **Food & Beverage Packaging** CREATIVE FIRM: **Drexel University Graphic Design Program, AWCoMAD - Philadelphia, PA** CREATIVE TEAM: **Olga Filipava - Student Designer; Sandy Stewart - University Instructor** CLIENT: **Drexel University Graphic Design Program, AWCoMAD**
6 CATEGORY: **Brochure, Consumer Products/Services** CREATIVE FIRM: **Savannah College of Art and Design - Davidsonville, MD** CREATIVE TEAM: **Kristen Mattes** CLIENT: **Savannah College of Art and Design**

1

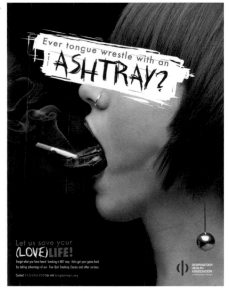

2

3

4

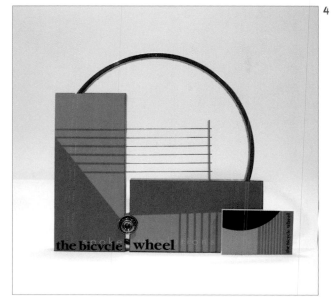

5

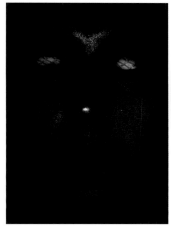
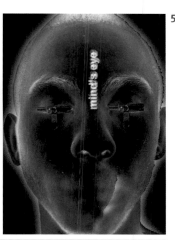

1 CATEGORY: **Magazine Ad, Public Service, Single Unit** CREATIVE FIRM: **Columbia College Chicago - Chicago, IL** CREATIVE TEAM: **Michael Murphy - Writer; Andrew Walenca - Art Director; Laurence Minsky - Faculty Advisor** CLIENT: **Respiratory Health Association of Met Chicago** 2 CATEGORY: **Annual Reports** CREATIVE FIRM: **Savannah College of Art and Design - Davidsonville, MD** CREATIVE TEAM: **Kristen Mattes** CLIENT: **Savannah College of Art and Design** 3 CATEGORY: **Food & Beverage Packaging** CREATIVE FIRM: **Drexel University Graphic Design Program, AWCoMAD - Philadelphia, PA** CREATIVE TEAM: **Trissie Harding - Student Designer; Mark Willie - University Instructor** CLIENT: **Drexel University Graphic Design Program, AWCoMAD** 4 CATEGORY: **Retail Packaging** CREATIVE FIRM: **Drexel University Graphic Design Program, AWCoMAD - Philadelphia, PA** CREATIVE TEAM: **Steve Nunes - Student Designer; Sandy Stewart - University Instructor** CLIENT: **Drexel University Graphic Design Program, AWCoMAD** 5 CREATIVE FIRM: **Purdue University - West Lafayette, IN** CREATIVE TEAM: **Li Zhang** CLIENT: **College of Liberal Arts**

creativity 38 annual awards

1

2

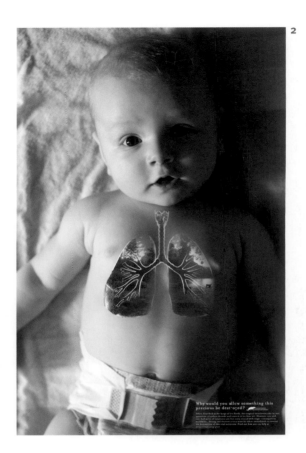

3

RODCHENKO_4
EXHIBIT ENTRANCE

4

5

1 CATEGORY: **Collateral Material, Campaign** CREATIVE FIRM: **Savannah College of Art and Design - Davidsonville, MD** CREATIVE TEAM: **Kristen Mattes** CLIENT: **Savannah College of Art and Design**
2 CATEGORY: **Collateral Material, Campaign** CREATIVE FIRM: **Savannah College of Art and Design - Davidsonville, MD** CREATIVE TEAM: **Kristen Mattes** CLIENT: **Savannah College of Art and Design**
3 CATEGORY: **Environmental Graphics, Single Unit** CREATIVE FIRM: **Drexel University Graphic Design Program, AWCoMAD - Philadelphia, PA** CREATIVE TEAM: **Julia Dobbins, Michele Kopec, Dan Steinberg - Student Designers; Jody Graff - University Instructor** CLIENT: **Drexel University Graphic Design Program, AWCoMAD** 4 CATEGORY: **Branding, Campaign** CREATIVE FIRM: **Tyler School of Art - Piermont, NY** CREATIVE TEAM: **Mark Sposato - Designer (student); Stephanie Knopp - Professor** CLIENT: **Stephanie Knopp** 5 CATEGORY: **Food & Beverage Packaging** CREATIVE FIRM: **The University of Texas at Arlington - Arlington, TX** CREATIVE TEAM: **Alexander Pierce - Designer** CLIENT: **Whipper Snapper Brewery (fictional)**

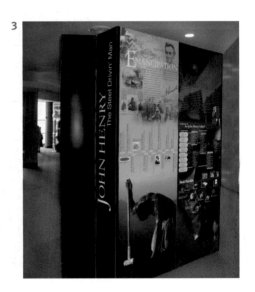

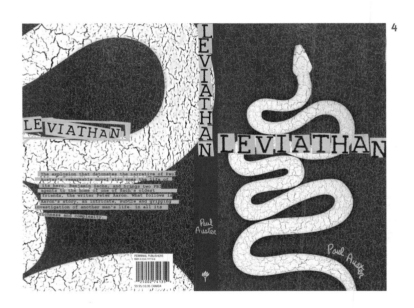

1 CATEGORY: **Magazine Ad, Consumer, Campaign** CREATIVE FIRM: **SIUC - Carbondale, IL** CREATIVE TEAM: **Micheal Williams** CLIENT: **BIC** 2 CATEGORY: **Poster, Single Unit** CREATIVE FIRM: **The Design Studio at Kean University - Union, NJ** CREATIVE TEAM: **Steven Brower - Director of the Design Studio; Thomas Sinnott - Student Designer** CLIENT: **The Department of Theater at Kean University**
3 CATEGORY: **Trade Show Display/Graphics** CREATIVE FIRM: **West Virginia University - Morgantown, WV** CREATIVE TEAM: **Carla Witt-Ford, Graham Curry, Brad Robertson, Lauren Lamb, Scott Taylor - Students; Eve Faulkes - Professor** CLIENT: **West Virginia Humanities Council** 4 CATEGORY: **Book Design, Jacket** CREATIVE FIRM: **Drexel University Graphic Design Program, AWCoMAD - Philadelphia, PA** CREATIVE TEAM: **Julia Dobbins - Student Designer; E. June Roberts-Lunn - University Instructor** CLIENT: **Drexel University Graphic Design Program, AWCoMAD** 5 CATEGORY: **Book Design, Jacket** CREATIVE FIRM: **Drexel University Graphic Design Program, AWCoMAD - Philadelphia, PA** CREATIVE TEAM: **Ruslan Khaydarov - Student Designer; E. June Roberts-Lunn - University Instructor** CLIENT: **Drexel University Graphic Design Program, AWCoMAD** 6 CATEGORY: **Book Design, Jacket** CREATIVE FIRM: **Drexel University Graphic Design Program, AWCoMAD - Philadelphia, PA** CREATIVE TEAM: **Ruslan Khaydarov - Student Designer; E. June Roberts-Lunn - University Instructor** CLIENT: **Drexel University Graphic Design Program, AWCoMAD**

creativity 38 annual awards

stop and smell the design

arne jacobsen

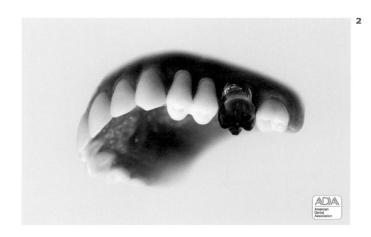

PETCO
you're all they know.

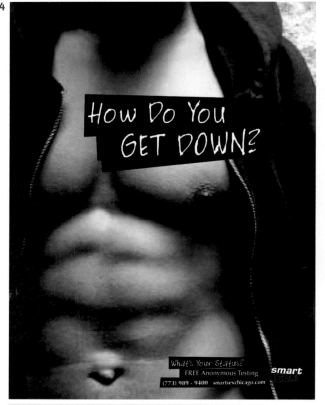

HOW DO YOU GET DOWN?

What's Your Status?
FREE Anonymous Testing
(773) 989 - 9400   smartsexchicago.com
smart

WEARING FUR DOESN'T

OIL KILLS

1 CATEGORY: **Magazine Ad, Consumer, Single Unit** CREATIVE FIRM: **Radford University - Christiansburg, VA** CREATIVE TEAM: **Radford University** CLIENT: **Arne Jacobsen Furniture** 2 CATEGORY: **Magazine Ad, Consumer, Single Unit** CREATIVE FIRM: **Parsons The New School for Design - Jersey City, NJ** CREATIVE TEAM: **Ryan Wi - Art Director** CLIENT: **American Dental Association** 3 CATEGORY: **Magazine Ad, Consumer, Campaign** CREATIVE FIRM: **Parsons The New School for Design - Jersey City, NJ** CREATIVE TEAM: **Ryan Wi - Art Director, Copywriter** CLIENT: **PETCO** 4 CATEGORY: **Magazine Ad, Public Service, Single Unit** CREATIVE FIRM: **Columbia College Chicago - Chicago, IL** CREATIVE TEAM: **Michael Murphy - Writer, Art Director; Laurence Minsky - Faculty Advisor** CLIENT: **Test Positive Aware Network** 5 CATEGORY: **Magazine Design, Interior** CREATIVE FIRM: **RIT - Rochester, NY** CREATIVE TEAM: **Denis Defibaugh, Lorri Freer - Professors** CLIENT: **RIT**

1

2

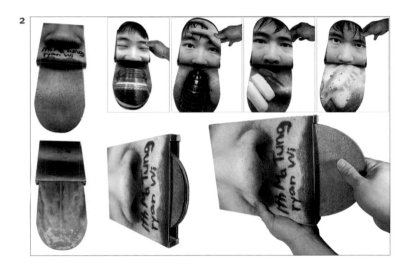

3

4

CHAPTERONE

5

1 CATEGORY: **Corporate TV, Single Unit** CREATIVE FIRM: **Illusion and Mirrors - Los Angeles, CA** CREATIVE TEAM: **Jennava Laska - Director; Mattew Lim - Cinematographer** CLIENT: **Betty Crocker** 2 CATEGORY: **Book Design, Jacket** CREATIVE FIRM: **Parsons The New School for Design - Jersey City, NJ** CREATIVE TEAM: **Ryan Wi - Art Director, Designer** CLIENT: **A specific part of my body** 3 CATEGORY: **Magazine Ad, Public Service, Single Unit** CREATIVE FIRM: **Columbia College Chicago - Chicago, IL** CREATIVE TEAM: **Michael Murphy - Writer; Andrew Walenca - Art Director; Laurence Minsky - Faculty Advisor** CLIENT: **Respiratory Health Association of Met Chicago** 4 CATEGORY: **Logos and Trademarks** CREATIVE FIRM: **Pratt Institute - Astoria, NY** CREATIVE TEAM: **Pratt Institute** CLIENT: **Chapter One** 5 CATEGORY: **Magazine Design, Cover** CREATIVE FIRM: **Baruch College-CUNY - Flushing, NY** CREATIVE TEAM: **Tong Wu** CLIENT: **Encounter Magazine - New York**

1

2

3

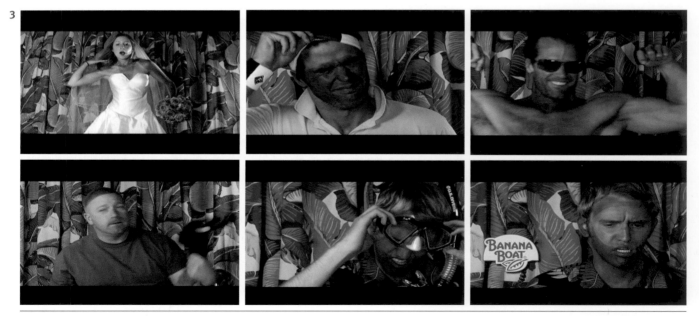

1 CATEGORY: Consumer TV, Campaign CREATIVE FIRM: Illusion and Mirrors - Los Angeles, CA CREATIVE TEAM: Jennava Laska - Director; Hunter Metcalf - Cinematographer CLIENT: Match.com 2 CATEGORY: Consumer TV, Campaign CREATIVE FIRM: Illusion and Mirrors - Los Angeles, CA CREATIVE TEAM: Jennava Laska - Director; Mattew Lim - Cinematographer CLIENT: Converse Tennis Shoes 3 CATEGORY: Consumer TV, Single Unit CREATIVE FIRM: Illusion and Mirrors - Los Angeles, CA CREATIVE TEAM: Jennava Laska - Director; Hunter Metcalf - Cinematographer CLIENT: Banana Boat